The Politics of Neglect:
Urban Aid from Model Cities to Revenue Sharing

A Publication of the Joint Center for Urban Studies of the Massachusetts Institute of Technology and Harvard University

The Politics of Neglect:
Urban Aid from Model Cities to Revenue Sharing

Bernard J. Frieden
and Marshall Kaplan

The MIT Press
Cambridge, Massachusetts, and London, England

34305

This book was set in IBM Composer Press Roman
by Techdata Associates Incorporated,
printed on Mohawk Neotext Offset,
and bound in Columbia Millbank Vellum
by The Colonial Press, Inc.
in the United States of America.

Library of Congress Cataloging in Publication Data

Frieden, Bernard J.
  The politics of neglect.

  Includes bibliographical references and index.
  1. Cities and towns—Planning—United States. 2. Urban renewal—United States. 3. Federal-city relations—United States. I. Kaplan, Marshall, joint author. II. Title.
HT167.F74   309.2'62'0973   75-6792
ISBN 0-262-06061-2

To the memory of
CHARLES ABRAMS—
teacher, colleague, and friend

Contents

Acknowledgments

This study would not have been possible without the generous cooperation of many people who themselves were key participants in the design and management of the Model Cities Program. We are most indebted to those present and former officials of the Department of Housing and Urban Development who permitted us to make use of their extensive files on the history of the program and who gave us the benefit of their review of portions of the manuscript: Robert Wood, Floyd Hyde, H. Ralph Taylor, Walter G. Farr, Jr., and John McLean. Edward C. Banfield also shared with us the files of the White House Task Force on Model Cities, which he chaired, and Sidney Gardner made available materials concerning his former participation in the program on behalf of the Department of Health, Education, and Welfare. Other present and former HUD staff members who assisted us by supplying information or reviewing chapters of this work in draft form are Sherry Arnstein, Robert Baida, Warren Butler, Joseph Crane, Richard Langendorf, Meredith Potter, Bernard Russell, and George Williams.

Interviews are acknowledged specifically in the text. We want especially to thank Daniel P. Moynihan, Joseph A. Califano, Jr., and John Price for sharing with us their perspective from the White House, Richard C. Van Dusen for his views from the office of the Under Secretary of Housing and Urban Development, and Richard P. Nathan, whose insights reflected his experience in both the Office of Management and Budget and the Department of Health, Education, and Welfare. We are also indebted to Charles Haar, formerly Assistant Secretary of HUD for Metropolitan Development, with whom we discussed the Model Cities Program on many occasions while we worked as coinvestigators on a study of the program sponsored by the Ford Foundation.

We have also drawn extensively on notes and observations made during our personal participation in several phases of the Model Cities Program. Bernard Frieden was a member of the staff of President Johnson's 1965 Task Force on Urban Problems, chaired by Robert Wood, and was a member of President Nixon's 1969 Task Force on Model Cities, chaired by Edward C. Banfield. Marshall Kaplan, as a principal in the consulting firm of Marshall Kaplan, Gans and Kahn, directed several evaluation studies of the Model Cities Program under contract to the Department of Housing and Urban Development; these are cited in the text. In addition, while on leave from his firm, he served as on-site adviser to Assistant Secretary Floyd Hyde in Washington in 1970-71. Because of our own involvement, as well as our personal commitments to the social goals of the Model Cities Program, we can make no claim to scholarly detachment. This work is in part participant history and in part more traditional research and analysis. Responsibility for inaccuracies and interpretation is, of course, solely our own.

Robert Fogelson and Martha Derthick made many perceptive comments on an earlier draft of this study; their reactions and suggestions were extremely helpful.

We are grateful to Sheldon Gans and Howard Kahn of Marshall Kaplan, Gans and Kahn for making available background data from their firm's many studies of the Model Cities Program and for their continuous helpful comments on our efforts. Leigh Boyd of Marshall Kaplan, Gans and Kahn, Audrey Ginsberg of the Joint Center for Urban Studies, and Callie Struggs of Flower Mound New Town, Ltd., handled ably the administrative and secretarial work that kept the project moving smoothly.

Karla O'Brien, Director of Publications for the Joint Center for Urban Studies, made many important contributions to this work that went far beyond her nominal role as editor. We are especially appreciative of her patient and good-humored handling of the complex problems posed by joint authorship and by the distance between the authors, who worked in Cambridge, San Francisco, and Dallas.

We owe a special debt to the Ford Foundation and to Louis Winnick, Deputy Vice President, Division of National Affairs, whose support made our research possible.

Finally and customarily for works of this kind and duration, our deepest gratitude goes to our wives and families for bearing with many inconveniences and forgone vacations so that we could complete this study.

Cambridge, Massachusetts   Bernard J. Frieden
Dallas, Texas   Marshall Kaplan
October 1974

Part I
Origins

Chapter 1
Introduction

For most Americans concerned with the quality of life in the nation's cities, the decade of the 1960s was filled with both opportunities and frustrations. It was a time of contradictions: the noble sentiments of Martin Luther King's "I Have a Dream" with Bull Connor's police dogs, the idealism of black and white youth singing "We Shall Overcome" with the ready resort to assassination as a form of politics. The nation rediscovered the problems of poverty and redefined urban problems to give prime emphasis to the plight of the poor living in the central cities. Yet many people could not understand the reasons behind ever-frequent urban riots in light of what appeared to be constantly increasing federal attention to the poor and the minorities.

This was an exceptionally fertile period for the invention of programs. The social vision of the New Frontier, followed immediately by the legislative achievements of the Great Society, vastly accelerated federal involvement in the problems of the cities. The number of federal grant authorizations grew from 161 in 1962 to 429 by 1969. New programs, each with its own budget and statutory requirements, generated a massive federal administrative structure and a significant transformation of federal-state-city relationships.

The steady growth of federal programs, despite the war in Vietnam, may be seen in itself as evidence of great responsiveness of government to perceived domestic problems. The ultimate test of responsiveness, however, is not the passage of laws but their implementation. In this respect the record is less than satisfactory. In retrospect, much was attempted, much was promised, but the achievements fell far short of expectations. The gap between intentions and performance continues to puzzle the experts as well as the public at large and the groups who were expected to benefit most from new federal activities.

The authors were among those who participated directly in the development of national efforts to remedy urban ills. We shared with others a perplexity over the pressure of unexpected events, as well as a commitment to act in behalf of social goals even on the basis of imperfect knowledge. In today's perspective, the central question for us is the capacity of the federal government to respond to the needs of the poor and minorities in the cities. That capacity was put to an extreme test in the Model Cities Program, which attempted a series of federal reforms aimed ultimately at improving living conditions for the residents of a series of poverty neighborhoods across the country. We have chosen to explore the nature and limits of federal performance through an analysis of this program.

We both played several roles in the design, implementation, monitoring, and review of the Model Cities Program from 1965 through the early 1970s. We continue to believe in the validity of the goals of this program. The people who remain trapped in the poverty of the inner city continue to receive less than a fair share of public resources or attention. Until they do, the "urban problem" will not go away.

Our assessment of the model cities experience, therefore, is not free of bias. We hope, however, that it is an informed and critical one. We have deliberately limited our perspective to the federal management of the Model Cities Program, leaving to others the analysis of local activities. A careful reading of the federal implementation effort should help to define a future role for the federal government in reducing poverty and inequality, drawing on the experience of the 1960s but without repeating the overly optimistic assumptions and mistakes of that decade.

Federal Bureaucracies: The One and the Many

In studying the capacity of the federal government to respond to the needs of cities, we are concerned above all with the performance of the federal bureaucracies charged with responsibility for administering urban aid programs. Federal agencies began to operate programs of assistance to the cities in the 1930s. Their number and functions grew slowly but steadily through the early 1960s. Significantly, they operated on a piecemeal basis, each pursuing a different activity with its own conception of public purpose. Some, such as public housing, were aimed at alleviating the plight of the poor, but most were not. The majority supplied aid for general urban development, such as highways, airports, hospital construction, and waste treatment works. By 1962, the Advisory Commission on Intergovernmental Relations made a conservative definition of federal urban development programs and counted forty of them.[1] Other grant programs created by then had to do with the provision of services rather than physical facilities, so that by the early 1960s the federal urban aid inventory already involved more than a dozen agencies and well over one hundred programs.

But growth in the number and variety of federal aid programs did not seem to bring with it the relief of urban woes. Proliferating federal aid led to extreme confusion and long delays that threatened to deplete the limited energies of city

[1] U.S. Advisory Commission on Intergovernmental Relations, *Impact of Federal Urban Development Programs on Local Government Organization and Planning*, U.S. Senate Committee on Government Operations, 88th Cong., 2nd Sess., Committee Print, May 30, 1964, p. 2.

administrators, who had been seduced into the maze of federal review and approval processes by the lure of "free" federal money. By the mid-1960s, a chorus of complaints sounded in Congress and in the city halls, as well as in the studies of political scientists. Federal officials and local grantsmen alike were caught in the red tape of programs that seemed to be both underfunded and overregulated.

Something new was needed, given the laudable desire of both President Kennedy and President Johnson to act on the nation's increasingly obvious urban difficulties. Two answers emerged. First was the creation of a Department of Housing and Urban Development (HUD), as a new federal instrument to give more deliberate policy direction to the earlier scattered efforts. President Kennedy repeatedly urged the establishment of this department, starting in 1961; in September 1965, Congress finally enacted legislation to create the department at the request of President Johnson. Congressional considerations focused mainly on the question of how best to achieve coordination of the many federal functions affecting urban development. Part of the solution was to gather together within the new department a number of programs formerly administered by separate housing agencies. But the Senate Committee reporting out the final legislation emphasized that many relevant programs would continue to be administered by other departments and agencies. It charged the Secretary of Housing and Urban Development with responsibility to negotiate with these other agencies to achieve needed coordination and policy consistency across departmental lines.

Before the ink was dry on the law establishing HUD, President Johnson appointed a task force to advise him on how to organize the new department and what new programs it should have. The task force, too, saw an urgent need to coordinate and concentrate scattered federal efforts in urban affairs, but with a new emphasis on focusing these aids in the poverty areas of central cities. Working in secrecy and reporting directly to the White House, the task force came up with the Model Cities Program as the grand unifier and coordinator of all federal urban grants, within a new department whose overall mission gave high priority to precisely such coordination.

The task force's strategy for implementing this program was simple. With strong backing from the White House, HUD would channel the existing flow of federal resources from other agencies into selected poverty neighborhoods where a great concentration of effort could demonstrate significant results. Thus the President and the Secretary of HUD would see to it that the full inventory of federal grants contributed to a comprehensive attack on the problems of poverty and at the same time would equip local governments for the task of carrying out a sustained program. As HUD officials later refined this strategy, it came to include the promise of federal reform to streamline grant processing for participating cities, earmark funds in advance from other grant-in-aid programs, establish the local model cities agency as the single point of entry for all federal resources affecting the model neighborhood, and supply technical assistance from all relevant federal agencies.

Although the strategy was relatively simple to conceive, it added up to a formidable assignment. Were the bureaucracies capable of reforming and unifying their policies, given pressure from the White House and HUD to make them move? Nobody had asked for their cooperation in advance, nor were they even represented on the task force that proposed the program. Within a year, Congress adopted legislation setting up the Model Cities Program with only minor changes from the task force's conception. But Congressional acceptance did not necessarily mean that the program had enough political support to ensure successful implementation later. Many legislative enactments result from the pressure of interest groups that continue to look after particular programs after they have been established. In these cases, an organized constituency first presses Congress for legislative action, then keeps up the pressure on federal agencies to operate the program effectively. Model cities, however, did not emerge out of conventional interest group politics. The legislation was a result of Presidential politics: created out of ideas proposed by a White House task force, drafted in the White House without discussion among affected agencies, and pushed energetically as a key part of the President's legislative program when he had an exceptionally large majority behind him in Congress.

Defining the Implementation Issues

The literature on bureaucracy is helpful in supplying a framework for understanding what happened as HUD set about putting the Model Cities Program into operation. It raises persistent and fundamental issues still underlying current controversies over federal urban policy. They have to do with the limits of Presidential power and White House control over federal aid programs; with the operational consequences of power widely dispersed and shared among the White House, Congress, the federal bureaucracies, and state and local governments; with the difficulties of securing increased resources for politically weak minorities; and with a political culture that reflects a high degree of pluralism in American society, coupled with the lack of consensus on a proper strategy for coping with the problems of urban poverty.

Anthony Downs's provocative book, *Inside Bureaucracy*, notes that shifts in economic and political conditions often generate expanding areas of a bureaucratic no-man's-land, where many different agencies carry out newly important functions in a partial and fragmented way. No agency is dominant. In such policy-dense areas, new bureaus often arise.[2] This was precisely the case with increasing activity in urban affairs through the early 1960s, followed by the establishment of HUD and of the Model Cities Program as coordinating instruments for a major piece of this territory.

Downs contends that the boundaries of a bureau's territory are usually ambiguous as a result of complicated interdependencies in modern societies. Such interdependencies are particularly evident in the case of urban poverty, which most analysts view as a condition arising from multiple causes requiring a series of many different policy interventions.

Bureaus recognize and deal with interdependencies in two contrasting ways. Some narrow their purposes and actions so that they affect relatively few external agents. Downs terms this approach the "shrinking violet syndrome."[3] Some agencies thus pursue a sharply defined course of action, such as highway departments that concentrate on building roads and give minimal attention to the indirect effects of their actions on others. This approach may fail to take advantage of genuine interdependencies and fail to cope adequately with external effects of programs. In contrast, some agencies make very comprehensive proposals and ignore the interests and likely behavior of other affected bureaus. Downs terms this the "superman syndrome" and illustrates it by citing the frequent preparation of city master plans that call for unrealistic behavior on the part of others.[4]

These distinctions suggest a series of questions. How did HUD move into the no-man's-land of urban policy making? Did its component parts—the Office of the Secretary and the Model Cities Administration—follow a consistent strategy? What were the consequences of HUD's tactical decisions for the behavior of other agencies, and what were their consequences for the implementation of the Model Cities Program?

[2] Anthony Downs, *Inside Bureaucracy* (Boston: Little, Brown, 1967), p. 220.
[3] Ibid., p. 217.
[4] Ibid., p. 218.

Many groups outside the federal bureaucracies have strong influence over their behavior, particularly Congress and organized interest groups among the public. Downs points out that people often hold conflicting perceptions of bureaus, which in turn affect the demands they make of the bureaucracies. At one extreme, popular criticism holds that government bureaus are bungling, narrow-minded, and fail to coordinate their activities with those of other agencies. The implication of this view is that there is not enough intelligent, centralized coordination of government's many bureaus. Another view, however, holds that bureaucracies are a threat to individual liberty, that they are monolithic organizations where a few powerful men at the top concentrate control over a vast range of activities. The implication of this view is that efforts to strengthen coordination among agencies are potentially dangerous, because they may upset the existing balance of power that permits considerable freedom of action for many interest groups.[5]

These contrasting views reflect a commonly perceived ambivalence about bureaucracies in American society. Often the same people hold both views, depending upon which agencies they have in mind and on particular circumstances or points of time. Many people who advocate government reform through improvements in coordination also worry about excessive concentrations of power in federal agencies or in the executive branch as a whole. For this study, an important issue is the extent to which either of these views created pressures that affected the ability of HUD to carry out the mandate of the Model Cities Program. In particular, how did these views influence the task force, Congress, and HUD when they set ground rules for the Model Cities Program?

Forms of Coordination

Among political scientists who have studied interagency relationships, Charles E. Lindblom has formulated a very helpful theoretical framework for understanding alternative methods of coordination and the conditions under which they are likely to work. In *The Intelligence of Democracy*, he distinguishes two basic types. In central coordination, individual decision makers adapt to one another on instructions from a central regulating authority. At the other end of the spectrum is a process of mutual adjustment, in which no central decision maker exer-

[5] See ibid., pp. 132-133.

cises any coordinating responsibility. The most familiar mutual adjustment process is negotiation among independent agencies.[6]

Among other types of coordination that Lindblom identifies, one is cooperative discussion among decision makers, in which the group as a whole plays the role of the central regulator. In this form of coordination, decision makers are in substantial agreement on criteria for resolving their problems, and they cooperate rather than bargain or negotiate with each other.[7]

Coordination by cooperative discussion represents one of the strategies that could conceivably have been used in the Model Cities Program. It was, however, a road conspicuously not taken, for reasons that Lindblom's comments suggest. This form of coordination requires the participants to agree on common values and purposes, and to maintain that agreement over time. In a pluralistic system, where federal agencies reflect the interests of many different client groups, this degree of consensus and commitment is rare. The Model Cities Program did not in fact emerge from cooperative discussions among interested agencies. It originated in a Presidential task force made up almost entirely of people from outside government; Presidential pressure made possible its passage through Congress; and the White House and HUD only then attempted to secure the cooperation of other federal agencies.

The designers of the Model Cities Program envisioned a different relationship: central coordination, with the White House and HUD exercising coordinating responsibility. Two key questions are apparent: Was this conception workable? Was it compatible with the way the federal government operates?

Lindblom gives most of his attention to a process he terms partisan mutual adjustment, which appears closest to the reality of typical interagency relationships in Washington. In this form of coordination, each participant makes decisions calculated to serve his own goals, not goals necessarily shared by other interdependent decision makers. He may make decisions counter to his own goals only to the extent that he is in turn controlled by other partisans or by central supervision. For this process to work, the participants need only agree on a course of action at a particular time. They do not have to reach consensus on goals or values in order to reach an agreement on what to do. Each may subscribe to a common decision for his own reasons.

[6] Charles E. Lindblom, *The Intelligence of Democracy* (New York: Free Press, 1965), pp. 25-26.
[7] Ibid., p. 28.

Partisan decision makers may operate in several different ways. One type of partisan, according to Lindblom, assumes his interests are seriously in conflict with those of the other decision makers. He adopts an overtly hostile stance and attempts to prevail. Another type is reluctant to take the position of an avowed partisan but pursues his own purposes under a veneer of harmony and cooperation. Still another has a conception of the public interest that guides his own decisions but knows that others do not share this particular conception of the common good.

Thus partisanship is not necessarily synonymous with unprincipled behavior to protect or expand one's own bureaucratic turf. Nor does it necessarily reflect advocacy of the interests of a narrow client group. But decision makers who pursue their own versions of the public interest, in relationships with others who define the general welfare differently, are partisans, in Lindblom's terminology. All the recognized pressure groups in American government, he notes, are thus partisan decision makers; as indeed on many occasions are the President, all members of Congress, and all administrators.[8]

Partisanship contrasts sharply with coordination through a cooperative search for decisions. Partisan negotiators may have some common purposes while conflicting on others, or they may have very limited knowledge of one another's purposes. Their relationships proceed on the basis of negotiation, bargaining, and chance. Partisan adjustment is entirely compatible with centrally regulated coordination. A central decision maker often attempts to coordinate the actions of others who are themselves partisans. Lindblom comments perceptively that in many cases what appears to be central coordination is actually a process of partisan mutual adjustment.[9]

Lindblom argues that the process of partisan mutual adjustment is a helpful and appropriate method of policy making, frequently superior to attempts at central decision making. Granting that its value varies in different circumstances, Lindblom still points out a series of arguments in its favor: It disperses otherwise dangerously concentrated political power; it encourages widespread participation in the political process; it is likely to produce action and initiative (rather than the resistance usually generated by central decision making or the deadlock of two-party negotiations). Beyond these arguments, however, he states the case for partisan mutual adjustment as a method for "calculated, reasonable, rational, intelligent, wise" policy making.[10]

[8] Ibid., pp. 28-30.
[9] Ibid., p. 31.
[10] Ibid., pp. 293-294.

It is clear to even a casual observer that partisan mutual adjustment—in combination with limited central direction—is an apt description of the way the federal government tried to implement the Model Cities Program. Our study aims at finding out whether this process was as productive as Lindblom claims it to be, and whether it was productive in ways relevant to the purposes of the Model Cities Program. Our analysis is concerned with the varied elements of federal action undertaken as part of the Model Cities Program. In each phase, we attempt to clarify the relative roles of central regulation and of partisan behavior and to consider the policy outcomes of this combination.

Strategies for Redistribution

Model cities tried to do more than improve federal coordination, however. This program sought deliberately to redistribute resources, and hence power, to the urban poor and minority groups. Conceivably a method of implementation that is workable where redistributive issues are not involved might be inappropriate to cope with the additional resistance to such redistribution of resources to the poor.

Lindblom considers this possibility as an objection that may be raised against relying on partisan mutual adjustment for policy making. Partisan adjustment is likely to produce decisions that reflect the relative power of the participants. Although allocations of authority can be changed formally, such as through legislation, the underlying distribution of power in society has a way of reasserting itself as mutual adjustments are worked out.

Where the intended beneficiaries of a coordination process are weak politically, as the residents of poverty neighborhoods in the cities are, those who want to block redistributive measures can do so by using their power in the course of partisan mutual adjustment. Does this not argue, then, for outside intervention by a central decision maker on behalf of the powerless? Lindblom contends it does not. If the status quo distribution of power is deeply entrenched, he maintains, those who hold power will be equally able to block change that a central regulator attempts to impose.

Lindblom derides the notion that central decision making is "a kind of button to press where reform is needed," while the diffusion of policy making through mutual adjustment leaves no opening for reform. "If there were anything analogous to a button to press in a central system," he argues, "almost no one would be allowed to press it." Partisan mutual adjustment, in contrast, permits anyone to press at least one button, to enter into policy making, and to transmit impulses to decision makers whose participation in reform is required.[11] Whether this process can change the balance of power to benefit the poor remains to be seen.

The model cities experience is rich on this particular point, and our account of it focuses on three key questions: What were the limits of Presidential intervention on behalf of the poor? What buttons did the White House push to increase the leverage of the poor, and who resisted? To what extent did partisan processes of interagency negotiation block attempted reform and redistribution? Writing at a time when the events associated with Watergate have persuaded many people of the need to curtail and bound Presidential authority, we consider it important to review a recent effort to use that power for the sake of redistributing resources to the poor.

Organization of the Study

We started our analysis by investigating the underlying aims and strategies of the program as these emerged from the intellectual and political context of the 1960s and as they were shaped by the process of legislative enactment. Chapters 2 and 3 present our findings on these subjects.

From the origins, we move in Part II to an analysis of what happened to the intentions and the promises of federal reform. The five chapters of this section consider the several implementation strategies that were pursued by the Model Cities Administration (MCA) and the ways in which they were modified by the course of events. The main task here is to clarify the sources of difficulty in meeting the federal promises. The resistance of administrators, the rigidities of programs and procedures, and the competing claims of other constituencies all interacted in varying ways to frustrate the early hopes for success. But these factors are not all to be weighed equally: a close examination shows that there were different degrees of resistance and greater progress on some fronts than on others.

In applying this body of experience to the design of policies for the future, we attempt in Part III to answer a number of basic questions. What are the most important lessons to be derived from seven years of effort in Washington? How serious was the national commitment to the purposes of this program, and how serious a commitment is needed for success? Which barriers seem most formid-

[11] Ibid., pp. 301-302.

able for the future? Where was progress made? What new opportunities came to light, even if model cities failed to grasp them? What are the most pressing priorities for future federal urban policy? What can be done to assure a reasonable base of political support? How can federal aid best be applied to the range of urban problems for which the Model Cities Program was designed? The answers can serve to test the legislative proposals of the 1970s against the realities of our federal system and can point the way toward constructive next steps in the evolution of national policies for the cities.

Chapter 2
Defining the Urban Problem

The Model Cities Program, like most Great Society innovations of the late 1960s, was both a response to the special conditions of that turbulent period and the product of a long lineage of prior federal actions. It came into being because of a perceived crisis of the cities. Yet this undertaking illustrated with particular clarity that in recent times most new federal programs have arisen out of the shortcomings of earlier ones—in this case, out of the poor coordination of previous programs as well as the specific disappointments with urban renewal. Starting with the New Deal, Congress enacted a series of programs to help cope with housing and urban problems. But during the 1960s the country became sharply aware of the continued severity of those problems, as they were described in the press, broadcast on television, analyzed in the new scholarly literature on urban studies, and reinforced by rising discontent among the urban poor and the black communities in particular.

These elements all suggested that existing federal urban programs were not doing an effective job. In addition, a growing number of critics, from right and left, were lacing into the major federal aid program designed to assist the central cities—urban renewal. Serious critical works began to appear in the early 1960s, at the same time that there was growing political protest from the victims of urban renewal in the cities. A new climate of opinion increasingly regarded criticisms of renewal as legitimate and well founded—criticisms that earlier were held to represent no more than opposition to progress.

There was also a new political context in the early 1960s, giving rise to a steadily growing number of urban aid programs conceived under unusual auspices. Both Presidents Kennedy and Johnson were eager to use federal resources to cope with the social problems of the cities, which were commanding increasing national attention. They did not wait for special interest groups to organize and make demands. Instead, they turned increasingly to staff advisers, White House task forces, and Presidential commissions to generate ideas for new programs. Experts in urban affairs became the designers of programs that activist Presidents could present to the Congress—and these urban experts drew many of their ideas from reform concepts advanced in the late 1950s and early 1960s.

Some of the reform ideas were concerned with administering federal programs more efficiently. Others had to do with the nature of urban poverty and the shortcomings of earlier attempts to alleviate it. At first, these streams of thought gave rise to separate proposals for public policy. But increasingly the designers of new programs began to combine ideas from both agendas in formulating, first, the War on Poverty, and later, the Model Cities Program.

The Critique of Federal Urban Programs

Two distinct points of view about the defects in federal urban policies shaped the initial conception of the Model Cities Program. The first stressed the growing difficulty of coordinating and managing the rapidly growing number of federal aid programs for the cities; the second focused on the neglect of social concerns in urban renewal and its failure to improve living conditions for the poor and for minority groups. Different people advanced these two viewpoints, basing them on different sets of values and concerns and on different political priorities.

Coordinating the Federal Effort

Analysts of federal aid programs had called attention to the problems of coordination long before, but these problems acquired a special saliency by the mid-1960s, for two reasons. First, both the cost and the number of programs had grown strikingly, beginning in the late 1950s. In 1950, federal grants-in-aid to state and local governments totaled some $2 billion, almost exactly the same figure as in 1940. By 1960, this figure climbed to $7 billion, and by 1965 to $11 billion.[1] The number of separate grant authorizations in force at the end of 1962 was 160; from 1963 through 1965, Congress authorized an additional 170 grant programs.[2] Further, by the 1960s, both the critics of federal programs and the public at large began to hold the government to higher standards of performance. As Charles Schultze and his colleagues at the Brookings Institution have pointed out, federal officials had to show not only that they were spending tax-payers' money for proper purposes but that their programs were actually producing results—that children were learning more in the schools, water was cleaner, medical care was better, and housing conditions were improving.[3]

Coincident with these changes, the demands for coordination grew more insistent. In 1955, President Eisenhower's Commission on Intergovernmental Relations (Kestnbaum Commission) reported in moderate tones on its study of federal grant programs. The commission concluded that federal grants did not constitute a system and were never intended to do so. Their varied characteristics resulted naturally enough from their "varied objectives and piecemeal devel-

[1] U.S. Advisory Commission on Intergovernmental Relations, *Fiscal Balance in the American Federal System* (Washington, D.C.: U.S. Government Printing Office, 1967), Vol. 1, p. 147.
[2] Ibid., p. 151.
[3] Charles L. Schultze, Edward R. Fried, Alice M. Rivlin, and Nancy H. Teeters, *Setting National Priorities: The 1973 Budget* (Washington, D.C.: Brookings Institution, 1972), pp. 449-452.

opment." The commission warned that without careful administrative coordination at the national level, federal programs might produce confusion at the local level, might fail to provide mutual support, or, in extreme cases, might work at cross purposes. It found "some evidence that these results have occurred in the past," and recommended a Presidential staff agency on intergovernmental relations to avoid such results in the future.[4]

By 1961, the carefully qualified findings of the Kestnbaum Commission were accepted as established facts. The newly established Advisory Commission on Intergovernmental Relations studied the impact of federal grant programs in metropolitan areas and observed: "The fragmented and conflicting impact at the State and local level of disparate Federal programs concerning urban highways, urban renewal, housing, airport and sewage facility construction, and so on, are well known." In sharper language, the Advisory Commission emphasized that intergovernmental relations with respect to urban affairs were "unnecessarily impaired because of inadequate coordination of Federal programs"; it urged "prompt and effective steps" to improve the situation.[5]

The concern over coordination was prompted mainly by a perceived need to improve the administration of federal programs. With better coordination, these programs would be more effective, federal expenditures would yield greater returns, and the process of urban development would become more efficient. As a later Advisory Commission report put it, "Coordination among Federal programs is essential if the objective of orderly urban development is to be attained."[6] This assessment was directed mainly at problems of waste, duplication, and misuse of resources. It could appeal to widely held public and Congressional concern with government efficiency and economy.

This point of view, which a growing number of mayors and other local officials also began to advance, was instrumental in persuading Congress to establish a Department of Housing and Urban Development. Before 1965, federal housing and community development programs were administered by the Housing and

[4] U.S. Commission on Intergovernmental Relations, *Message from the President of the United States Transmitting the Final Report of the Commission on Intergovernmental Relations*, 84th Cong., 1st Sess., House Document No. 198 (1955), pp. 118, 139.

[5] U.S. Advisory Commission on Intergovernmental Relations, *Governmental Structure, Organization and Planning in Metropolitan Areas* (Washington, D.C.: U.S. Government Printing Office, 1961), p. 52.

[6] U.S. Advisory Commission on Intergovernmental Relations, *Impact of Federal Urban Development Programs on Local Government Organization and Planning*, U.S. Senate Committee on Government Operations, 88th Cong., 2nd Sess., Committee Print, May 30, 1974, p. 7.

Home Finance Agency and several of its powerful constituent branches, such as the Federal Housing Administration and the Urban Renewal Administration, which often acted with considerable independence of the HHFA Administrator. President Kennedy made several attempts to win Congressional support for a Cabinet-level urban affairs department. President Johnson continued the effort, and Congress took action to establish the new department in 1965. The large Democratic majority that swept in with President Johnson's electoral victory in 1964 and also the widespread public perception of "the urban crisis" were undoubtedly the critical factors in this decision; however, the specific arguments advanced by supporters of this measure must also be taken into account.

Both the House and the Senate committee reports recommending enactment of the Administration bill were essentially in agreement. Both accepted President Johnson's contention that the severity of current urban problems demanded high national priority and that the volume of future urban development would be so great as to demand continued attention at the highest level of government. President Johnson's message to Congress in March 1965 made the latter point particularly vividly:

In the remainder of this century—in less than 40 years—urban population will double, city land will double, and we will have to build in our cities as much as all that we have built since the first colonist arrived on these shores. It is as if we had 40 years to rebuild the entire urban United States.[7]

In the reports of both committees, second only to the question of national priority was the need for improved coordination of urban programs. The House Committee believed that departmental status would "clarify jumbled lines of authority within the Housing and Home Finance Agency, knitting together its programs with better cohesion, and giving the whole a greater unity of purpose and objectives."[8] To support its position, the House Committee cited the frequent recommendations of mayors and municipal organizations that the executive branch establish a new department as a focal point for coordinating and correlating policies affecting housing and urban development.

The Senate Committee stated bluntly that it "was largely concerned with the problem of how best to achieve coordination of the many Federal functions that

[7] Message from the President of the United States, *Problems and Future of the Central City and its Suburbs*, 89th Cong., 1st Sess., House Document No. 99, 1965, p. 2.
[8] U.S. Congress, House Committee on Government Operations, *Report: Establishing a Department of Housing and Urban Development, and for Other Purposes*, 89th Cong., 1st Sess., House Report No. 337, 1965, p. 11.

importantly affect community development."[9] The purposes to be achieved by this improved coordination were the familiar ones of greater economy and efficiency. To the Senate Committee, coordination was essential because "uncoordinated programs result in duplication and in wasteful expenditures of administrative and program funds." The House Committee similarly claimed that savings would result not only from the increased effectiveness of program operations—such as the reduction of delays in urban renewal projects—but also from internal administrative economies made possible by centralization of services.

Both committees recognized that the creation of a Cabinet-level department consolidating the programs of HHFA would not in itself resolve the problems of coordination, because other Cabinet departments would continue to administer a large number of programs affecting urban development. The Senate Committee report noted that the President alone could settle conflicts among federal agencies, but it argued that a new department at Cabinet level would help the President exercise this responsibility. As a further safeguard, the Senate Committee recommended establishment within the new Department of Housing and Urban Development of an office specifically concerned with problems of coordination across departmental boundaries.

In the House, two minority statements within the Committee report posed the problem of interdepartmental coordination most sharply, and indeed spoke prophetically of what was to happen with the Model Cities Program. Seven members argued in their minority opinion that the bill would not in fact create "a Cabinet-level Department to coordinate the Federal programs geared to the needs of urban communities." Citing a report of the Advisory Commission on Intergovernmental Relations, the minority noted that there were more than 40 separate federal programs for urban development which among them involved some 13 departments and agencies. The Department of Housing and Urban Development, they contended, "at best would have jurisdiction over only a minor fraction of Federal activities and funds aimed at assisting States and municipalities to solve metropolitan problems."[10]

Four other members of the House Committee came forward with an interesting alternative proposal to establish an Office of Community Development within the Executive Office of the President as well as a Cabinet-level Community

[9] U.S. Congress, Senate Committee on Government Operations, *Report: Establishment of a Department of Housing and Urban Development*, 89th Cong., 1st Sess., Senate Report No. 536 (1965), p. 9.

[10] House Committee on Government Operations, *Report*, p. 39.

hoods. . . . Even now a very large percentage of existing buildings would make choice residences. Many were once the homes and apartments of the well-to-do and have real charm which would be a credit in any age to any city.[15]

The urban reformers who subscribed to this viewpoint, and to the proposals it generated, did not present themselves as advocates for any special interest group but rather as objective observers whose views reflected widely held values that were in the public interest: efficiency, economy, land conservation, beauty, a sense of community. But others began to question these underlying assumptions, and particularly the recommendations for restoring the vitality of the central city. One of the first was Raymond Vernon, director of the massive New York Metropolitan Region Study, which produced, between 1959 and 1961, nine scholarly volumes documenting and analyzing the massive changes taking place in the structure of the metropolitan area. After the New York study was complete, Vernon turned his attention from analysis and forecasting to asking who was benefiting and who was losing in the newly emerging metropolis.

In a notable series of lectures delivered at Princeton University in 1961, Vernon argued that both the middle-income group and the poor were improving their position because of the new opportunities offered by the spread of urban development. In moving to the suburbs, middle-income families were getting new housing with modern equipment, more outdoor space than they enjoyed in city neighborhoods, and good auto access to a growing number of industrial parks and shopping centers. They were strangely unmoved by the protests of the suburban critics. The poor, too, were taking advantage of wider options by moving into houses and neighborhoods left behind by the middle class. Most of these neighborhoods were in the central cities, but the poor were also able to enter some of the older suburbs. Both the middle class and the poor, Vernon contended, saw their lifetime experience as one of progress and improvement; they were living better than their parents, and they expected their children to do better still.

The well-to-do, on the other hand, found fewer pleasant options open to them than in the past. Fifty years earlier, the wealthy were able to live in mansions or town houses in exclusive city locations. They could live close to offices and theaters and enjoy promenades on the city streets, or they could buy a home in an exclusive community thirty minutes from downtown by new suburban trains. Over time, the in-town mansion became less feasible. Office and apartment de-

---

[15] Edward Higbee, *The Squeeze: Cities Without Space* (New York: Morrow & Co., Apollo Editions, 1967), pp. 83-84. This book was originally published in 1960.

velopments invaded the exclusive neighborhoods, and even most of the wealthy could no longer afford the cost of an in-town site for a single-family house. Then, too, the slums began to spread, and the city streets were no longer as safe as they used to be. At the same time, new suburban growth was threatening the outlying enclaves of the rich. As Vernon put it, "The inexorable tide of the middle class was surrounding the elite suburb, infiltrating the empty land where it could, crowding the little shopping centers, undermining the air of exclusivity and remoteness which had once prevailed."[16]

The wealthy still had their alternatives. Some chose to live in luxury apartments in town, others to move still farther away from their downtown executive offices, banks, and law firms. But the luxury apartments did not rival the earlier town houses, and the newer suburban locations required still longer commuting to jobs that mostly remained anchored to central locations.

More aggrieved than the wealthy, in Vernon's view, were the cultural elite who shared their attachment to the central city but were not in the same high income bracket. These were people who enjoyed the cosmopolitan environment of the big cities, the art galleries, museums, professional societies, political organizations. Many of them were writers and community leaders, influential in shaping public opinion. Lacking the ability of the rich to pay for luxury housing downtown, they found ways of communicating their unhappiness with the changes taking place in urban life.

Taken together, people with an economic interest in downtown and people with an interest in maintaining the central district as an intellectual and cultural focus represented a significant part of the leadership of an urban area. Vernon suggested that in their diagnosis of what was wrong with urban areas, these groups formulated the problems to reflect their own needs and proposed solutions to promote their own special values and priorities.[17]

The Attack on Urban Renewal

Vernon's interpretation offered a very unconventional view: the prevailing critique of urban development, he suggested, did not represent a "public interest" orientation, as its spokesmen claimed, but rather it mirrored the values of a limited elite group of users of the central city. The argument might have remained entirely academic except that a major and expanding public program ap-

[16] Raymond Vernon, *The Myth and Reality of Our Urban Problems* (Cambridge, Mass.: Harvard University Press, 1962, 1966), p. 48.
[17] Ibid., pp. 52-54.

peared to be acting on precisely those values that Vernon called into question. Urban renewal, begun in 1949 as a slum clearance program with the avowed purpose of improving living conditions for slum residents, was converted during the 1950s into a program for strengthening the central cities against suburban competition.[18]

As the largest federal grant-in-aid program available to the cities, urban renewal was bound to attract critical attention. By the late 1950s, several studies had begun, and the program was in sufficient use around the country to generate a mass of impressionistic observations. The critics—particularly those who subscribed to the early objectives of slum clearance—were shocked and angry with what they found. In essence, the cities were using urban renewal to refurbish the central business district, build housing for middle- and upper-income families, and bolster their property tax base. In the pursuit of such high-sounding objectives as saving the central city and revitalizing old neighborhoods, they were evicting the poor and doing little to relocate them. The intended beneficiaries of the program had become its victims ("refugees from civic progress"), while the actual beneficiaries were real estate developers, affluent residents of the new housing, and businesses located in new office space.

The issues raised by urban renewal figured importantly in the subsequent formulation of the Model Cities Program. Three points were of greatest relevance: (1) the choice of renewal project areas, (2) the impact of renewal activities on the city's housing supply, and (3) the attention given to the problems of the poor.

1. In deciding where to locate urban renewal projects, the cities were subject to conflicting pressures. Legally, they were required to select only areas that were "blighted," although there was no precise way to define or measure blight. But they also had to find sites that would attract private investors after the land had been cleared and made available for rebuilding. In city after city, the second consideration seemed to govern the choice of project areas. Local authorities often avoided the worst slum areas and instead designated neighborhoods that were marginal in quality but particularly well located for new and expensive housing—"the blight that's right," as Charles Abrams put it. In one of the early critical articles to appear, Staughton Lynd wrote:

We have come a long way from the intention of Senator Wagner when we permit

---

[18] For a definitive account of the early objectives and later transformation of urban renewal, see U.S. National Commission on Urban Problems, *Building the American City* (Washington, D.C.: U.S. Government Printing Office, 1968), pp. 152-169.

the businessman to build on a site which does not decrease the slums; pick up the tab for most of his land cost with taxpayers' money . . . ; and then let him charge up to $75-100 per room per month. Calling this "urban renewal" is just putting a fast buck between glossy covers.[19]

2. Because urban renewal projects cleared blighted neighborhoods and rebuilt them with middle- and upper-income housing, the program inevitably took more low-income housing off the market than it replaced. Further, because long delays were typical of the renewal process, many cleared sites remained vacant for years. As a result, the total impact was to reduce the housing supply in cities making use of the program. From 1949 through 1963, urban renewal demolished the housing of 177,000 families and another 66,000 single individuals, most of them poor and most of them black. During this period only 48,000 new housing units were completed in renewal projects, and another 18,000 were under construction; of this total, some 20,000 were low-rent public housing. [20] Scott Greer summarized the results aptly in the opening sentence of his book on urban renewal: "At a cost of more than three billion dollars the Urban Renewal Agency . . . has succeeded in materially reducing the supply of low-cost housing in American cities."[21]

3. Urban renewal demonstrated clearly that city governments gave low priority to the needs of the poor who were affected by their civic improvement programs. After taking over their neighborhoods for the benefit of others, the cities gave only belated and inadequate attention to the problem of finding decent relocation housing for the former residents. Lewis Mumford, who for years had advocated government programs to improve slum conditions, recognized that urban renewal was a betrayal of the reformers' hopes.

In the name of slum clearance, many quarters of Greater New York that would still have been decently habitable with a modest expenditure of capital have been razed, and their inhabitants, along with the shopkeepers and tavern keepers who served them, have been booted out, to resettle in even slummier quarters.[22]

[19] Staughton Lynd, "Urban Renewal—For Whom?" *Commentary*, Vol. 31 (January 1961), p. 36.
[20] U.S. Advisory Commission on Intergovernmental Relations, *Relocation: Unequal Treatment of People and Businesses Displaced by Governments* (Washington, D.C., 1965), p. 24; William L. Slayton, Commissioner, Urban Renewal Administration, Statement in U.S. Congress, House Subcommittee on Housing, *Hearings: Urban Renewal*, 88th Cong., 1st Sess. 1963, pp. 421, 428.
[21] Scott Greer, *Urban Renewal and American Cities* (Indianapolis: Bobbs-Merrill, 1965), p. 3.
[22] Lewis Mumford, "The Sky Line: Mother Jacobs' Home Remedies," *The New Yorker*, December 1, 1962, p. 148.

Social psychologist Marc Fried studied the aftermath of a 1958 clearance project in Boston's West End and found that half the displaced residents suffered from serious grief reactions and depression as much as two years later. Fried's research team also discovered that the city authorities covered their tracks: they reported to Washington that only 2 percent of the families had been relocated in physically substandard housing; yet Fried's independent survey revealed a figure of 25 percent.[23] A series of investigations by the General Accounting Office turned up numerous other instances of local evasion of federal relocation regulations and dishonest reporting of the results.[24] Less than one percent of the federal expenditures on renewal went for relocation expenses; local renewal officials viewed relocation as an incidental obstacle in a program whose primary goals had little to do with helping the slum resident.

Critical books and articles appeared in profusion in the early 1960s. Conservative critics objected to federal intervention in the cities, liberals to the Robin Hood in-reverse character of the program. To Martin Anderson, a critic from the right, urban renewal was "the federal bulldozer"; a review of Anderson's book by Nathan Glazer, a disappointed liberal, termed it "the asphalt bungle." [25] Some of the publications were balanced in their appraisal, others took extreme positions; some simply proposed reforms in the urban renewal program, others more radical alternatives.[26] Despite the varying viewpoints and uneven quality of the critical literature, it had a marked impact in persuading urban experts, elected officials, and the public that whatever the virtues of renewal, it was imposing great hardships on the urban poor.

The mounting criticism of urban renewal did not, however, create a consensus in professional circles. At the annual conferences of city planners, housing officials, and public administrators, the critics of renewal were in a small minority. Spokesmen for the professional societies as well as the Urban Renewal Administration repeatedly defended the program and did their best to rebut the hostile

---

[23] Chester Hartman, "The Housing of Relocated Families," *Journal of the American Institute of Planners*, Vol. 30 (November 1964), pp. 266-286.

[24] See Chester W. Hartman, "Rejoinder by the Author," *Journal of the American Institute of Planners*, Vol. 31 (November 1965), pp. 340-344.

[25] Nathan Glazer. "The Asphalt Bungle," *New York Herald Tribune Book Week*, January 3, 1965, p. 1.

[26] Critical works published at this time included Charles Abrams, *The City Is the Frontier* (New York: Harper & Row, 1965); Martin Anderson, *The Federal Bulldozer* (Cambridge, Mass.: M.I.T. Press, 1964); Bernard J. Frieden, *The Future of Old Neighborhoods* (Cambridge, Mass.: M.I.T. Press, 1964); Greer, *Urban Renewal and American Cities;* Jane Jacobs, *The Death and Life of Great American Cities* (New York: Random House, 1961); James Q. Wilson, ed., *Urban Renewal: The Record and the Controversy* (Cambridge, Mass.: M.I.T. Press, 1966).

books and articles. Renewal became more controversial than it was previously, but it continued to win widespread support and growing Congressional appropriations. Only as recently as 1970 did the Assistant Secretary of HUD responsible for the renewal program concede that the allegations of the early 1960s had had some merit and that even after years of effort to reform the earlier abuses, local agencies were still not living up to their responsibilities. Norman V. Watson, then Acting Assistant Secretary for Renewal and Housing Management, spoke to a conference of the National Association of Housing and Redevelopment Officials:

> It has often been said by our critics that we have been unresponsive to the relocation needs of project residents. It has been said, for example, that urban renewal is nothing more than Negro removal. It has been said that we consider relocation as no more than a hurdle which must be overcome to implement the urban renewal plan, and that we pay scant attention to relocation practices. We have been accused of violating the law and of contravening our own administrative regulations. And today we are being called "legal lawbreakers".
>
> It is time to be honest with each other and to admit that there is some validity to these allegations.[27]

Speaking of federal-local relations in the program, Secretary Watson urged the local administrators to stop dishonest reporting:

> We should not have to look continually over your shoulder to check the accuracy of your data. We should not have to act as a full time watchdog over your displacement activities. . . .
> When you prepare an urban renewal application, you should be honest about your relocation submission. . . .
> When, during the course of project execution, you find there are not adequate rehousing resources, you should admit it honestly. You should immediately restructure your project activities.[28]

In the early 1960s, federal officials were not prepared to agree with the critics of urban renewal. Nevertheless, a close look at the operation of this program shook the faith of many urbanists that the "public interest" was being well served by existing programs to rebuild the central cities. The public interest turned out to be a handful of very special interests, as Raymond Vernon had suggested, with the poor who lived in the central cities conspicuously left out. A few city planners began to urge that urban development plans be drawn up on

[27] Norman V. Watson, Acting Assistant Secretary for Renewal and Housing Management, Department of Housing and Urban Development, "Urban Renewal and the Relocation Process," remarks prepared for delivery at the Conference of the National Association of Housing and Redevelopment Officials, Sun Valley, Idaho, September 24, 1970.
[28] Ibid.

behalf of minority residents and of neighborhood groups threatened by renewal; these would be prepared in a spirit of advocacy and challenge to the official city plans, which presumed to represent the interests of all groups but in fact did not.[29] To many urban experts, the renewal experience was evidence that city government policies, if left unchecked, would continue to work to the disadvantage of the poor and minorities.

Rediscovering the Poor

While the analysts of urban development were pondering the discovery that urban renewal had boomeranged badly, other events were beginning to demonstrate the feasibility of public programs focused more directly on meeting the needs of the urban poor. During the 1950s, when city governments first began to turn urban renewal to their own purposes, the Ford Foundation embarked on its own very different approach toward the needs of slum residents. Staff members of the Foundation's Public Affairs Department were convinced that programs of physical renewal would not be sufficient to cope with the serious social problems of the central cities, and they also sensed that the federal government, under the Eisenhower Administration, was unlikely to attempt anything more ambitious.

They started with a series of grants to big-city school systems to fund innovative activities in slum neighborhoods, but the staff and their consultants were also interested in broader approaches to the human problems of these "gray areas." Beginning in 1961, the Foundation made sizable grants to city governments and independent social action agencies in Oakland, New Haven, Philadelphia, Boston, and Washington, and to a statewide agency, the North Carolina Fund. These six grants constituted the Ford Foundation's "gray areas program." In addition, the Foundation contributed to a similar project in lower Manhattan, Mobilization for Youth. All the projects directed their activities toward the general social environment of depressed neighborhoods, but they had a special focus on the problems of youth.[30]

[29] See Paul Davidoff, "Advocacy and Pluralism in Planning," *Journal of the American Institute of Planners*, Vol. 31 (November 1965), pp. 331-338; and Bernard J. Frieden, "Toward Equality of Urban Opportunity," *Journal of the American Institute of Planners*, Vol. 31 (November 1965), pp. 320-330.

[30] The most complete and incisive analysis of the gray areas projects, as well as similar projects sponsored by the President's Committee on Juvenile Delinquency and Youth Crime, is in Peter Marris and Martin Rein, *Dilemmas of Social Reform* (Chicago: Aldine Publishing Co., 1973), from which most of the present discussion is drawn.

Soon after John F. Kennedy's inauguration in 1961, the interest of the President and of Attorney General Robert Kennedy in youth and poverty led to the establishment by executive order of the President's Committee on Juvenile Delinquency and Youth Crime. Robert Kennedy chaired the Committee, whose members also included the Secretaries of Labor and of Health, Education, and Welfare. Their mandate was to review and coordinate federal activities bearing on juvenile delinquency and to stimulate experimentation and innovation in this field. Later that year, Congress enacted the Administration's Juvenile Delinquency and Youth Offenses Control Act of 1961, which authorized grants for demonstrations, research, and training as outlined in the Committee's recommendations. Community agencies responded quickly with proposals for funding. By the beginning of 1965, the Office of Juvenile Delinquency awarded $10 million to sixteen demonstration projects, including four that were also in the Ford Foundation's gray areas program. The Ford Foundation by then had committed some $20 million to experimental community projects.

The Ford Foundation and the President's Committee had many policies in common which shaped the projects they supported. Both focused on changing the institutions that affected slum residents and attempted to integrate their operations. Both decided to concentrate their resources in a few selected projects that they hoped would serve as demonstrations of new approaches. Both tried to build local constituencies by involving recognized leadership as well as poverty residents in planning their projects; both introduced a broad range of activities—in education, vocational training, youth employment services, legal aid, and community service centers.[31] These features had substantial influence on later antipoverty efforts, including the Model Cities Program.

The theory underlying these activities was that the causes of poverty are complex, circular, and self-perpetuating. As Marris and Rein have reconstructed these assumptions, they held that the children of the poor started school at a disadvantage, and their parents could give them little help when they fell behind their classmates. Because they performed poorly, school became a painful experience, and they dropped out before finishing. Without adequate education or confidence in themselves, they were only marginally employable. Some turned to crime; most remained poor. Without the ability to hold a decent job or earn a reasonable income, the young men lacked self-respect and were unable to become responsible husbands or fathers. Their children, in turn, suffered from

[31] Ibid., p. 24.

broken homes and a disadvantaged family life, which continued the cycle of poverty to the next generation.

If this theory was correct, it justified a broad range of interventions—in the schools, the employment system, the services that might strengthen family life. The interdependence of many aspects of poverty argued strongly for coordinated efforts among the public and private agencies affecting the poor; yet these agencies seemed to be independent in their actions and provincial in their views. Further, they were conservative in practice, failing to recognize changes in social conditions. Thus the planners of these programs emphasized the importance of innovative changes.[32]

Despite the impressive qualities of these new programs, their actual achievements, both in the neighborhoods where they operated and in their function as national demonstrations, appear to have been limited. Nevertheless, they demonstrated clearly to those who kept in touch with events that most of their starting assumptions were well founded. Sanford Kravitz, a social welfare professional involved in the design and early operation of the Office of Economic Opportunity's (OEO's) Community Action Program, concluded that both the gray areas and the juvenile delinquency projects drew national attention to the failures of the conventional services and programs constituting society's attempt to help the urban poor.

They demonstrated that many private agency "welfare" programs were not reaching the poor at all; of those that did, many offered services that were inappropriate. Services oriented toward the poor were typically fragmented and unrelated; each specialty worked without awareness of any related fields or of efforts to interlock. Professionals and community leaders alike had little realistic understanding of the problems poor people faced. Political leaders had minimal involvement in the decisions of voluntary social welfare agencies, and the poor themselves had little to do with planning or implementing the programs, which were managed by professionals and community leaders.[33]

OEO and Community Action

The programs of the Ford Foundation and the President's Committee also served a different purpose: they heightened public awareness that poverty remained a serious problem in the United States, and they also showed that there were new

[32] Ibid., pp. 39-41.
[33] Sanford Kravitz, "The Community Action Program—Past, Present, and Its Future?" in James L. Sundquist, ed., *On Fighting Poverty* (New York: Basic Books, 1969), pp. 56-57.

ideas in the air about how to deal with it. In this respect, they reinforced many other factors that were also moving the climate of opinion in the same direction: the growth of the civil rights movement, John F. Kennedy's exposure to rural poverty during the 1960 primary in West Virginia, the wide impact of Michael Harrington's *The Other America* and John Kenneth Galbraith's *The Affluent Society*.

Probably most important was President Kennedy's election promise that he would search for federal initiatives to get the country moving again. During a review of economic conditions in December 1962, President Kennedy told the chairman of his Council of Economic Advisers, Walter Heller, that he wanted to go beyond past accomplishments. He asked for facts and figures on the things still to be done: "For example, what about the poverty problem in the United States?" At the same time, Kennedy asked for copies of *The Other America* and for another recent study of poverty by Leon Keyserling.[34]

Heller assigned members of his staff to consider what might constitute a practical antipoverty program. By October 1963, the President was asking him to prepare proposals for action in 1964, and three days before his assassination Kennedy reiterated his intention of including antipoverty measures in the 1964 legislative program. The day after the assassination, President Johnson asked Heller to keep moving ahead with these proposals.[35]

The Council of Economic Advisers and the Bureau of the Budget considered many ideas as they worked in haste late in 1963. David Hackett, of the President's Committee on Juvenile Delinquency and Youth Crime, suggested that they utilize community organizations of the sort his committee had been funding. William Cannon of the Budget Bureau was quick to pick up the concepts as well as the philosophy of the President's Committee. He proposed the selection of ten demonstration areas and establishment of a development corporation in each. With federal funds the corporation would organize a wide range of programs and provide the coordinating mechanism for them. Among its several advantages, this proposal met a criterion advanced by Charles L. Schultze, then Assistant Budget Director, that resources should be concentrated geographically for maximum effectiveness rather than spread thinly across the country. Cannon's idea was welcomed with enthusiasm; it was named "community action,"

---

[34] James L. Sundquist, "Origins of the War on Poverty," in Sundquist, ed., *On Fighting Poverty*, p. 7.
[35] Ibid., pp. 20-21.

and in a pattern that foreshadowed the model cities experience, it was quickly transformed from ten demonstration areas into a national program.[36]

When President Johnson named Sargent Shriver to head his task force on the War on Poverty in February 1964, the leadership passed from the Council of Economic Advisers and the Budget Bureau to a more diverse group of program planners. The influence of the juvenile delinquency programs persisted, however, in continued support for a Community Action Program. As it came to be developed by the Shriver task force, this program had three principles in common with the earlier gray areas and juvenile delinquency projects. First, it proposed to redirect and coordinate the resources of government to concentrate on the most pressing social needs. Second, it sought to explore innovative ways of meeting these needs. Third, the people to be helped were to determine the needs and contribute to the planning.[37]

These principles made good sense to many people who had diagnosed the problems of poverty and the weaknesses of past approaches. Yet to some in government, the principle of coordination had an independent appeal, as noted earlier in this chapter. Daniel P. Moynihan attributed the support of the Budget Bureau for this feature of community action to its own deep concern with giving order and direction to the growing number of separate domestic programs:

The job of the Bureau of the Budget is to make the system work. "Coordination" is the ever-invoked, but never-achieved ideal: a system that would work with harmony and efficiency, that would protect the interests of the President, carry out the intent of Congress, and, if possible, get the most for the taxpayer's dollar. . . . True coordination, especially at the pinnacle of the system in Washington, is difficult if not impossible. . . . It would appear that in the community action agency a number of the leading budget examiners in the Bureau perceived the alluring, intoxicating possibility of doing it from the *bottom*.[38]

To the Shriver task force, it was clear that the complex causes of poverty required comprehensive changes in the environment where poor people lived. Changes were needed in employment services, health care, housing conditions, and education. Translated into operational terms, the goal of comprehensiveness required that funds and programs be drawn in from many different and inde-

[36] Ibid., pp. 22-25.
[37] Marris and Rein, *Dilemmas of Social Reform*, p. 240.
[38] Daniel P. Moynihan, *Maximum Feasible Misunderstanding* (New York: Free Press, 1969), pp. 77-78.

pendent federal agencies. Adam Yarmolinsky, deputy director of the task force, was aware of the problems ahead.

All of these programs operated under their own financial stringencies. None was designed specifically to help poor people. How would their resources be allocated between the demands of community-action programs and all the other demands pouring in on them? And what authority or influence would the new OEO have through its coordinating powers to assure that the poor received their fair share?[39]

The question was whether OEO could exert leverage for the poor by means of partisan negotiation alone without the help of strong central direction from the White House. The task force discussed this issue but came to no resolution.

As the antipoverty legislation emerged from the Administration and from Congress, community action represented only one thrust among several, including the Job Corps, work-training programs, special rural programs, and Volunteers in Service to America (VISTA). Yet community action was one of the most distinctive and original features of the War on Poverty. Certainly it had the clearest relevance for the subsequent design of the Model Cities Program.

The Economic Opportunity Act became law on August 20, 1964. The Community Action Program grew quickly. By September 1965, OEO had funded more than 500 Community Action Agencies across the country, with federal expenditures rising from $237 million in fiscal 1965 to $628 million in fiscal 1966.[40] Despite this rapid start, the program soon ran into trouble. Jack Conway, its first director, tried to strike a balance among the three local interest groups that had to be involved in community action: public officials, private agencies, and representatives of the poor. In his view, local programs were not to become the tools of city hall, although they needed effective support from elected officials.[41] But the three groups could not be reconciled, and bitter controversies erupted wherever the mayors viewed community action agencies as mobilizers of the poor against city hall.

As early as the spring of 1965, a group of mayors led by Mayor Daley of Chicago met with Vice President Humphrey to register their protests. The President

[39] Adam Yarmolinsky, "The Beginnings of OEO," in Sundquist, ed., *On Fighting Poverty*, p. 48.
[40] U.S. Advisory Commission on Intergovernmental Relations, *Intergovernmental Relations in the Poverty Program* (Washington, D.C.: U.S. Government Printing Office, 1966), p. 28; Sar A. Levitan, *The Great Society's Poor Law* (Baltimore: Johns Hopkins Press, 1969), p. 123.
[41] John G. Wofford, "The Politics of Local Responsibility," in Sandquist, ed., *On Fighting Poverty*, p. 77.

and Vice President sided with the mayors, and the Budget Bureau soon passed the word to OEO to reduce the role of the poor in policy making. With domestic political troubles on the increase, President Johnson's interest in community action began to cool. In September, he cut deeply into the poverty program's budget request and at about the same time appointed a federal team to investigate and straighten out the management of OEO.[42]

The Political Context: 1965

What had been established in the progression from gray areas programs through juvenile delinquency projects through community action which could guide the designers of subsequent urban programs? Despite the mayors' early complaints about OEO, it was clear that the political environment had changed strikingly between 1960 and 1965. Before 1960, poverty was simply not a direct and open subject of national political concern. People who formulated programs to aid the poor had to do so in the name of other and more politically attractive causes, such as reviving the economy, preventing juvenile delinquency (which would in time threaten the rest of society), or rebuilding the central cities.

By 1965, the Administration and the Congress were willing to enact legislation and appropriate money for the open purpose of reducing poverty in the United States. Further, numerous experts appeared to have acquired a stock of plausible, but still unproved, ideas on how to proceed. Yet the early experience with community action also indicated the need for caution. If the War on Poverty was not organized with great care, the new political support that had just emerged might disappear abruptly.

At the same time, pressure was mounting to attend to the problems of black neighborhoods in the cities, where disproportionate numbers of the poor were concentrated. Between 1963 and 1965, the civil rights movement was turning from the problems of segregation in the South to the living conditions of black residents in the cities of the North. And the pattern of summer riots was shifting ominously from the South to the North.

In 1963, the most serious conflicts took place in Birmingham; but there were also disorders in Cambridge (Maryland), Chicago, and Philadelphia. By 1964, the list of cities experiencing racial violence was considerably longer: Cleveland, New York, Rochester, Jersey City, Elizabeth, Paterson, Chicago, and Philadelphia.

[42] Moynihan, *Maximum Feasible Misunderstanding*, pp. 144-145; Robert A. Levine, *The Poor Ye Need Not Have with You* (Cambridge, Mass.: M.I.T. Press, 1970), pp. 62-63.

During 1965, civil rights demonstrations led to violence in the southern communities of Selma, Alabama, and Bogalusa, Louisiana. But in August, the worst riot in the United States since the Detroit riots of 1943 erupted in the Watts area of Los Angeles. The police were soon overwhelmed and had to ask for help from the National Guard. After several days of fighting, 34 people were dead, hundreds injured, and 4,000 arrested.[43]

Whether ideas or events are more potent in shaping federal policy is a question that gave rise to some debate during the 1960s. There may be no conclusive answer, but ideas and events were mutually reinforcing at that time. Analysts of urban affairs gave fresh recognition to the unsolved problems of poverty and race in the cities and studied ways of intervening. Simultaneously, the increasing outbreaks of civil disorder were a sign of growing anger and frustration with poverty and discrimination. To respond to the needs of the poor and the blacks was no longer a matter of simple justice. To ignore them threatened to tear apart the fragile social fabric that was holding the cities together.

Plans for urban reform were irrelevant to the newly perceived problems of the mid-1960s if they dealt only with civic improvement and developmental efficiency. They had to face up to issues of racial and economic inequities as a first priority. Urban renewal, which lacked any commitment to a redistribution of resources or power, was no answer. Besides, the black and the poor were its most conspicuous victims.

The War on Poverty, especially the Community Action Program, was more in keeping with the new climate of informed opinion. At the same time, rising protest in the black communities reinforced the need for this program. But its strategies of implementation had not yet passed the tests either of political feasibility or of relevance to its intended clients. Without strong central direction, which could come only from the White House, the intent of community action to coordinate and focus federal resources on the problems of poverty might well fail. Further, the mandate of community action to organize and mobilize the poor had already begun to undermine the political coalition needed to make coordination work through a process of partisan negotiation.

Thus, despite the intellectual redefinition of the urban problem, and despite the visible evidence of a need for more decisive action in the cities, the search for an effective policy had to continue.

[43] U.S. National Advisory Commission on Civil Disorders, *Report* (Washington, D.C.: U.S. Government Printing Office, 1968), pp. 19-20.

Chapter 3
From Task Force to Legislation

By 1965, the climate was ripe for further federal action to meet the recognized needs of the central city poor and minority groups. An activist President had just been elected in his own right by a landslide vote, with an exceptionally large majority behind him in Congress. President Johnson had announced the beginning of the War on Poverty early in 1964, and soon afterward Congress had created the Office of Economic Opportunity to lead it. By the summer of 1965, OEO was already in some trouble; but whether or not OEO faltered, the President wanted to respond to the widely perceived "crisis of the cities" in other ways, as well.

Although the War on Poverty set out to include a very broad scope of operations, it did not give much attention to the physical environment of cities: housing, community facilities, and transportation systems. Its ideas and program content came primarily from fields such as education, manpower training, community organization, and social welfare. In 1965, Congress established the Department of Housing and Urban Development, which was designed to pull together the federal programs concerned with the environment of cities. How the new department would be organized, and what it would do beyond operating the existing federal programs, remained to be determined. The newness of the agency and the uncertainty of its mandate opened the possibility that, like OEO, it would give special recognition to the poverty groups concentrated in the central cities.

President Johnson's desire to have a major new housing program, coupled with the practice of going outside the established bureaucracies for legislative ideas, led him to appoint a task force in the fall of 1965 to advise on organization and programs for the new department. The task force recognized its unusual opportunity to redirect federal urban programs and considered at length ways of bringing the social concerns of the War on Poverty into the Department of Housing and Urban Development.

Drawing on ideas that were current at the time, the task force came up with a program for the President. It had much in common with community action and its predecessors, but it also incorporated the less controversial objectives of reform and coordination of the federal grant-in-aid system. Besides drawing from the two separate agendas of helping the poor and coordinating federal programs, the task force made an effort to build in safeguards against the abuses of urban renewal.

The task force's main proposal—the Model Cities Program—was an imaginative advance over earlier thinking, but it was faulty in numerous ways that will emerge later in this analysis. The underlying problem, however, was not in the technicalities of program design. It was, rather, a domestic counterpart of the same illusions that led the Johnson Administration deeper and deeper into the tragedy of Vietnam. Members of the task force, in common with many of their contemporaries, had a naïve belief in the power of the President to reshape not only the federal government but the world outside Washington. They counted heavily on a sustained White House commitment to social reform and placed great faith in the ability of rational planning to find solutions to the problems of the cities. They also accepted White House assurances that substantial new funds would be available for domestic programs, despite the competing claims of the Vietnam War. If national recognition of the legitimacy of action against poverty was not sufficient in itself to win over political opposition, control the federal bureaucracy, and move the cities to redress the inequities of the past, the President himself could step in and take charge. The stubborn facts of interest group politics, limited budgets, bureaucratic resistance to change, and the extreme pluralism of American society faded away before the image of a well-conceived federal blueprint for the slums, backed by a President with enormous power.

This view of the world could not be sustained very long. Even the course of Congressional debate and enactment of the legislation began to reveal the limits of the power of the Chief Executive. Congress accepted the program only after a long struggle and only after reshaping it to protect the needs of interest group politics. Reactions in Congress gave early signals that the Model Cities Program was unlikely to achieve the extensive federal reform that its designers had in mind, and thus foreshadowed the difficult problems of implementation that were to emerge later.

The Task Force on Urban Problems

Both the Kennedy and Johnson Administrations made extensive use of task forces to recruit help from outside government in formulating their legislative programs. President Johnson was convinced that he could not rely on federal officials alone to produce fresh ideas. "The bureaucracy," he wrote, ". . . is too preoccupied with day-to-day operations, and there is strong bureaucratic inertia dedicated to preserving the status quo. . . . Moreover, the cumbersome organization of government is simply not equipped to solve complex problems that cut across departmental jurisdictions."[1]

[1] Lyndon B. Johnson, *The Vantage Point* (New York: Popular Library, 1971), pp. 326-327.

Late in 1965, President Johnson told his Special Assistant Joseph A. Califano that he wanted a big, imaginative housing program, and that the ideas of federal housing officials were not good enough. Califano's assignment, therefore, was to organize a task force.[2] The President wanted his task forces to have "a broad balance of thinkers and doers, . . . representative groups that would be familiar with all the elements of the special areas assigned to them, so that we could look at our problems whole."[3] In September, he selected Robert Wood, head of the Political Science Department at M.I.T., to chair the new Task Force on Urban Problems. Califano, in consultation with Wood, put together a diverse list of members: Kermit Gordon, President of the Brookings Institution, who had recently served as Director of the Bureau of the Budget; Charles Haar, a professor at the Harvard Law School and an expert on land use law; Edgar Kaiser, Chairman of Kaiser Industries; William Rafsky, an urban renewal administrator who had been development coordinator for Philadelphia; Walter Reuther, President of the United Auto Workers; and Whitney Young, Executive Director of the National Urban League. To represent still other perspectives, President Johnson personally added railway executive Ben W. Heineman and Senator Abraham Ribicoff.[4] White House Special Counsel Harry McPherson was assigned to work closely with the task force as the President's liaison. The membership was in keeping with President Johnson's desire for broad balance and representation, with one conspicuous exception. None of the members represented the federal bureaucracy itself or had had much personal experience with its internal administration. Kermit Gordon had seen the bureaucracy from the special viewpoint of the Budget Bureau, as had Wood himself years before as a staff member of the Budget Bureau. Senator Ribicoff was the best qualified in this respect, because he had served as Secretary of Health, Education, and Welfare; but he was only an occasional participant in the work of the group.

The task force began its work in October 1965 with a mandate to recommend new programs for the Department of Housing and Urban Development; later the assignment was expanded to include recommending an organization plan for the new Department. Like other Johnson task forces at the time, it worked in great secrecy, and it deliberately avoided contact with federal agencies in its field of concern. The White House made provision for a small full-time staff to be hired from outside the federal government, as well as funds for additional consultants. Wood promptly hired Chester Rapkin, a housing specialist and professor of city

---

[2] Patrick Anderson, *The Presidents' Men* (Garden City, N.Y.: Doubleday, 1968), p. 369.
[3] Johnson, *The Vantage Point*, p. 327.
[4] Interview with Robert Wood, July 3, 1974.

planning at the University of Pennsylvania, as staff director. Rapkin assembled a team of five, opened an unmarked office in the Federal Maritime Commission building, and began to commission consultants to write special papers. Even with these resources, which were exceptional among White House task forces, there was little time for independent studies or careful assessment of past experience. The final report was due before the end of the year.

The White House gave definite direction to the task force's deliberations. The top priority, President Johnson wrote, was "to attack the problem of rebuilding the slums."[5] Joseph Califano indicated special interest in two ideas: to have major demonstrations in the rebuilding of entire neighborhoods, and to make federal funds available to the cities in the form of block grants that could be spent flexibly and unhindered by normal federal grant-in-aid restrictions.

Both these ideas were in vogue among professionals in urban affairs. The demonstration concept, as noted earlier, was prominent in the development of the Ford Foundation gray areas program and the projects of the President's Committee on Juvenile Delinquency and Youth Crime. It also came to the task force through a more direct route. Robert Wood had chaired a similar White House task force in 1964. In the final report he had included a proposal submitted to the group by Leonard Duhl and Antonia Chayes of the National Institute of Mental Health. Their memorandum, "Demonstration Cities," proposed the selection of three major cities for comprehensive experiments in the rebuilding of slums. All federal agencies with suitable programs would be asked to join in preparing plans for social and environmental improvement, and they would then concentrate their resources to carry them out. The 1964 task force did not actually endorse this proposal, but one of its members, Mayor Jerome Cavanagh of Detroit, later showed it to Walter Reuther. Together they prepared a proposal, entitled "Detroit, a Demonstration City," which they discussed with Robert Weaver, then Administrator of the Housing and Home Finance Agency, and with President Johnson. The President and his staff were sufficiently interested in the idea to urge the new task force to consider it further.[6]

The White House staff communicated something else of even greater importance to the task force: a sense of President Johnson's determination to deal decisively with the problems of the cities and a sense of the power he could bring to bear. Like many others who saw Lyndon Johnson in action, his aides

---

[5] Johnson, *The Vantage Point*, p. 330.
[6] Edward C. Banfield, "Making a New Federal Program: Model Cities, 1964-68," in Allan P. Sindler, ed., *Policy and Politics in America* (Boston: Little, Brown, 1973), pp. 129-131.

regarded him with awe. David Halberstam caught the mood well when he wrote: "He was a man of primal force. . . . His genes were seemingly larger and more demanding than those of other men; he dominated other men, leaning on them, sensing that every man had his price or his breaking point." Yet in 1965 this was a benevolent force, not one to be feared: "His ability to drive men to a program and policy beyond what they themselves considered wise was considered a national asset, since the men he was manipulating were largely old tired conservative Southern congressmen who headed committees and thus blocked progress. A powerful Presidency was still considered very desirable in those days; the problem was seen as too much power in the Congress and too little in the executive branch. . . ."[7]

Two brief examples illustrate the attitudes of the White House staff. At an early task force meeting in the White House, members asked whether they should consider the prospects for Congressional acceptance when they recommended new programs. Presidential aide Jack Valenti brushed aside any doubts on political feasibility, urging the task force to come forward with its best ideas and "leave the driving to us." Later, task force members began to wonder whether, in view of the escalating war in Vietnam, funds would be available for the massive urban program the President seemed to want. Wood reassured them by reporting what the President had said at a dinner in July 1965, organized for members of the 1964 task forces. In Lyndon Johnson's view, Roosevelt's New Deal was never completed because it ground to a halt on the battlefields of World War II; he was absolutely determined that his Great Society was not going to be chewed up on the battlefields of Vietnam. Together with other, less expert citizens, the task force members believed these things and set aside their doubts.

Accounting for Past Failures
Because federal programs had been multiplying in the early 1960s, and yet the cries of discontent from the cities had become louder all the time, anyone proposing new programs had first to explain why the old ones were not producing better results. Several members of the task force believed that the programs and the bureaucracy that HUD was about to take over were oriented excessively to commercial real estate considerations and showed too little sensitivity to social issues.

Strong backing for this view came from Jack Conway, who had become an

[7] David Halberstam, *The Best and the Brightest* (Greenwich, Conn.: Fawcett Crest, 1973), pp. 529, 369.

active participant in the task force proceedings. Conway was a former aide to Walter Reuther, who introduced him into the task force as an adviser. Since leaving the UAW, Conway had first been Deputy Administrator of the Housing and Home Finance Agency and then became director of OEO's Community Action Program (CAP). Conway described the bureaucracy of the Federal Housing Administration, which would constitute by far the largest and most influential branch of the new HUD, as "FHA commercials." He and Reuther took the lead in arguing that the new department would have to have a strong social orientation if urban development programs were to become more effective in coping with problems of the central city. To establish this sense of social purpose, they contended, HUD would need major programs directed at the urban poor, and these programs would have to be comprehensive and not rely solely on "brick-and-mortar" solutions.

Starting with this premise, Reuther and Conway proposed that the Community Action Program be transferred from OEO to HUD. At an early task force meeting they had a pointed exchange on this issue with Kermit Gordon. Gordon argued that the CAP was a national and not an urban program. It was intended to focus on the factors that make people chronically poor, and these factors fell mainly in areas that were the concern of the Department of Health, Education, and Welfare. The Community Action Program was intended to focus the services from several federal departments on the problems of poverty, and about 80 percent of the resources it needed came from HEW. Why put it in HUD, Gordon asked, rather than HEW, which supplied the tools? To put the CAP in a more parochial department—and Gordon conceived of HUD's concerns as limited to physical development—would run the risk of distorting the program, interfering with a comprehensive attack on poverty, and overemphasizing HUD's own programs within it.

Reuther and Conway countered that the CAP was primarily an urban program, with about 80 percent of its funds going to the cities. In order to improve overall living conditions in the cities, it was necessary, they asserted, to tie in housing with CAP's social measures. The two also argued the need to develop participation and leadership in the core communities and maintained that the agency best able to do this was the one with responsibility for housing and relocation. The Department of Health, Education, and Welfare, they noted further, worked through the states and not directly with local communities. The new Department of Housing and Urban Development, with its broad focus on the cities, would be better equipped to proceed with the Community Action Programs.

Jack Conway further distinguished the CAP from other OEO programs. The others, such as the Job Corps and VISTA, were properly delegated to operating departments. But the CAP was not a program in the same sense: it was rather a process for mobilizing resources and coordinating other programs. It would give the new HUD Secretary precisely the coordination role he needed. William Rafsky supported this position; he pointed out that the CAP dealt with problems that were concentrated in special local areas and therefore needed the skills of people who knew slum neighborhoods and how to deal with them.

In general, the task force reached its decisions on the basis of consensus, or a sense of the meeting as summarized by its chairman, Robert Wood. Only rarely was there unanimity, but there was enough agreement to permit the group to make recommendations. In this instance, most members endorsed the position that Reuther and Conway had developed, primarily because they believed the CAP would force HUD to be attentive to social purposes. Although two members notified Wood in writing of their dissent, the task force's first report to the White House, on an organization plan for the new department, recommended transferring the CAP to HUD on the basis of a rationale that had more to do with HUD than with the CAP.

Community Action Programs . . . deal directly with the social environment of the City. Such programs could and would add important "human" dimensions to a Department that would otherwise be excessively preoccupied with the physical environment alone. Moreover, the Department with its funds, programs, and new status would lend needed strength and protection to the Community Action Programs.

. . . OEO programs must soon find permanent homes in Executive Departments. A number already have. In the judgment of the task force, the Community Action Programs are vital to the performance of the New Department's total responsibilities and should be transferred to it.[8]

The White House staff soon notified Wood that this transfer was unlikely. (Wood learned later that President Johnson made a point of not relieving any of President Kennedy's appointees of their responsibilities. Sargent Shriver, as head of OEO, was one of Kennedy's most prominent appointees.) The task force, however, determined in any event to incorporate some of the basic ideas of the Community Action Program into its own recommendations for HUD. Its diag-

[8] Task Force on Urban Problems, "Department of Housing and Urban Development: Proposed Plan of Organization," December 7, 1965, p. 4. The task force also recommended transferring responsibility for metropolitan transportation planning from the Bureau of Public Roads to HUD, and metropolitan planning responsibility for air and water pollution control and solid waste disposal from other agencies to HUD.

nosis that past failures resulted from insufficient attention being paid to social factors led the task force to have high hopes for what might be achieved through a combination of environmental and social strategies. Thus the task force moved toward recommending very comprehensive programs as a way to avoid past errors.

Several task force members put forward other explanations for the failures of earlier programs. Walter Reuther contended that the underlying problem with urban renewal was that it lacked a large-scale construction program to rehouse the people it displaced; what was needed, therefore, was a massive housing program to complement renewal. Kermit Gordon believed that earlier programs had not been more effective because they did nothing to cope with obsolete practices in the building industry and with obsolete local regulations, particularly restrictive labor practices, building codes, and zoning regulations. His position led to a recommendation for demonstration programs that would permit a waiver of customary regulations within the special project areas. Most task force members believed that the federal programs themselves were overly rigid in their regulations and that a new approach should provide greater flexibility for local government. Because of federal restrictions, the members contended that there were gaps between existing programs—needs for which no federal aids were available—and that the time needed to carry out activities under federal programs was unnecessarily prolonged. These views, too, contributed to the idea of suspending established rules as part of a demonstration program.

The task force also subscribed to the widely held belief, noted earlier, that federal aids were spread too thin to be very effective. There were two key points to this critique: first, that federal aid programs were too small in total size to meet the needs of the cities, and second, that the limited resources available from several different programs were not well coordinated with each other. Out of this critique came recommendations both for an increase in the scale of federal aid and for a more deliberate concentration of resources in selected target areas.

The task force did not give serious attention to another explanation of past failures that some critics of urban renewal were advancing at the time. According to these critics, the objectives of city governments were in conflict with the national purposes of the War on Poverty. The central cities were still striving to meet the needs of the middle class and to protect their residential and commercial tax bases through renewal projects designed to attract middle- and upper-income residents. The cities, these critics held, gave low priority to the poor and thus exacerbated urban social problems. Federal aid resources were admittedly not great, but the cities were not directing them to the advantage of the poor in any case. This line of thinking could have led to a further tightening of federal regulations in order to get cities to align their development programs more closely with national goals.

Because the task force had begun its deliberations with the idea of promoting a limited number of demonstrations, there was, perhaps, no need to question the purposes and motives of city governments in their application of the urban renewal program. Whatever the motives of most cities had been in the past, some of them, surely, would be willing to participate in a new federal program that emphasized the needs of the poor. Indeed, the fact that cities were quick to make use of the OEO programs gave further assurance on this score.

The task force nevertheless proceeded to define the ways in which it intended to depart from the programs of the past. The final report summarized its various criticisms of previous programs by emphasizing the points of difference in its own proposals:

Thus the demonstration program differs sharply from the present package of programs such as urban renewal by stressing:
—*massive additions* to the total supply of low and moderate-cost housing, providing decent housing for families now living in substandard conditions,
—a *total approach* combining physical rebuilding with human concerns and social programs,
—*increased flexibility* for local governments to operate outside existing administrative structures and other customary constraints,
—*willingness to change traditional patterns* of building regulation and trade practices.[9]

Proposals for a Demonstration Program
Drawing on the many ideas that the task force had discussed, Wood and Haar prepared a draft report in early December. After a last meeting to review the proposals and incorporate a few changes, they sent a final report to the White House just before Christmas. It proposed a new "demonstration city program" based on three main principles:

—the *concentration* of available and special resources in sufficient magnitude to demonstrate swiftly what qualified urban communities can do and can become.
—the *coordination* of all available talent and aid in a way impossible where

[9] U.S. President's Task Force on Urban Problems, "Proposed Programs for the Department of Housing and Urban Development," December 1965.

assistance is provided across the board and men and money must be spread thin.

—the *mobilization* of local leadership and initiative to assure that the key decisions as to the future of American cities are made by the citizens who live there, and to commit local leadership . . . to a comprehensive attack on urban problems, freed from the constraints that have handicapped past efforts and inflated their costs.[10]

Wood and Haar were well aware of the criticism that cities through urban renewal had pursued objectives inimical to the interests of the poor. They had to find a way of ensuring that cities did not distort the intended priorities of their new program, while still respecting the task force's wish to avoid close federal regulation of city operations. During the course of the task force's work, Lyle Fitch, President of the Institute of Public Administration, had suggested a means for reconciling these two objectives. As a consultant to staff director Chester Rapkin, he submitted a paper entitled "Proposal for a Program of Competitions for 'Best Programs' of Urban Improvement." Fitch argued that the federal government was capable of mobilizing local and private resources in complex undertakings if it defined clear objectives and offered sufficient incentives. Programs such as the space effort and the competition to build a giant electron accelerator combined, in his view, clearly stated objectives with large prizes in the form of federal funds. He also emphasized another feature common to these programs: although the objectives were clearly defined, the means of achieving them were left to be worked out by the participants. His argument pointed to a workable strategy for the new program. If the federal government invited cities to enter a competition for funds, and if it spelled out firm criteria for selecting the winners, it could determine the general nature of local operations without imposing excessive regulations or limiting local flexibility.

This strategy was attractive for still another reason. Many people who took part in the design of federal programs in the early 1960s believed strongly in home-grown approaches to urban problems. In their view, local communities were capable of coming up with ingenious and workable ideas; and Washington should not attempt to impose national solutions. This perspective had been influential in shaping the Community Action Program, which attempted to mobilize and support local initiatives. In presenting the Economic Opportunity Act of 1964 to Congress, the White House cited several stories of local success in helping the poor and claimed there were "countless additional examples of imagina-

[10] Ibid.

tive community programming to expand opportunity and break the cycle of poverty."[11] Many members of the Wood task force also believed that if the federal government encouraged the cities to try new approaches toward the rebuilding of slum neighborhoods, local talent would produce fresh and innovative ideas.

In the final task force report, Wood and Haar proposed a national competition in which all cities, including small ones, would be invited to submit their proposals; the best of these would be selected for federal assistance. They stated their decision not to propose specific program content, but they proceeded to spell out numerous criteria to establish the purposes and general character of the proposals that would be selected.

The demonstration as defined would have to be large enough in its physical and social dimensions to improve entire neighborhoods and have a substantial impact on the total city; it would have to help close the gap between the living conditions of the poor and minorities and those of the rest of the community; it would have to foster local leadership and widespread citizen participation; incorporate measures to reduce construction costs; make major improvements in the physical environment; improve on past relocation practices where relocation proved necessary; establish appropriate administrative mechanisms to bring in both public and private resources and community leadership; provide adequate municipal and private financial resources to complement federal aid; and maintain a predominantly residential character in the area. It would also have to extend for at least five years and provide for significant achievements within the first two years.

The report developed each of these criteria in somewhat greater detail but refrained carefully from prescribing how the cities ought to meet these objectives. The proposed criteria, together with related parts of the report, gave primary emphasis to a focus on poverty neighborhoods, mounting broad programs to improve living conditions for the residents of those neighborhoods, and developing and testing approaches that might later be extended to other cities.

For the cities that submitted the most promising programs in keeping with these objectives—as judged by "a special Presidential commission"—the task force proposed two forms of federal aid. First, they advocated making available "on a priority basis" the full array of existing grants under all relevant federal

[11] U.S. Senate Committee on Labor and Public Welfare, *The War on Poverty: The Economic Opportunity Act of 1964, A Compilation of Materials Relevant to S.2642*, 88th Cong., 2nd Sess., Senate Document No. 86, July 23, 1964, p. 52.

programs in such fields as housing, transportation, education, and welfare. To bring these aids together effectively, the task force proposed assigning a federal coordinator to each participating city. And to increase the flexibility of the existing programs, the task force proposed that their funding be merged in a common account from which the city would be able to draw money as its program required, subject to certification by the federal expediter.

In addition to giving the cities this special priority in the use of existing categorical grants, the task force recommended that federal supplemental funds be made available to cover 80 percent of the remaining costs that could not be met out of other federal programs. The supplemental fund allocations would be subject to a maintenance-of-effort provision to ensure that the cities did not cut back their own expenditures in order to take advantage of the new federal assistance.

This two-part formulation of federal aid offered the distinct advantage of minimizing new federal appropriations. Only the supplemental grants would require new appropriations; the bulk of federal support would come from the large federal aid budget already available under existing programs. Tapping these programs on a priority basis, and providing them for the cities in a coordinated way, represented precisely the sort of grant-in-aid reform that had been advocated earlier by those who believed strongly in the benefits of coordination, for example, the Advisory Commission on Intergovernmental Relations and the Congressional committees that had approved creation of the Department of Housing and Urban Development. The supplemental grants went still further in offering local communities flexible federal funding exempt from the usual restrictions and available for a wide variety of activities. This provision represented an early and major step toward "block grants" or revenue sharing, a concept that was already on the horizon of proposals for federal aid reform in the mid-1960s.

By proposing to focus a combination of federal resources on the needs of poverty neighborhoods, the Wood task force was also drawing inspiration from the concepts underlying the War on Poverty. Although the mechanisms for delivering federal aid came directly from the agenda developed by the critics of the categorical grant-in-aid system, the beneficiaries were to be the newly identified constituency of the urban poor whose problems required a comprehensive and flexible approach. Thus the task force adopted ideas from both agendas of urban reform described in the preceding chapter, and it could hope to attract the support of people who wanted to test innovations in intergovernmental relations as well as those who wanted to address the neglected problems of urban poverty.

In terms of the issues Downs posed in his analysis of bureaucracy, the task force conceived of a very broad set of boundaries for HUD to try to maintain in its relations with other federal agencies. Most task force members were not concerned about an excessive concentration of power either within HUD or within the executive branch. On the contrary, they welcomed this concentration of authority and saw it as the way to deal effectively with the country's urban problems. At the same time, the task force attempted to tackle the difficult combination of problems Lindblom had described: achieving a high degree of coordination among independent agencies while simultaneously shifting the balance of power to redistribute resources to the poor. To do this, they pinned their hopes on central direction as the basis for coordination, with President Johnson pushing the right buttons to accomplish their program. If Lindblom was correct in doubting the effectiveness of central decision making to accomplish basic reforms, the task force's strategy would not carry the program very far.

How Many Cities and How Much Money?

The notion of city demonstrations originally implied the selection of a small number of communities in which governments would be able to suspend some of their customary regulations for the sake of testing new ideas. The memorandum by Leonard Duhl and Antonia Chayes, "Demonstration Cities," which had been appended to the 1964 task force report, proposed three cities. Walter Reuther and Mayor Cavanagh subsequently suggested Detroit as a single demonstration city. During the 1965 task force discussions, the number expanded steadily, much as William Cannon's earlier concept of ten demonstration areas for community action had grown into a national program under the wing of the Shriver task force on poverty.

The Wood task force wanted to concentrate funds in a small number of cities, principally the largest. In the first draft of their report, Wood and Haar proposed the selection of six cities with populations over 500,000, ten cities with populations between 200,000 and 500,000, and twenty cities with populations below 200,000. During the task force review of this draft, Senator Ribicoff recommended the addition of another category of small cities, with populations between 2,500 and 100,000. He suggested the desirability of including some fifty cities in this grouping, so that Senate members could feel that every state might have at least one participating city.

The prospect of an enlarged program prompted several members to raise questions. Ben Heineman asked whether the managerial techniques were known for so large and complex a program. Rafsky and Wood conceded that the appropriate techniques had been tried only on a small scale and that there was a shortage of skilled technical personnel. Kermit Gordon suggested that the demonstration program was a potential successor to urban renewal, but he questioned whether it could still be considered a test if the number of cities were expanded.

The task force gave surprisingly little attention to the question of whether the federal government would be able to redirect the resources from its inventory of existing grant programs into the city demonstrations, particularly if the number of demonstrations was increased further. Earlier, in discussing an organization plan for HUD, the members recognized that the Secretary would carry considerable responsibility for coordinating housing and urban development programs with those of the other domestic agencies. Accordingly, they recommended establishing a Council on Interdepartmental Coordination, which would consist of the Secretaries of Commerce, Defense, Interior, Labor, and Health, Education, and Welfare, with the Secretary of HUD serving as chairman. With this mechanism in mind, plus great faith in the ability of President Johnson to knock heads together, most members were convinced that HUD could take the lead in securing necessary program coordination. Kermit Gordon remarked that the Secretary of HUD would have to be a superman to achieve what the task force expected of him, but the majority believed otherwise.

As far as the budget was concerned, task force members were under the impression that a great deal of new money would become available for domestic programs. When Califano first called Wood to the White House in September to ask him to head the task force, he told him the White House anticipated normal economic growth to generate a "fiscal dividend" of some $12 billion under existing tax rates during the coming year. Of this total, some would be needed for Vietnam, some might go for tax reduction, but about $4 billion was likely to go into federal aid programs.[12] Califano, together with other domestic advisers, was among many victims of deception as to the greatly accelerating requirements of the Vietnam War. Walter Heller, Chairman of the Council of Economic Advisers from 1961 through 1964, also counted on substantial continuing increases in federal revenues resulting from economic growth in the late 1960s. His widely publicized proposal for revenue sharing, presented at Harvard University's Godkin Lectures in March 1966, was premised on the need to allocate $7-8 billion a year generated automatically by economic growth.[13] In late 1965 and early 1966, however, the military planners were already contemplating massive increases in troop levels and in expenditures, but they kept their calculations se-

[12] Interview with Robert Wood, July 3, 1974.
[13] See Walter W. Heller, *New Dimensions of Political Economy* (Cambridge, Mass.: Harvard University Press, 1966), p. 105.

cret from White House domestic aides and economic advisers and greatly understated the cost of the war in their budget estimates. As David Halberstam put it, "one part of the government was lying to another part." In March 1966, President Johnson consulted with Congressional and business leaders on the basis of this misleading budget information, and then decided not to seek a tax increase at that time. As a result, the subsequent escalation in Vietnam not only wiped out the expected fiscal dividend but left a deficit in its place.[14]

Wood, meanwhile, assumed that the injection of $4 billion in domestic federal program funds would, like a rising tide, float all ships. Thus he passed word to the task force that there would be a great deal of money in the pipeline of most federal aid programs, and that the volume of grant applications would not press severely against appropriation limits. Indeed, in the case of HUD, he noted that even in 1965 applications for urban renewal and other programs were not coming in fast enough to create a backlog of demand. Further, a quick look at the large budgets of agencies such as Health, Education, and Welfare persuaded most people that the Secretary, with a little pressure from the White House, could surely come up with considerable support for the city demonstrations out of discretionary funds. The task force staff, working under severe time pressures to prepare background papers on the nature of possible demonstration programs, undertook no study of grant programs outside HUD.

When they came to write the final report, Wood and Haar increased the recommended number of participating cities with populations below 200,000 from twenty to fifty, thus raising the total number of cities from thirty-six to sixty-six. Although the six largest and ten middle-sized cities would still presumably get a disproportionate share of the funds, the task force itself was no longer on record as favoring a major concentration of resources within a few demonstration areas. The final report did not deal head-on with the question of how much money would have to come from existing programs. It contained a budgetary estimate only for supplemental funds, based on hasty staff calculations, proposing a five-year cost of $2.3 billion, of which the federal share would be approximately $1.9 billion.

Congressional Acceptance—With Reservations

President Johnson, his staff, and HUD lost no time translating the task force recommendations into a legislative proposal. They did so in the same climate of

[14] Halberstam, *The Best and the Brightest*, pp. 736-739.

haste and secrecy that had surrounded the work of the task force itself. The deliberations, and even the existence, of the task force surfaced only through a few leaks to the newspapers, one of which prompted Republican Congressman Charles Mathias of Maryland to charge the Administration with "bungling in secrecy" to cover the "absence of top-level foresight."[15] To minimize the risk of premature disclosure, Wood sent the manuscript of the completed task force report directly to the White House for final typing, where a clean version was prepared for internal distribution on December 22, 1965.

This curious preoccupation with secrecy characterized most of the Johnson task forces. As President Johnson later explained it, he insisted on strict confidentiality because he wanted candid, objective advice and believed that public disclosure of task force recommendations would make the members cautious and reluctant to take critical positions. Also, he had observed that President Kennedy's opponents took advantage of early public information on 1960 task force recommendations to begin their campaign against his program even before the President made up his mind which proposals to accept.[16] Still another reason may well have been President Johnson's wish to avoid possible criticism for ignoring task force recommendations that were not to his liking. Whatever the reasons, however, he paid a price for secrecy. In the case of model cities, it prevented the extensive consultations with Congressional leaders and executive departments which would normally have contributed to the formulation of a program of this importance. Further, it put HUD's lawyers under tremendous time pressures to draft a bill the President could present to Congress, when they were not familiar with the thinking that had gone into the task force proposal.

Within a single hectic month after receiving the task force report, President Johnson filled the top positions in the Department of Housing and Urban Development and prepared his legislative program for the Congress. After what had been a long search, he appointed Robert C. Weaver, Administrator of HHFA, as Secretary of HUD and turned over the task force report to him for implementation. Maintaining continuity with the task force, Johnson appointed Robert Wood as Under Secretary and, a few weeks later, Charles M. Haar as Assistant Secretary for Metropolitan Development. With Wood's consent, Chester Rapkin had kept Weaver aware of the task force recommendations in a general way. During January, Weaver entered more directly into the planning of the program, as HUD's general counsel and his staff took responsibility for translating the task force recommendations into an Administration bill.

[15] "Sweeping Shifts Mapped for Cities," *New York Times*, November 15, 1965, p. 1.
[16] Johnson, *The Vantage Point*, pp. 327-328.

Although there was little time for review or debate within the Administration, Califano did discuss the proposed program with Secretary of Labor Willard Wirtz. Wirtz did not think the idea of concentrating federal resources in a few selected poverty neighborhoods would work. He warned that statutory restrictions allowed federal administrators little discretion to reallocate funds from existing grant programs, and they would use what discretion they had in ways acceptable to Congressmen and interest groups who supported their own programs.[17]

Nevertheless, on January 26, 1966, President Johnson delivered to the Congress a special message and a bill for city demonstration programs which embodied the major task force proposals, as interpreted and, in some respects, amended by the HUD legislative team. His message, drafted originally by Harry McPherson with help from Wood and Haar, paralleled the task force's sense of priorities and its explanation of the weaknesses of past programs. He presented a picture of the widening gap between "the suburban affluent and the urban poor, each filled with mistrust and fear one for the other" and specified the unmet needs of the central cities: chronic shortages of decent low- and moderate-income housing; "the special problem of the poor and the Negro, unable to move freely from their ghettoes, exploited in the quest for the necessities of life"; rising pressures on municipal budgets; and the high human costs of "crime, delinquency, welfare loads, disease and health hazards."

Acknowledging some of the weaknesses of urban renewal, he argued also that "the size and scale of urban assistance has been too small, and too widely dispersed." Further, existing programs were "often prisoners of archaic and wasteful building practices." The President's message recognized the extreme complexity of central city problems and thus the need for comprehensive solutions. His goal was nothing less than building "cities of spacious beauty and lively promise, where men are truly free to determine how they will live." In characteristic Johnsonian rhetoric, he urged: "Let there be debate over means and priorities. Let there be experiment with a dozen approaches, or a hundred. But let there be commitment to that goal."[18]

The following day, the Administration bill was formally introduced by Representative Wright Patman, Chairman of the House Banking and Currency Committee, and by Senator Paul Douglas with fifteen cosponsors. Its declaration of purpose left no doubt about the redistributive intent of the program and its consistency with the objectives of the War on Poverty:

[17] Banfield in Sindler, ed., *Policy and Politics in America*, pp. 135-136.
[18] U.S. President, *Message Transmitting Recommendations for City Demonstration Programs*, 89th Cong., 2nd Sess., House Document No. 368, January 26, 1966.

The Congress hereby finds and declares that improving the quality of urban life is the most critical domestic problem facing the United States. The persistence of widespread urban slums and blight, the concentration of persons of low income in older urban areas, and the unmet needs for additional housing and community facilities and services arising from rapid expansion of our urban population have resulted in a marked deterioration in the environment of large numbers of our people while the Nation as a whole prospers.[19]

Similarly, the bill gave clear expression to the second part of the task force's agenda: concentrating and coordinating federal aids in poverty neighborhoods. (Another part of the report, not dealt with in this analysis, extended the same agenda to the remainder of urban areas, as well, in the form of a proposal for demonstration projects in metropolitan planning and development.) One of the stated purposes was "to assist cities to coordinate activities aided under existing Federal programs with other public and private actions in order to provide the most effective and economical concentration of Federal, State, local, and private efforts to improve the quality of urban life." And the bill defined a "comprehensive city demonstration program" as one "for rebuilding or restoring entire sections and neighborhoods of slum and blighted areas through the concentrated and coordinated use of all available Federal aids and local private and governmental resources . . . necessary to improve the general welfare of the people living or working in the areas."[20]

Safeguards that the task force had devised to prevent the new program from following the course of urban renewal were retained in the Administration bill. There were three main faults of urban renewal, in the eyes of its critics: first, project areas in many cities were not hard-core slums; second, the net effect of the program was to reduce the supply of low-cost housing; and third, the needs of the poor living in project areas received only secondary attention. Statutory language dealt with all three points. Programs proposed by the cities would be eligible for federal aid under the act only if the Secretary of HUD determined that they would "make marked progress in serving the poor and disadvantaged people living in slum and blighted areas" and would also "provide a substantial increase in the supply of standard housing of low and moderate cost." Several stipulations in the bill made it clear that the intention was to improve living

---

[19] U.S. Congress, House Subcommittee on Housing of the Committee on Banking and Currency, *Hearings: Demonstration Cities, Housing and Urban Development, and Urban Mass Transit*, 89th Congress, 2nd Sess., 1966, Part 1, p. 1.
[20] Ibid., p. 2.

conditions for the residents of project areas. The declaration of purpose, for example, stated that the act was to provide "assistance to enable cities . . . to plan, develop, and carry out programs to rebuild or revitalize large slum and blighted areas and expand and improve public programs and services available to the people who live in such areas."

The main features of the task force's strategy remained intact, but they were combined with a number of new provisions that HUD's legislative draftsmen had inserted to make the program more acceptable to Congress and more inviting to the cities. The bill contemplated a competitive program in which cities would be selected only if their proposals met a demanding series of criteria, most of which had been contained in the task force report. But where the task force had suggested a special Presidential commission to select cities for participation, the Administration bill authorized the Secretary of HUD, who was more accessible to members of Congress, to make this determination. (This change also suited HUD's more immediate purpose of establishing its own authority in the program.) The task force had proposed tapping funds from other federal programs on a priority basis and merging them in a common account. HUD's lawyers were more cautious. Their bill claimed no special priority, went along with the task force proposal to establish an office of the federal coordinator to help achieve maximum grant-in-aid coordination under the direction of the Secretary, but noted carefully that the Secretary would have no authority to exercise any function vested in other federal agencies. The bill made no mention of a Council on Interdepartmental Coordination but merely called on the Secretary of HUD to consult with other federal agencies.

For the cities, the task force had proposed supplemental grants for model cities projects on a cost-sharing basis (80 percent federal, 20 percent local). The Administration bill instead offered full federal funding with no local matching but set an upper limit based on 80 percent of the local shares required by other federal grants used in a community's Model Cities Program. And the bill defined the City Demonstration Agency clearly as either the city government itself or a local public agency, while the task force had suggested that the administering agency might be a development authority that was not necessarily a formal unit of government.

Lacking time to recalculate program costs based on any new assumptions, the HUD team simply adopted the task force's rough cost estimate for five years of supplemental grants, eliminated the local share, and stood by the total of $2.3 billion in federal funding. Although the bill did not specify the number of cities to be included, Secretary Weaver's initial presentation to the House Subcommittee on Housing confirmed their understanding that sixty to seventy cities would be selected—just as the task force had proposed.[21]

Congressional Reaction

Within a month after Wood put his final report in the mail, the demonstration program designed by his task force had undergone its first revision and was now in the hands of Congressional committees. The 89th Congress, with its huge Democratic majority, offered an exceptionally friendly climate for White House initiatives; and Johnson's White House team had built up formidable skill in securing Congressional backing for the President's legislation. Yet despite these favorable conditions, the Administration bill had a reception ranging from cool to hostile. During a complicated legislative struggle that lasted through the following October, the bill "endured as many perils as Pauline, required frequent rescue, and on two occasions was pronounced stone dead, beyond even the resuscitative powers of the President."[22] Eventually Congress did enact the model cities legislation, but only after making a number of changes based on a different conception of how this program ought to proceed.

The long tale of legislative maneuvers, White House pressures, and negotiated settlements has been told elsewhere and is not central to this analysis.[23] The nature of the Congressional objections, however, and the compromises that were finally struck are important elements in appraising the model cities experience. They reveal significant differences of perspective between a task force aiming at the reform of federal aid policies and a Congress attuned to the pressures of constituencies and interest groups. More fundamentally, they raise serious questions about the political feasibility of implementing the Model Cities Program as the task force had conceived it.

Congressional reluctance to accept the Administration bill had little to do with open disagreements over the purposes or even the main substantive elements of the contemplated program. Although there was undoubtedly some Congressional hostility toward the use of federal resources to help the urban poor, very little came to the surface. The Watts riot of the summer before and the riots in Chicago and in the Hough area of Cleveland during the summer of 1966 strength-

[21] Ibid., pp. 68-69.
[22] Robert B. Semple, Jr., "Signing of Model Cities Bill Ends a Long Struggle to Keep It Alive," *New York Times*, November 4, 1966, p. 1.
[23] See ibid.; Banfield in Sindler, ed., *Policy and Politics in America*, and Suzanne Farkas, *Urban Lobbying* (New York: New York University Press, 1971), pp. 207-216.

ened, on the whole, the sense of legitimacy and urgency behind this purpose, although a few Congressmen were opposed to measures that might "reward" the rioters. Administration strategists managing the legislation never sensed serious Congressional reservations about the redistributive purpose of the program. Even several members of Congress who raised objections to the bill were careful to register their agreement with its goals. Representative William Widnall of New Jersey, a key Republican member of the Subcommittee on Housing, stated his strong support for the social purposes of the new bill, but he argued that these same purposes should be written into the existing urban renewal law.

If a city qualifies for demonstration city assistance, then why should it be permitted to continue at the same time with residential urban renewal projects completely inconsistent with the goals set forth for the new program? And why should only demonstration projects in demonstration cities be required to produce "a substantial increase in the supply of standard housing of low and moderate cost and result in marked progress in serving the poor and disadvantaged people living in slum and blighted areas"?[24]

Widnall proposed the revision of urban renewal as an alternative to mounting a new program. He urged the restriction of urban renewal grants to cities "interested in housing the poor instead of accommodating the rich." He further commented: "Had we kept our urban renewal program on the right track all these years, possibly millions of our citizens of all races and backgrounds would not be living in fear for their very lives and properties this summer." Subsequently, Widnall successfully introduced an amendment from the floor which required residential urban renewal projects to meet the housing criteria that the Administration had proposed for the Model Cities Program.

Congressional objections centered on a series of other issues. In a memorandum to Lawrence O'Brien, who was managing Congressional relations for the White House, Weaver summarized the problems that were already evident by early April 1966.[25] First, there was widespread opposition to starting any expensive new program. Second, Congressmen were concerned that only a limited number of cities would be permitted to participate in the program. Compounding the concern that many cities would be left out was the fear that cities included in the program would also divert a substantial amount of money from

[24] U.S. Congress, House Committee on Banking and Currency, *Report: Demonstration Cities and Metropolitan Development Act of 1966*, 89th Cong., 2nd Sess., Report No. 1931, September 1, 1966, pp. 149-150.
[25] Robert C. Weaver, Memorandum for Larry O'Brien, "Easter Recess Analysis," April 6, 1966.

existing grant-in-aid programs, to the detriment of other communities. Thus the cities that were excluded might lose on two counts. As a result, many who supported the model cities legislation believed it would be necessary to provide additional funding for other programs to cover grants given to participating cities. Further, there were objections to the broad discretion given to the Secretary of HUD to select the participants and to require them to meet such criteria as counteracting the segregation of housing by race or income.

Other parts of the Administration's proposed housing and urban development legislation, particularly those sections concerned with grants to encourage planned metropolitan development, raised still greater Congressional fears of White House control over local government decisions. But these fears extended to the model cities proposals, as well. The minority view contained in the House Committee report on the Senate bill contended that the city demonstration program would "give away much of the national legislative controls belonging to the Congress and also those local controls which belong to the communities of the Nation." The minority statement warned of "the great danger of the program as proposed—that it will be used as a political 'lure' to entice political support in the hope of generous Federal bequests."[26]

A Hesitant Constituency

The appearance of a strong constituency backing the Administration's bill might have prompted many Congressmen to reconsider their early doubts. But the secrecy and haste of the bill's origins prevented extensive Administration consultation with political interest groups just as it had with the Congress itself. Influential spokesmen for various urban interest groups did come forward to testify in support of the bill, but almost all of them qualified their support by also noting reservations.

The mayors of the nation's cities, speaking individually as well as through their organizations, provided the most visible and favorable support, before both the House and Senate subcommittees. Among the individual spokesmen were Mayors Hugh Addonizio of Newark, Jerome Cavanagh of Detroit, Richard Daley of Chicago, John Lindsay of New York, and Ralph Locher of Cleveland. Almost all of them warned that the funding the Administration had proposed—$2.3 billion over a five-year period—would be inadequate. Mayor Addonizio proposed an in-

[26] House Committee on Banking and Currency, *Report: Demonstration Cities . . .* , pp. 135-136.

crease to $10 billion, and Mayor Lindsay estimated that New York City alone would need approximately $1 billion for urban renewal activities and another $1 billion for social services. Mayor Cavanagh further objected to the competitive nature of the program and recommended no limit on the number of cities that could participate. Mayor Daley, testifying before the House Subcommittee on behalf of the U.S. Conference of Mayors, called attention to the "obvious inadequacy" of $2.3 billion and suggested that the only way to estimate the funds needed for the program was to wait for the cities to submit their plans. Mayor Locher warned also of funding shortages in the other federal programs that cities were expected to utilize, and he urged Congress to make available adequate appropriations for these complementary programs on a schedule to coincide with the city demonstrations.

Representatives of other housing and urban interest groups gave similar support to the bill: the National Association of Home Builders, the National Association of Housing and Redevelopment Officials, the National Housing Conference, the AFL-CIO. Several reiterated the point that existing grant-in-aid programs would require additional appropriations, and Boris Shishkin, speaking before the House Subcommittee on behalf of the AFL-CIO, termed the Administration proposal an "auspicious step in the right direction" but "unduly modest in magnitude."

The hearings thus produced a sizable body of favorable testimony, but with qualifications that were troublesome. If the Administration's cost estimates were in fact unrealistically low, model cities could indeed become a more expensive program than many Congressmen were willing to fund at a time when expenditures on the Vietnam War were beginning to escalate. But if the mayors and other spokesmen had no assurance of additional funding, particularly for existing grant-in-aid programs that were important to them, their support might waver.

The visible constituency that came forward at the hearings was heavily dominated by the mayors. During the next few months, the White House staff and HUD officials attempted to activate a broader base of support. They turned to traditional friends of housing legislation, such as builders and mortgage bankers, as well as to other groups concerned with urban poverty: labor, civil rights, religious, and health and welfare organizations. This new coalition, chaired by John Gunther, executive director of the U.S. Conference of Mayors, began to meet regularly in Washington to plan its Congressional strategy. Andrew Biemiller, the veteran legislative aide of the AFL-CIO, began to play an active role; and the Administration succeeded in organizing a supportive committee of business leaders including David Rockefeller and Henry Ford II.[27]

As the constituency broadened and began to press individual Congressmen for their votes, the bill's prospects improved. But two points were clear. The core of the committed remained the mayors and their organizations: in deciding on legislative changes, as well as in the subsequent implementation of the program, the Administration would have to be attentive to the mayors' needs. And the interest groups themselves, as well as the Congress, wanted to see some changes in the Administration's bill.

Legislative Changes

The process of Congressional consideration offered numerous opportunities for making alterations in the original bill. The Administration took the initiative in proposing some changes based on the hearings and on early discussions with members of Congress; the House and Senate committees made certain changes in the course of reporting out the legislation; Senator Edmund Muskie insisted on several key alterations before he agreed to manage the bill in the Senate; and still others came in the form of amendments from the floor of the House and Senate.

Despite the numerous Congressional objections and the long campaign necessary to win majority support, Congress did not make radical changes in the Model Cities Program. The Administration got most of what it wanted from Congress; and what it wanted was reasonably close to the task force proposal. Congress did continue a process that had begun within the task force itself and been maintained within the Administration: adjusting an initial conception of how to cope with slum problems to a political context and to the competing claims of constituents who stood behind other grant-in-aid programs. Thus Congressional action reduced the possibility for aggressive use of the Model Cities Program to promote racial integration, it increased the number and geographic spread of cities that could participate, and it set limits on the ability of the Administration to draw funds away from other grant programs in order to concentrate them in the demonstration neighborhoods.

General Purposes Congress did not challenge the basic redistributive aim of the program—to send additional federal resources into poverty neighborhoods—but it did weaken the Administration's concern with helping minority groups to

[27] Semple, "Signing of Model Cities ..."; Banfield in Sindler, ed., *Policy and Politics in America*, p. 138; and Farkas, *Urban Lobbying*, pp. 211-213.

move out of segregated areas. The task force proposed that city demonstrations be required to include "measures to eliminate social and racial segregation, including assurance of equal opportunity in housing." The Administration bill, following this suggestion, included in the selection criteria consideration of whether "the program will encourage good community relations and counteract the segregation of housing by race or income," and added a second requirement "to assure maximum opportunity in the choice of housing accommodations by all citizens." Senator Muskie replaced the two stipulations, which had drawn the fire of opponents, with a single, less threatening requirement of "maximum opportunities in the choice of housing accommodation for all citizens of all income levels," and this was retained in the final enactment.

A second racial issue had to do with busing for purposes of school integration. Representative Paul A. Fino of New York contended that the Secretary of HUD could—and would—require school integration measures as a condition of model cities aid. After an acrimonious floor debate on this point during final House consideration, the Administration decided to agree to an amendment prohibiting the Secretary from requiring pupil transfers as part of a demonstration program or from offering financial incentives to encourage such transfers.

Congress altered the priority given to another purpose of the program as well. Both the task force and the White House hoped to encourage local innovation in the city demonstrations, but neither proposed a specific directive to that end. Again at Senator Muskie's suggestion, the Administration accepted a statement requiring localities first to use model cities supplemental funds for new activities not covered under other federal grant programs, and permitting their use as part of the local contribution to other federal aid programs only after the new activities were fully funded. Similarly, Senator Muskie redrafted the statement of purpose to stipulate assistance for city demonstration programs "containing new and imaginative proposals"—a modifier not present in the original bill.

The Number of Cities The task force itself began the process of diluting the early conception of concentrating funds in a limited number of large cities when it recommended a total of sixty-six cities in different size categories. The White House accepted this recommendation. The Senate Subcommittee on Housing went beyond the Administration's intentions by authorizing $12 million in planning funds for each of two years, thus declaring its intention to double the number of participating cities by adding a second round of competitions. Senator Muskie's redraft of the Administration bill inserted deliberate references to the provision of assistance to cities *of all sizes*, and the Senator gave assurances during the floor debate that small cities would be included in the program. The House later removed any remaining doubts on this subject by adding, after "cities of all sizes," the phrase "with equal regard to the problems of small as well as large cities." To further ensure geographic spread, Senator John Tower of Texas succeeded in adding an amendment from the floor limiting the allocation of model cities funds in any one state to 15 percent of the total authorization.

In effect, Congress was willing to support a redistributive program, but only if it could slice the shares thinner in order to accommodate more districts. While doubling the number of cities, Congress reduced the program's funding authorization from the Administration's request of $2.3 billion over six years (one year for planning and five for operations) to $900 million for two years.

Coordination of Other Federal Programs Improved coordination of federal aid was central to the entire conception of the Model Cities Program; the task force gave this reform goal specific meaning by calling for a concentration of federal resources in selected poverty neighborhoods and for the allocation of existing grants to the participating cities "on a priority basis." They also proposed two mechanisms: the designation of a federal coordinator for each city who would bring together the relevant resources in a common fund and make them available according to the program needs and timetable of the community; and a federal Council on Interdepartmental Coordination chaired by the Secretary of HUD.

The Administration bill proposed the concentration and coordination of all available federal aids within the demonstration areas; but neither its provisions nor its spokesmen were clear on how they proposed to bring about the needed coordination. Secretary Weaver's opening statement to the House Subcommittee on Housing seemed to deny that participating cities would have any special claim on the resources of existing programs.

The fact that a particular project, eligible for grants under an existing Federal program, is undertaken as part of a demonstration program will in no way affect its eligibility under the existing program. The city will apply to the Federal agency which administers the existing program, and the application will be subject to all the existing rules, regulations, and priorities governing that program.[28]

One of the first questions put to Weaver was whether the effect of the Model Cities Program would be to increase the drain on authorizations for existing programs, such as urban renewal, and whether, as a result, cities not included in the demonstration program would find less money available to them. Weaver's

[28] House Subcommittee on Housing, *Hearings: Demonstration Cities* . . . , p. 35.

answer was "a definite no. . . . We are not robbing Peter to pay Paul in this program."[29] Yet, at about the same time, when Weaver addressed the National League of Cities on the merits of the new program, he assured them that

The Federal Government, for its part, will commit its total resources to help the city. It will do this by making available the whole range of Federal urban programs. It will do it by meaningful infusions of money and technical help.[30]

How the federal government would make available its full inventory of aids to participating cities without giving them special priority over other applicants was a great mystery. At one point in his testimony, Weaver implied that the massing and coordination of federal aids would be primarily a local responsibility, spurred on by an incentive formula that based the supplemental grant to a city on the total volume of federal aid it brought into the demonstration. (Supplemental grants were expected to equal 80 percent of the total local share of all federally aided activities that were part of the demonstration program.) This conception of coordination from the bottom suggested that cities that were good at grantsmanship would earn an extra reward in supplemental funds. Cities with only average grant-getting talent, however, would have an incentive to focus most of their resources on a single neighborhood. "Those cities which can concentrate their resources," Weaver said, ". . . will be the first aboard."[31]

One way to interpret Weaver's comments to Congress is that they implied a program that would not attempt to change the allocation of federal funds *among* cities but would seek only to concentrate the grant funds normally available to any participating city within a designated poverty neighborhood of that city. Yet the Administration's proposal to appoint a federal coordinator for each participating city seemed to imply more than this. As Weaver explained the function of the coordinator, he would help cities carry out their programs by offering technical advice, providing access to other federal agencies, and applying negotiating skills to bring together relevant federal aids. If he could not get the cooperation of other federal agencies at the local or regional level, he would call on HUD in Washington for assistance.[32] But surely this coordinator would seek special advantages for the city he was trying to help; if he was at all effective, he would give the participating city an edge over other competitors by influencing federal agency allocations, funding schedules, or processing time.

[29] Ibid., p. 69.
[30] Robert C. Weaver, "Joint Ventures to Build Great Cities," Address to National League of Cities, Washington, D.C., March 30, 1966.
[31] House Subcommittee on Housing, *Hearings: Demonstration Cities . . .* , p. 35.
[32] Ibid., pp. 76-77, 99.

Congress responded to this ambivalence over coordination and its meaning with an ambivalence of its own. First, both the House and Senate committees declared their intention not to change priorities within existing federal programs. The House version stated:

Your committee . . . wishes to make very clear its intent that the demonstration cities program will not in any way change the flow of funds, as among cities, under existing grant-in-aid programs. The demonstration cities program does not provide any priority in the use of existing Federal grant-in-aid programs for cities which participate in the demonstration program.[33]

The Administration, meanwhile, recognized the fears of mayors and of Congressmen that the participating cities would draw heavily on urban renewal funds, leaving too little for other applicants, regardless of the assurances and declarations made all around that there would be no change in aid priorities among cities. At a meeting of urban renewal administrators in Washington during the winter, Edward J. Logue, one of the country's leading practitioners of renewal, succeeded in persuading Wood and other HUD officials that there was solid justification for these fears. Logue demonstrated by simple arithmetic that because the Administration cost estimate of $2.3 billion was based on a proposed formula setting supplemental grants equal to no more than 80 percent of the local share of other federal programs being used in the city demonstrations, this implied local matching shares of some $3 billion over five years. In urban renewal, which was expected to be the main existing program drawn upon for the demonstrations, the matching formula was one-third local to two-thirds federal contributions. Thus the implied volume of urban renewal was close to $6 billion in federal allocations over a five-year period—more than enough to exhaust all federal urban renewal appropriations at the then current level in the selected cities alone, leaving nothing for the rest of the country. Logue's assumptions were extreme, because he did not figure in substantial federal inputs from programs other than urban renewal, but he nevertheless made his point effectively.[34]

In June, Weaver announced to the U.S. Conference of Mayors meeting in Dallas that he was prepared to press for special urban renewal appropriations for participating cities. The Administration then requested an additional $600 million in urban renewal authorizations to be earmarked for use in demonstration city programs, and the House Subcommittee on Housing added this provision

[33] House Committee on Banking and Currency, *Report: Demonstration Cities* . . . , p. 15.
[34] Interview with Robert Wood, July 3, 1974.

before reporting out a bill in late June. The Senate Subcommittee on Housing subsequently retained this provision but cut the amount to $250 million.

The proposal to designate federal coordinators ran into trouble on other grounds. Some Congressmen and some mayors voiced concern that this official would wield great power over local governments; far from assisting them, he might intrude into local affairs through his manipulation of federal funds. Representative Paul Fino, during the House hearings, called him "a commissarlike coordinator" and "this commissar or czar or coordinator." The House Subcommittee, in revising the Administration bill, eliminated provision for a mandatory federal coordinator and authorized, instead, the appointment of a "metropolitan expediter" to be appointed only at the request of local officials. The Senate version retained this optional expediter, but during the floor debate in the House, backers of the bill agreed to delete the section. Finally, the House-Senate Conference Committee restored this feature, but with a further stipulation that the central city in any metropolitan area would have to request the appointment of a metropolitan expediter. The House members of the Conference Committee stated their intention that the expediter was to be "the servant of the cities in the metropolitan area," with his functions "limited to providing information, data, and assistance to local authorities. . . ."[35] Even this diluted version never came to life, however, because future Congresses refused to appropriate funds for the metropolitan expediters.

Still, many in Congress believed strongly in the benefits that would flow from improved coordination, and believed the city demonstration program offered an important opportunity to achieve this goal. Senator Muskie's revision of the Administration bill added a requirement that the Secretary of HUD shall

. . . in conjunction with other appropriate Federal departments and agencies and at the direction of the President insure maximum coordination of Federal assistance . . . , prompt response to local initiative, and maximum flexibility in programming, consistent with the requirements of law and sound administrative practice.[36]

This language was retained in the final legislation; and the same Senate and House committee reports that declared a clear intention not to interfere with the priorities of existing programs simultaneously called on the Secretary of HUD to

---

[35] U.S. Congress, House, *Conference Report: Demonstration Cities and Metropolitan Act of 1966*, 89th Cong., 2nd Sess., House Report No. 2301, October 18, 1966, p. 44.
[36] U.S. Congress, Senate, "Comprehensive City Demonstration Programs and Metropolitan Development Programs As Approved by the Senate Subcommittee on Housing," 89th Cong., 2nd Sess:, July 26, 1966, Sec. 103(b)(2).

look after the necessary coordination of these programs. In the House version, the committee stated its conviction that the demonstration program would require "far more effective coordination of existing Federal programs than has been achieved in the past." The committee, therefore, "expects the Secretary to utilize his existing authority to assure that cities' comprehensive demonstration programs are not disrupted by a failure to coordinate activities under existing Federal grant-in-aid programs."[37]

The model cities bill presented Congress with a problem that neither the War on Poverty task force, the model cities task force, nor the White House had been able to resolve earlier: how to concentrate existing federal aids in poverty areas, make them conform to local priorities and schedules, and yet not take funds away from cities that wanted to utilize existing programs in more traditional ways. The Wood task force assumed there would be no conflict between cities selected for the new program and other users of federal aid, as they believed there would be a surplus of funds sufficient to take care of both groups. Congress believed differently, and thus undertook a bizarre combination of steps:

1. It declared a clear legislative intent not to permit the demonstration program to alter the allocation of funds among cities.
2. Just in case nobody was listening to declaration 1, it authorized special appropriations for urban renewal, the other program that it expected to be most directly affected by competing claims.
3. It gutted the Administration proposal to appoint federal coordinators who could help participating cities to get the resources they needed from existing programs.
4. It called on the Secretary of HUD to find some way, within his existing powers, to arrange for the coordination necessary to allow locally designed demonstrations to succeed.

Implications: Conflicts Postponed

Both the House and Senate quickly accepted the legislation as reconciled in the conference report, although the votes were relatively close in both cases (142 to 126 and 38 to 22). President Johnson signed the bill into law on November 3, referring to the new program as "model cities" rather than "demonstration cities" as in the title of the bill. By that time city demonstrations had an unpleas-

[37] House Committee on Banking and Currency, *Report: Demonstration Cities . . .* , p. 13.

ant overtone, and HUD immediately switched to "model cities" for all future references to the program.

The invention of the Wood task force had been translated into law in less than a year, with numerous changes of detail but the major ideas intact. Thanks to the skill and muscle of the Johnson White House and to the large Democratic majority in Congress, it had passed its initial test of political feasibility. Yet the difficulties of passage did not augur well for the future of the program. An internal study of the legislative history prepared by the HUD staff concluded that the act was "pressed upon a surprised and reluctant Congress. A Congress like the 'Fabulous 89th' comes once in a generation; but only practiced Administration maneuvering secured passage even in this friendly climate."[38]

The legislative history brought to the surface numerous conflicts within the original conception of the Model Cities Program. Was it a demonstration or a national program? Was its main purpose to test innovations or to help the slum dweller catch up with the rest of society? Could it secure the necessary federal resources without raising havoc among other users of the grant-in-aid programs? Did it require an exceptional delegation of authority to the executive branch, or could it operate within the normal terms of Congressional-White House relations? Did it require steady central direction from the White House to keep federal agencies in line, or could HUD operate in "superman" style to implement an interagency program? Could it achieve its redistributive intent through partisan negotiations among equal agencies, or did it require special provisions for federal coordination?

Congressional action did not create these issues, but neither did it resolve them. To have attempted a clear resolution of each point would probably have destroyed the program's base of support. Even within the nine-member Wood task force, a certain ambiguity was necessary to preserve a consensus, because different members sought different objectives. The success of the task force in bringing together diverse notions of reform and avoiding clarification of the most difficult conflicts gave the program a chance of political acceptance; and the same process was repeated in Congress. The conflicts would have to be dealt with later. Certainly, Congressional action provided no mandate for an ambitious reform of the federal grant-in-aid system. Instead, it revealed deep Congressional uneasiness about changing that system.

[38] Richard Cherry and Kent Watkins, "History of Congressional Action Relative to Model Cities 1966-1967," Department of Housing and Urban Development, October 3, 1967, p. 43.

If Congressional decisions did not resolve conflicts within the program, they did nevertheless send warning signals to HUD, which would have the job of translating the law into an operational program. HUD officials followed events closely and began to draw conclusions. Staff members assigned to study the legislative history reported to their superiors that the program Congress had in mind was not exactly the same program HUD had in mind.

We keep telling Congress that Model Cities is a demonstration program, not a program program. At least part of Congress does not understand that. Do we understand what we mean by it? . . . Do we hope to demonstrate 70 approaches or one approach 70 times? . . . As it is the program is of sufficient magnitude that Congressmen tend not to treat it as a demonstration and continually expect it to operate like a categorical grant-in-aid program.
KEEP ON JIVING, BUT KEEP IT COOL![39]

The task force conceived of a program in keeping with its perception of urban problems and their solutions. The Administration and the Congress then redefined the program to balance the objectives of the task force against the political needs of Congressmen and of constituents. Next, the program had to be passed to HUD, which would need to find its own way through the still unresolved conflicts over purposes and strategies, give clearer definition to such concepts as coordination and concentration, and find ways to put its new mandate to work in the cities.

[39] Ibid., p. 45.

Part II
The Federal Response—Promise and Fulfillment

Even in its embryonic stages, the Model Cities Program meant many things to many people. Some saw it as the millennium in federal programming; some as merely one more categorical program. To most, model cities would permit the creation of a national laboratory within which a relatively few cities could demonstrate innovative urban strategies that other cities might later follow. Yet, to others, the program's chief virtue was its potential for bringing to cities increased amounts of federal resources.

The majority, by far, of the program's early supporters saw that it would require a well-orchestrated federal response toward the participating cities—a response demanding, in effect, nothing more nor less than a basic reform in traditional departmental behavior and federal-city relationships. Not too surprisingly, however, considering the atmosphere of crisis that surrounded the program's passage through Congress and the related requirement that departmental priorities for categorical programs not be upset, more rhetorical than strategic attention was given to the issue. Even though phrases such as "coordination of federal assistance," "prompt response to local initiative," and "maximum flexibility in programming" were included in the statute, they were clearly devoid of real operational content at the inception of the program. In effect, they reflected more the expressed hopes and desires of the program's supporters than the specific marching orders of Congress or the White House.

To HUD, as the department responsible by statute for administering the program, fell the lead role in defining the specific details of the federal response to model cities. That HUD was to work in *conjunction* with its sister agencies and at the *direction* of the White House was clear. However, its position as one Cabinet department among several of equal standing, meant that it had to accept as a general rule, negotiation, adaptation, and bargaining, rather than fiat, in seeking action from other members of the federal establishment; moreover, constant attention was required to the kind and degree of White House involvement and support.

Subsequent pages illustrate that model cities was a trying, often a frustrating, experience for most federal participants. Development of a federal response took place concurrently with, and often second to, numerous other activities associated directly with the initiation and administration of the program. HUD's many model cities mandates appeared at times to conflict with the statutory mandates of other programs in other departments; and their model cities constituencies seemed to conflict with the constituencies of other categorical programs.

Given these constraints, the federal response developed, understandably, by evolution, not revelation. Priorities were difficult to define and sustain for more than a short period of time. Agency interests or, more important, the interests of individuals within those agencies, determined that only momentary goals could be set. Five related areas of concern, however, gradually dominated discussion between HUD, the White House, and the participating departments. These areas included

1. The establishment of guidelines for the role of city hall and of resident groups within the program.
2. The development of ground rules for the application of existing federal categorical programs within each participating city.
3. The development of planning regulations to govern the submission of model city plans and the use of model city funds.
4. The definition and provision of technical assistance to the participating cities.
5. The initiation of an evaluative effort that would be in keeping with the demonstrative nature of the program in each city.

The way in which the federal government reacted to each area of concern is discussed in detail in the following chapters. Taken together, these reactions illustrate the major institutional and political obstacles to an effective federal response to urban problems. Certainly they testify to the difficulties involved in translating pleas for coordination into realistic terms or operational strategies. They suggest the surprising impotence of the President in dealing with departments on key issues and, conversely, the ability of the bureaucracy to resist White House as well as Secretarial direction. Further, they suggest the marginal effect on cities of a federally imposed planning model and related review processes, and they call into question the capacity of the federal bureaucracy to provide helpful technical assistance to cities asking for such help. Finally, they require us to consider whether the currently popular notion that federal assistance should be provided without strings is compatible with an unfinished national agenda for the elimination of poverty and the reduction of blight.

Model cities was serviced by good, and sometimes very able, men and women. As shown in the remainder of this text, however, the federal system and its decision-making process repeatedly blocked a sustained and effective response to the needs of our cities, and particularly to the needs of poverty neighborhoods. Many important lessons emerged about the federal capacity to respond to city priorities. Based on these lessons, new approaches are in order.

Chapter 4
A Local Government Strategy: Rechanneling
Federal Aid

From the outset, one part of the strategy of the Model Cities Program was to use federal leverage to bring about major improvements in the performance of local government. Not only were local governments to be induced to give higher priority to the problems of their poorest neighborhoods; they were also to be strengthened for the new tasks that would follow. In its diagnosis of the weaknesses of past federal aid programs for the cities, President Johnson's Task Force on Urban Problems (the Wood task force) noted their narrow orientation to specific functions and their tendency to encourage a division of authority among specialized agencies, which then impaired the effectiveness of local government in making use of federal funds. The new approach recommended by the task force promised

... the mobilization of local leadership and initiative to assure that the key decisions as to the future of American cities are made by the citizens who live there, and to commit local leadership both public and private to a comprehensive attack on urban problems, freed from the constraints that have handicapped past efforts and inflated their costs.[1]

Ways of achieving this mobilization were to be generated over the first few years of the program's operation. The Wood task force, and the legislation itself, laid down only the basic principles. Each city was to create an appropriate mechanism to bring together the local political leadership and the citizens of the area. The task force proposed that each city establish "an appropriate development authority and administrative mechanism, not necessarily a formal unit of government," which would provide for the necessary participation of the citizens and for the mobilization of resources. Each city would have to show that there was "a serious commitment to the demonstration program" by the mayor, the city council, and the relevant state government, and other local authorities.

As the program was translated into legislation, it became increasingly clear that the local agency that was to take responsibility for the program would be an arm of general government rather than a special-purpose authority. The City Demonstration Agency (CDA) was defined as "the city, the county, or any local public agency established or designated by the local governing body . . . to administer the comprehensive city demonstration program." The citizen role remained less clear, covered by the ambiguous requirement of "widespread citizen participation in the program."

A firmer stance on the involvement of local government took shape through

[1] U.S. President's Task Force on Urban Problems, "Proposed Programs for the Department of Housing and Urban Development," December 1965.

the work of the Advisory Committee on Demonstration Program Development that Secretary Weaver had commissioned even before final passage of the legislation. This committee was chaired by William Rafsky, a member of the Wood task force and an able technician and local program administrator in Philadelphia. Its staff was directed by George Williams, special assistant to HUD Under Secretary Wood and later to become principal author of the first Model Cities Program planning guide.

The Rafsky committee took a strong position on how the demonstration agency should operate. Under the legislation then before Congress, the CDA had to be a public agency. The committee further insisted that it should be directly accountable to the responsible elected officials of the community and should be closely related to governmental decision making. Elected officials, the committee felt, should exercise leadership in setting the agency's policies, plans, and programs. The City Demonstration Agency was to be given sufficient authority to administer both the social and physical aspects of the program, and this would include the power to ensure that the proposed program was carried out. It was not to assume operating control of projects that existing agencies could handle but instead to enter into contracts with these agencies and integrate their work. Special administrative machinery would be needed to coordinate and direct programs for the model neighborhood: this might include policy or advisory boards representing other agencies and interests, interagency agreements, "checkpoint" procedures, and authority to reconcile conflicting plans, programs, or priorities.

The cities also had an obligation to create a mechanism whereby residents of the area could become involved in planning and carrying out the program. Residents were to have opportunities to contribute ideas and to review and comment on its operation. But the emphasis here was clearly on improved communication between citizen groups and public officials, not on a sharing of power between the two.[2]

The advisory committee was also clear about its long-term intention to "strengthen the capability of cities to deal with urban problems." In their view, the demonstration program was to pull together the fragmented authority of numerous autonomous and semi-autonomous agencies of government into a new administrative structure that would out-last model cities itself and equip cities to handle their problems more effectively on a continuing basis.[3]

[2] HUD Advisory Committee on Demonstration Program Development, "Report to the Secretary on the Proposed City Demonstration Program," September 1966, pp. 14-16, 29-30.
[3] Ibid., pp. 14-15.

These ideas were to become the basis of the program's strategy for local government reform. They marked a sharp reversal of earlier trends in federal-city programs. HUD's own programs were typical. Public housing, for example, was administered by semi-independent housing authorities with their own commissioners. Similarly, urban renewal was generally handled by a local public agency with its own board rather than a municipal department responsible to the mayor. Thus the federal aid programs themselves were limiting the capacity of city government to respond to citizen pressure for change as this might be expressed through the normal political channels. The agencies that handled federal funds were insulated from political pressures focused on city hall, a reflection of earlier reformers' beliefs that it was necessary to keep "politics" out of urban programs. As a result, mayors and other elected officials had very little control over the federal funds that began to flow into their communities in an increasing volume in the 1950s and 1960s. Data collected by a study in Oakland showed that only about 12 percent of all federal money spent in Oakland in the mid-1960s was subject to control by local government.[4] Now the reformers proposed to give the mayors and other elected officials new authority and resources, in the hope that they would prove more responsive to the poor than the earlier system had been, and also in the hope that they would undertake more comprehensive programs than had been possible before.

The aims of the original White House Task Force and the subsequent HUD Advisory Committee dovetailed neatly. The first wanted to find a way to achieve better results from federal aid expenditures in the cities, while the second aimed more directly at a strengthening of city government capabilities that could lead to precisely that goal. Bringing about changes in the local implementation of federal programs, however, first required interagency agreement in Washington on new procedures. HUD not only would have to bring its own prior programs in line with the model cities strategy but would have to persuade other agencies with relevant urban aid programs to do the same.

This strategy posed more severe problems than its originators anticipated. It called on other agencies to assign a major role in their programs to a new group of clients, the mayors and the residents of model neighborhoods. Most federal administrators were accustomed to working with other groups through their own

---

[4] Marshall Kaplan, Technical Director, Oakland Task Force. Findings of the Oakland study are reported in Oakland Task Force, San Francisco Federal Executive Board, *An Analysis of Federal Decision-Making and Impact: The Federal Government in Oakland*, Vol. 1 (Oakland, Calif., 1968), and Vol. 2 (1969).

channels. Moreover, it called on them to recognize the special claims of poverty neighborhoods to a share of their programs.

A further complication arose from the desire of HUD officials to give citizen groups a significant voice in making decisions about the uses of federal aid in model neighborhoods. This role was difficult to define, because in many cases resident groups were in conflict with city hall for control of Model Cities Programs. Also, some HUD officials favored a sharing of power between the two, while others wanted the residents to have only an advisory role.

The resolution of competing claims between residents and city hall depended in part on a clarification of the purposes of the Model Cities Program and the ideological beliefs underlying it. Although HUD never officially endorsed an equal sharing of power between city hall and resident groups, during the Johnson Administration it did put pressure on city hall to work out accommodations with neighborhood groups. The new HUD team that came in with the Nixon Administration shifted the conception of the program away from a redistribution of power to neighborhood groups and toward structural reform within local government. As a result, it applied pressure on city hall not to go too far in sharing power with citizens, so that what emerged was more clearly than ever a mayor's program.

Confusion about the citizen role added to the difficulty of getting interagency cooperation. At first, HUD was in the position of asking other agencies to give both city hall and residents control over the use of their funds in model neighborhoods. Later, they were asking for this control solely on behalf of city hall. Either way, other agencies were reluctant.

The purposes of this chapter are to examine, first, the strategy that HUD developed for implementing the Model Cities Program at the local government level, and, second, the attempt to win interagency support for this strategy. HUD officials tried to accomplish their plan for federal aid reform through a combination of White House pressure and direct negotiation with other agencies. Their attempt to rechannel federal aid put to the test Lindblom's theories of interagency behavior as described in Chapter 1. HUD's experience confronted the major themes posed by Lindblom's theoretical analysis: How effective is central direction? What are the strengths and limitations of "partisan mutual adjustment" as a way to make policy? What special resistance is generated by a program that tries to redistribute federal resources from existing interest groups to a newly recognized constituency of the mayors and the urban poor?

First Ground Rules: The Balance between
Residents and City Government

The details of HUD's local government strategy were hammered out over a period of several years in the course of preparing guidelines, reviewing city proposals, and making decisions on individual city requests for HUD approval of local plans and procedures. The first program guide issued to the cities, explaining how to enter the model cities competition, followed the tone of the Rafsky committee recommendations but gave only general guidelines and left considerable room for local choice. It adopted language from the Advisory Committee report, requiring the City Demonstration Agency to be a public agency and to be "closely related to the governmental decision-making process in a way that permits the exercise of leadership by responsible elected officials."[5]

While the cities worked on their applications, the newly appointed top officials of HUD were becoming firmly committed to the belief that the Model Cities Program should be associated with the mayor's office. Ralph Taylor, Assistant Secretary in charge of the Model Cities Program and a former local urban renewal official himself, gave the news to his onetime colleagues in November 1966 at a meeting of the National Association of Housing and Redevelopment officials. He informed them that urban renewal agencies would not be permitted to administer the Model Cities Program. Their interest in land development and physical facilities was too narrow to encompass the social goals of model cities, which was to be more than an enlarged urban renewal program. As special-purpose, usually semi-independent bodies, they could not fill the need for an agency close to the mayor and capable of pulling together the necessary range of public agencies and private interests. Taylor now began to speak of model cities as a "mayor's program."

HUD's position on the structure of the CDAs was made known to the cities, and the initial applications demonstrated that the latter were making an effort to comply. A major test of the policy was developing, however, around the issue of citizen participation. Taylor wanted elected officials to be accountable for the program but also wanted neighborhood residents to have a voice in it. A conflict was inevitable over the balance of power between residents and the local govern-

[5] U.S. Department of Housing and Urban Development, *Improving the Quality of Urban Life: A Program Guide to Model Neighborhoods in Demonstration Cities*, December 1966, p. 11.

ment. If citizens were invited to participate in the program, how could their role be limited so that the city government would still be firmly in charge? The mood of the times, particularly in black and other minority communities, was one of distrust of local government and its institutions. As Robert Wood later observed, "We let the genie of citizen participation out of the bottle with OEO programs, and now there was no way to put the cork back in." Further, the Model Cities Program was intended for precisely those neighborhoods where city government had been most negligent in the past and where reasonable people had good cause to mistrust the intentions of the city fathers. If the cities needed the people's participation in order to get federal funds, a price was going to be exacted for it: that price was some measure of power for the residents over the Model Cities Program.

The first program guide to the cities was vague in its citizen participation requirements. It called on participating cities to provide neighborhood residents "a meaningful role" in policy making, to encourage a "flow of communication and meaningful dialogue" between residents and the CDA, and to develop "means of introducing the views of area residents in policy making" and opportunities for residents "to participate actively in planning and carrying out the demonstration program."[6] Those instructions left most of the definitions as well as the details to the cities.

As applications began to arrive, HUD staff members learned that citizens had not played a major role in this early stage. With tight schedules and demanding application requirements, that would have been difficult in any event. But more significantly, in their statements of intentions for the subsequent planning year, only a fifth of the cities judged likely to receive funding proposed to include residents on the CDA's executive or steering committee. Only about half the cities explained how they intended to select citizens for participation in the planning; and of these most proposed to do it by appointment rather than election.[7]

Taylor's chief staff adviser on citizen participation, Sherry Arnstein, was particularly dissatisfied with this early performance and began to move for a tightening of HUD's requirements on citizen participation. First, she developed methods for characterizing different degrees of resident involvement, ranging from cities informing citizens of plans through a series of gradations to delegating

[6] Ibid., p. 14.
[7] Memorandum from Bernard Russell, Model Cities Administration, "Content Analysis of Planning Grant Applications," November 6, 1967.

planning responsibilities to resident groups and including them in decision-making organizations.[8] This scale helped sensitize other HUD staff members to the range of involvement cities accorded their residents and set the terms of an ensuing debate.

HUD officials arranged for interagency teams to screen and review the city applications and to recommend cities for inclusion in the program. By including representatives of other agencies from the outset, they hoped to establish a basis for future cooperation on an implementation strategy. This early step meant that the Model Cities Administration would allow representatives of other agencies to influence its decisions, in order to set the stage for later "partisan mutual adjustments." Sherry Arnstein served as HUD's chief reviewer of citizen participation proposals, and she managed to have specialists with an orientation similar to her own review them on behalf of HEW, OEO, and the Justice Department's Community Relations Service. The reviewers gave strong reinforcement to Mrs. Arnstein's views. They all argued that HUD should ensure a greater role for local residents, and they entered into a long series of negotiations over the content of new HUD regulations on citizen participation with Ralph Taylor and Walter G. Farr, Jr., director of the Model Cities Administration.

OEO's representative, Donald Hess, proposed a prescriptive approach similar to his agency's own regulations. (OEO's *Community Action Program Guide* stated a clear requirement that local programs were to be "developed, conducted, and administered with the maximum feasible participation of the residents" and went on to spell out a dozen different ways in which this participation could be achieved.) Taylor and Farr favored more open performance standards that would put pressure on city hall to give the residents a voice in Model Cities Programs without prescribing specific forms of citizen participation. Arnstein pressed particularly for the reimbursement of residents for expenses connected with their participation and for independent technical assistance to the resident boards through sources outside local government. These interagency discussions were influential in shaping HUD policy. Taylor also listened to other points of view, however. When draft regulations had been prepared, he discussed them as well with two spokesmen for the mayoral point of view, John Gunther and Alan Pritchard of the National League of Cities-U.S. Conference of Mayors, who expressed their satisfaction with the outcome.

[8] See Sherry Arnstein's working paper for HUD, "Citizen Participation: Rhetoric and Reality," later revised as "A Ladder of Citizen Participation," *Journal of the American Institute of Planners*, Vol. 35 (July 1969), pp. 216-224.

A letter on citizen participation was issued on October 30, 1967, as a result of the deliberations, which established performance standards rather than prescriptive requirements. Cities would have to provide an organizational structure that brought neighborhood residents into the process of planning and implementation; positions of leadership would have to be held by persons whom neighborhood residents accepted as representative of their interests; and the structure for citizen participation would be required to give them direct access to the decision-making processes of the CDA, with sufficient time to consider and initiate proposals, and some form of acceptable technical assistance. Where financial problems were a barrier to effective participation, citizens were to be reimbursed for expenses and compensated for their service on boards or committees. The cities would be allowed flexibility in meeting these standards through their own organizational devices, but the standards had become clearer and more demanding than the earlier guidelines.

This early conflict over the citizen role resulted mainly from the pressures of model cities staff members and of other federal agency representatives who held strong views on the subject and used the interagency review process to advocate a change in HUD policy. After the first round of cities had been selected, however, resident groups across the country created additional pressure for change as they began to battle with city hall for control of the program. Neighborhood demands for power were far more insistent than either the cities or most HUD officials had expected. In many communities, the struggle for control consumed the bulk of effort and set the dominant tone of the planning year far more than did the pressure from HUD for careful problem analysis and rational, comprehensive planning.

Most cities established an organizational structure that seemed to offer neighborhood groups opportunities for real influence in the program. Typically, the local model cities organization included a mix of resident authority and city government authority. Most cities had a policy-making body including both residents and city officials, a neighborhood council, which sometimes had its own professional staff, and a CDA director and staff. Usually the CDA director and staff were closely associated with city hall, but sometimes not. In a few cases the CDA director identified strongly with the model neighborhood and attempted to serve as its advocate within the local government. Dayton, Ohio, went furthest in the direction of citizen control. There a planning council composed entirely of residents was the key policy-making body. A few other cities had resident majorities on the policy board, and still others had some form of neighborhood veto over plans. Most cities interpreted the HUD standard on citizen representation as a call for elections to choose policy board members. The voting turnout was usually around 10 percent of eligible residents but in a number of place: reached 25 percent or more. In virtually all cases, voting participation was much greater than it had been in earlier elections for Community Action Agency members.[9]

What did these developments mean? Some mayors felt that HUD's policy was pushing them into giving residents greater authority over the program than they themselves approved. To one mayor, a strong role for the residents meant that "all my good ideas can be shot down by one loudmouth who can carry people with him just because he says I represent the establishment."[10] Yet to Sherry Arnstein, still serving as Taylor's chief adviser on the subject, resident participation was not producing a real sharing of power. In the spring of 1968, Mrs. Arnstein and Daniel Fox, a consultant to HUD, went into the field to discover what was happening in the local programs. They were led to the conclusion that a large number of city officials were committed to participation only as a ritual and as a way of engineering the consent of the residents to plans drawn up by city officials.[11]

Arnstein and Fox argued for a further strengthening of the citizen role. Their conception of model cities varied from that underlying Taylor's strategy. Arnstein and Fox maintained that the goal of the program was "massive change in the quality of life in urban neighborhoods." For this to occur, residents would have to play a major part in the planning and administration of local programs. Only with strong resident involvement would the plans be relevant, sensitive, and effective in meeting citizen needs, as the citizens defined them. Local governments had often been wrong in their assessment of what was important to the

[9] James L. Sundquist and David W. Davis, *Making Federalism Work* (Washington, D.C.: Brookings Institution, 1969), pp. 85-113; Roland L. Warren, "Model Cities First Round: Politics, Planning and Participation," *Journal of the American Institute of Planners*, Vol. 35 (July 1969), pp. 245-252; Sherry Arnstein and Daniel M. Fox, "Citizen Participation in Model Cities: Developments, Dynamics and Dilemmas," draft No. 3, September 3, 1968 (unpublished HUD document); a summary version of this was later published as HUD Technical Assistance Bulletin No. 3, "Citizen Participation in Model Cities," December 1968; HUD, *The Model Cities Program: A History and Analysis of the Planning Process in Three Cities* (Washington, D.C.: U.S. Government Printing Office, 1969), prepared by Marshall Kaplan, Gans and Kahn; HUD, *The Model Cities Program: A Comparative Analysis of the Planning Process in Eleven Cities* (Washington, D.C.: U.S. Government Printing Office, 1970), prepared by Marshall Kaplan, Gans and Kahn.

[10] Sundquist and Davis, *Making Federalism Work*, p. 92.

[11] Sherry Arnstein and Daniel Fox, "Developments, Dynamics, and Dilemmas," unpublished draft circulated within Department of Housing and Urban Development, August 9, 1968, p. 28.

poor and insensitive in their administration of programs. Citizens had to be in a position of strength if they were to negotiate successfully with city officials. The key measure Arnstein and Fox proposed was independent technical assistance for citizen groups so that they could have staff and funds under their own administrative control for program development.

The strategy developed by the Rafsky Advisory Committee, and later by Ralph Taylor, implied less concern with the sensitivity and relevance of local programs to citizen needs, and much greater concern with the ability of cities to implement plans. Taylor's policy nevertheless did assign an important role for citizens. This role had to be built into the model cities process so that citizens could communicate their needs and priorities to city officials. In Taylor's view, the resident role was not to be taken to the point where it would impair the capacity of public officials to direct and coordinate the activities of public agencies. If city officials gave up too much of their authority to citizen groups, there was the risk that neither they nor the residents would be able to bring the local fiefdoms into line.

Taylor himself had been attracted to the idea of independent technical assistance as a means of building citizen capacity, and was persuaded of its effectiveness in the Dayton Model Cities Program. Nevertheless he decided against a direct requirement. Instead, he issued an abbreviated version of the Arnstein and Fox memorandum as Technical Assistance Bulletin No. 3, "Citizen Participation in Model Cities," in December 1968. Thus the Arnstein proposals were offered to the cities in the form of advice, not regulation. Still HUD was now encouraging cities to provide independent staff or consultants to citizen groups. At about this time, Mrs. Arnstein, who had seen her mission as that of persuading HUD to promote strong resident involvement, became convinced that Taylor would do nothing further in this direction. She resigned from HUD in September. By December, however, the efforts that she and others had made to secure support for technical assistance through interagency negotiations paid off to some extent when OEO decided to commit $4 million for training and technical assistance in model neighborhoods.

Taylor's evolving position on citizen participation was best expressed in a speech he gave to the National Association of Housing and Redevelopment Officials in September 1968. He wanted model cities to build citizen capability as well as city hall capability, but he needed a system for setting priorities.

The work that has to be done can only be accomplished by various public and private forces working together. In the Model Cities program, the responsibility for marshalling the public and private forces through political leadership, is placed on the Chief Executive of local government.

Citizen participation works best when, despite the rhetoric of control, citizens and city government negotiate a sharing of power that permits the people of the neighborhood to participate effectively in determining the use of the resources that affect the quality of life in the neighborhood.

In this partnership, the city is clearly the dominant partner . . . this does not mean the partners should not negotiate out rights and obligations that clarify their respective roles.

. . . the purpose of the power sharing must be positive—to identify and meet real needs, and to develop the capacity to function effectively in a society where coalitions, not absolutes, control.[12]

Taylor left no doubt that city officials were to have final responsibility, but he was prepared to pressure them into accommodating with neighborhood residents. Such accommodation could include a dominant role for residents in those communities where city government was prepared to accept it, as in Dayton. "In some communities," he noted in the same speech, "action may not be acceptable until the dominant minority is in apparent control of at least part of the structure." But for model cities to succeed, the citizen role had to lead to coalition, not to separation or to a prolonged deadlock.

Connecting Federal Agencies to City Hall

Having placed their bets on the mayors, while also making some concessions to the views of representatives of other departments, Weaver, Wood, and Taylor now had to bring the other federal agencies into line with their local government strategy. In the spring of 1968, when the first-round cities were a few months into their initial year of planning, Taylor and his staff had worked out the details of a federal interagency arrangement to meet the commitments made or implied as part of the Model Cities Program. These details, which form the themes of this and the following chapters, amounted to a series of requests that the Model Cities Administration would make of HUD and of the other federal agencies.

One of these requests sprang directly from the strategy that was evolving. This was to arrange for review by the City Demonstration Agencies and approval by the mayor of all federally assisted projects affecting model neighborhoods. What the HUD leadership wanted was explained in some detail in an internal memorandum from Under Secretary Robert Wood to the Assistant Secretaries in

[12] Remarks by H. Ralph Taylor to the National Association of Housing and Redevelopment Officials, Minneapolis, September 27, 1968.

charge of other HUD categorical programs. All parts of the department were to provide for CDA review and mayoral approval of programs affecting the model neighborhood. Both review and approval were to be more than perfunctory. The local executive (mayor, city manager, or county executive) was to have an opportunity to influence the planning, and in the case of the CDAs, review was to include participation in planning both by the CDA staff and by the local residents in whatever way they had been incorporated into the local structure. Thus HUD wanted the citizens and the CDA, as well as the mayor, to have substantial review authority over the total flow of resources into the model neighborhood or into programs that had a substantial impact on the neighborhood.

To establish this review authority, HUD officials were going to have to negotiate with the administrators in charge of all federal programs that supplied aid to the cities. Negotiations started first within HUD itself, and even there the Model Cities Administration ran into trouble. Its main target was urban renewal, HUD's largest grant program and one of considerable significance for the model neighborhoods. Congress had gone so far as to appropriate special urban renewal funds, earmarked for use in model neighborhoods, as a way to forestall any pressures to divert renewal funds away from other recipients and into the model neighborhoods. In many ways, urban renewal officials viewed the Model Cities Program as a threat. The latter had originated, in part, as a reaction against their own program and an effort to correct its abuses. Its orientation toward mixed social and environmental programming was a challenge to the continuing physical focus of renewal. Further, its commitment to improve housing conditions for the poor was a challenge to the earlier use of urban renewal to improve the tax base of cities by attracting high-value real estate investments.

Model cities now posed an additional threat to the local operation of urban renewal. Renewal projects were usually planned and implemented by local public agencies with their own commissioners or policy boards, established under state enabling legislation, which were relatively independent of elected public officials and of citizen groups. They had their own forms of resident involvement, but these usually relied on city-wide citizen advisory groups and gave little authority to project area residents. It is true that local government approval of each project was usually required. The significant new demand that model cities made was that renewal projects be reviewed by the citizen participants within the structure of the CDA.

Assistant Secretary Don Hummel, in charge of the renewal program, was reluctant but eventually acceded to pressure from the top HUD leadership. By April 1968, Hummel informed the regional administrators that renewal grant applications for projects in model neighborhoods would require special handling. The local CDA director was to work with the local renewal director to coordinate renewal activities with the model cities plan. More significantly, renewal proposals would be subject to the same citizen review as the other parts of the Model Cities Program. Where local arrangements provided for a resident veto, this would apply as well to urban renewal.[13] Inside HUD, the Secretary and Under Secretary supplied the needed central direction when a process of negotiation was not sufficient to produce agreement on the model cities strategy.

Negotiations with other federal agencies got under way in the spring of 1968, when HUD representatives brought up the subject of special review arrangements at meetings of an Inter-Agency Coordinating Committee that had been established early in 1967. At the same time, top HUD officials reached for central direction when they discussed federal program review as part of their entire Model Cities Program with White House aide Joseph Califano and the Budget Bureau staff. Califano and Budget Director Charles Zwick agreed to help prod the other agencies to meet HUD's terms for review, and included this request in a series of memoranda and telephone calls throughout that summer and the following fall. Negotiations dragged on for months and continued into the Nixon Administration. For different reasons, each of the principal federal agencies did not comply fully with HUD's requests. The reasons reveal a great deal about the limits of White House power as well as the failure of partisan negotiations to bring about major change in the grant-in-aid system.

At HEW, the response was generally favorable, but there were problems. James Alexander, director of the Center for Community Planning, obtained an opinion from the HEW General Counsel to the effect that the department could legally insist on a grant project being closely linked with the model neighborhood and having the approval of the CDA whenever grants were made directly from the federal to the local government. The bulk of HEW's grant funds, however, flowed through the states and were allocated in accordance with state plans and statutory formulas. These federal-state programs gave little discretion to the federal administrator; as a rule, he was required to make grants if certain conditions were met. As a result, the General Counsel advised that there would be few opportunities to relate state plan grant programs to model cities.[14]

[13] Memorandum from Don Hummel, Renewal and Housing Assistance, to all Regional Administrators, "Urban Renewal in Model Cities," April 9, 1968.
[14] Memorandum from Alanson W. Willcox, General Counsel, to James P. Alexander, Director, Center for Community Planning, "Model Cities Grant Control—Legal Questions," June 18, 1968.

For those programs where HEW could ask for reviews by the CDA and the mayor, it began to make the necessary arrangements during the summer of 1968. The Secretary, however, had to deal with his traditionally independent bureau chiefs. They in turn were asked to inform their field staff that funds for any federal-local demonstrations, service delivery, and training grants that affected model neighborhoods were not to be committed without the approval of the HEW regional director. He, in turn, would be responsible for calling these grant proposals to the attention of the CDA and for obtaining the latter's endorsement. HEW promised to develop detailed procedures later that would strengthen the new position of the regional directors. Although HEW's policy would obtain review by the CDA alone and not by explicit approval by the local chief executive, the Model Cities Administration (MCA) seemed satisfied with this response. The CDA would presumably serve as surrogate for the mayor. Ways would have to be explored later to give the CDAs some voice in the allocation of the much larger state formula grants. The problem here was a structural one involving federal-state relations that neither White House pressure nor interagency negotiations could change; and the MCA had not yet fashioned a strategy for dealing with the states.

In the case of the Office of Economic Opportunity, the effort to establish review by the CDA and the chief executive conflicted with the basic philosophy of its antipoverty program. OEO's own strategy was to deal directly with independent Community Action Agencies responsive to the poor and not subject to mayoral control. Under the Green Amendment of 1967, Congress had given the mayors an option to take over control of the Community Action Programs, but very few had actually chosen to do so. HUD was now asking OEO, in effect, to put a piece of its action—that affecting the model neighborhood—under mayoral control regardless of any prior commitments to resident groups. Further, it was asking OEO to work with the CDA citizen organizations rather than with OEO-funded community action citizen boards on any matters affecting the model neighborhoods.

Citizen review was an integral part of HUD's model cities strategy. An MCA memorandum prepared in March 1968 had noted:

Neighborhood residents have responded enthusiastically to the call for citizen participation and count on influencing *all* programs that affect their lives. Yet most Federal programs bypass the city and flow to independent agencies oftentimes without the Mayor's knowledge. And the model cities' citizen participation structures as yet have no assured role in any activities except those funded solely by city taxes or Model Cities supplementary grants. Indeed many other Federal programs support rival citizen groups.[15]

HUD was not opposed to OEO's philosophy in the sense of being anticitizen. Rather the question was: Whose citizens were to have the dominant review authority, HUD's or OEO's?

There was a difference, attributable mainly to the very different ideologies surrounding the origins of community action and of model cities. Community action, from the outset, meant different things to different people, several of whom took the trouble to try to set the record straight in their books a few years later. Through the various gradations, however, there was an underlying theme of opposition to local government and especially local agencies that dealt with the poor. As one insider described it afterward, the role of the Community Action Program as of 1965 was "advance guard for the overthrow of local establishments."[16] To others of moderate views, the purpose of community action was to reform local bureaucracies by organizing the poor as a pressure group for change; conflict was to lead to constructive results. By 1967, some of the militance was gone, but Community Action Agencies still understood that they were to organize the poor and serve as their advocate, perhaps in cooperation rather than in conflict with the establishment.[17] The Model Cities Program, however, was intended to create agreement and partnership between residents and city government. Even though the participating residents did not always share this view, the nature of the program itself pushed them increasingly toward a cooperative stance with local government after the initial ground rules had been established. Organizing the poor was never a major purpose of the program as HUD administered it.

So the question of whose citizens were to dominate was still an important one in early 1968, reflecting very different conceptions of the public interest. After initial exchanges of memoranda and meetings in June and July, OEO expressed its willingness to make some compromises. Theodore Berry, Director of the Community Action Program, offered to require Community Action Agencies (CAAs) to build closer working relationships with the mayors and the CDAs.

[15] HUD MCA memorandum, "The Federal Response to Model Cities," March 1968.
[16] Robert A. Levine, *The Poor Ye Need Not Have with You* (Cambridge, Mass.: M.I.T. Press, 1970), p. 65.
[17] Ibid., p. 85.

The Community Action Agencies would be asked to review their programs within the model neighborhood with the CDA or the mayor. Prior to final action, the CDA or the mayor would be asked to indicate their approval or disapproval at this review, and any objections they might raise would be forwarded to the OEO regional offices for further consultation and final decisions.[18] Taylor was not satisfied. He continued to press for a mayoral veto power.

> Local government must have final authority over Federal programs affecting the lives of residents of model neighborhoods. . . . Mayors and other community chief executive officers cannot be expected to bargain as an equal (or less) with CAA's or other OEO funded local organizations.[19]

OEO and HUD each consulted their respective General Counsels to discover whether OEO could require mayoral approval of grant applications in model neighborhoods. Not surprisingly, OEO's Counsel found that such a requirement would be inconsistent with Congressional intent; HUD's General Counsel, on the other hand, found that OEO's enabling legislation and the 1967 amendments presented no legal barriers.[20]

Discussions continued through the early fall, with Secretary Weaver, OEO Director Harding, and Joseph Califano all taking a direct hand in the negotiations. On September 27, Weaver and Harding sent a draft agreement to the President for review. On October 29, HUD and OEO announced the terms of their agreement. Both agencies urged local government to exercise its right to appoint one-third of the membership of the CAAs and the CDAs to achieve common policy board membership, to exchange staff and citizen representatives, and to work toward eventual consolidation of the resident organizations covering the model neighborhood. OEO and HUD would require CAAs and CDAs to keep each other informed of projects affecting the other's programs. The CAAs would be required to develop their projects in close cooperation with the CDA. Wherever local government, the CDA, or the citizen structure of the CDA questioned the consistency of an OEO-funded proposal with the plans for the model neighborhood, the boards of sponsoring local agencies would attempt

[18] Theodore M. Berry, Director, Community Action Program, memorandum to H. Ralph Taylor, "Mayoral Concurrence or Veto," July 9, 1968.
[19] H. Ralph Taylor, memorandum to Theodore Berry, "OEO Programs in Model Neighborhoods," July 15, 1968.
[20] Donald M. Baker, General Counsel, memorandum to Bertrand M. Harding, Acting Director, OEO, "Mayor's Veto," July 19, 1968; Otto J. Hetzel, Associate General Counsel, HUD, memorandum to H. Ralph Taylor, "OEO Response, Mayoral Veto," August 23, 1968.

to resolve the issue; and HUD and OEO representatives would try to conciliate any local differences. If local government still refused to approve a CAA proposal, the matter would be referred to the OEO and HUD regional offices and, if necessary, to Washington for resolution.[21]

The agreement was promptly attacked by a national meeting of CAA directors, board members, staff, and citizen representatives. The conference on model cities held by the National Association for Community Development, which met in Washington on November 23-24, condemned the agreement and the process that led up to it as a disavowal of OEO's basic principles. A field study of the relationships between Community Action Agencies and City Demonstration Agencies, which was conducted by the Urban Institute at this time, found that the CDAs were not taking advantage of the new policy, and that "community action agencies view it as a document of capitulation which they are not about to implement of their own initiative, without the threat of sanctions from Washington."[22] Agreement had been reached in Washington, but it was a long way from taking effect in the cities.

The other principal federal agency that HUD tried to draw into the model cities program was the Department of Labor. Its manpower programs were obviously relevant to the purposes of model cities, but like HEW this department worked mainly through state agencies. The Department of Labor, however, had already made special arrangements with OEO to fund Concentrated Employment Programs (CEPs) for poverty areas. Community Action Agencies were to be the "presumptive sponsors" of these programs, although other agencies could conceivably serve as sponsors in some circumstances. Much of HUD's effort centered on defining the boundaries for the CEPs to include model neighborhoods, and on securing mayoral and CDA veto powers over those CEPs in model neighborhoods.

The Department of Labor was cooperative on the first point, and CEP areas in model cities were usually drawn to include the model neighborhood. But the second request would have required a drastic departure from its normal mode of business. In December 1967, the Department of Labor asked its manpower ad-

[21] Walter G. Farr, Jr., Director, Model Cities Administration, and Donald K. Hess, Associate Director, Office of Program Policy and Rural Affairs, Community Action Program, memorandum, "HUD-OEO Agreement on Coordination of All OEO Assisted Programs that Affect Model Neighborhoods," October 29, 1968.
[22] Melvin Mogulof, "The Community Action Agency and the Model Cities Agency: A Study of their Local Relationships and Recommendations for Changes," prepared for the Urban Institute, January 17, 1969, unpublished manuscript.

ministration representatives to work with officials of the CDAs and the CAAs on the Concentrated Employment Program. To improve CEP coordination with other programs, they were also told to seek the involvement and concurrence of local government.[23] Involvement and concurrence were not the same as mayoral veto, however, and Taylor, with Califano's help, continued to press for a larger role for the CDA and city government. In September, he proposed an arrangement similar to the one worked out with HEW for those situations when either the local government, the CDA, or the CDA citizen structure was not satisfied that a Concentrated Employment Program was meeting the needs of the model neighborhood. Attempts were to be made locally to resolve such differences; if they failed, the matter was to go to regional officials of the concerned federal agencies or to Washington to be resolved on an interagency basis.[24]

But the Department of Labor was unwilling to go as far as HEW. Its directives to the field continued to express concurrence, consultation, and cooperative participation, but it still expected final decisions to be made by the regional manpower administrator whenever local participants disagreed. As Secretary Wirtz put it in response to Joseph Califano,

The Department of Labor's implementing instructions require consultation with the local chief executive prior to the approval of the Comprehensive Work and Training Program. These instructions also provide for consultation with the chief executive when any substantive modifications are made in the program.[25]

Within those federal agencies that were reluctant to agree to a mayoral veto the key staff members were seldom unanimous in their views. Thus the official line taken by any agency might suggest a more one-sided response than was actually the case. Further, some who opposed the veto did so on principle rather than to protect their own turf. As some staff members of the Model Cities Administration saw it, their counterparts in the Department of Labor who shared their commitment to the social goals of the Model Cities Program were simply not persuaded that a mayoral veto was desirable. Many mayors, in their view, could not be counted upon to endorse programs that would achieve needed so-

[23] Jack Howard, Manpower Administration, Department of Labor, Memorandum for All Regional Manpower Administrators and Manpower Representatives, "Development of Concentrated Employment Programs in Model Cities," December 27, 1967.

[24] H. Ralph Taylor to Bertrand M. Harding, Office of Economic Opportunity, Stanley H. Ruttenberg, Department of Labor, William Gaither, White House, William D. Carey, Bureau of the Budget, "Process for Assuring that Model Cities Can Coordinate Manpower Programs that Affect Model Neighborhoods," September 20, 1968.

[25] Willard Wirtz, Secretary of Labor, memorandum for Joseph A. Califano, Jr., October 7, 1968.

cial change in their cities. While a mayoral veto might be eminently logical for the implementation of the Model Cities Program, it was not necessarily the best way to improve job and training opportunities for the poor.

By the end of the Johnson Administration, the Model Cities Administration had thus made some headway; but where agencies other than HUD were concerned, the task had proved to be formidable. The effort to build up city government capability, with White House backing, had run up against statutory problems in the case of federal-state programs, and problems of agency policy in those cases where agencies were asked to channel their funds for traditional client groups through a new local structure. In most cases the traditional clients were state agencies, but in the case of OEO they were citizen-dominated local organizations. Further, even where department Secretaries were willing to institute changes, they had to work through bureaus that were not fully subject to their control and through regional bureaucracies that were not noted for their prompt compliance with policy changes in Washington. The model cities strategy seemed to call for a major overhaul in the administration of federal programs as well as for fundamental changes in federal-state-local relations. There was no apparent way for either central direction from the White House or partisan interagency adjustments to make these changes in the federal structure.

The New Administration: Changing the Balance

During the Johnson Administration, the strengthening of city hall had been one goal of the Model Cities Program. The underlying purpose had not been to bring about a general improvement in city government but to equip cities to deal more adequately with the problems of poverty areas. This was not a matter of capability alone. One of Farr's last memoranda to Taylor, who stayed on a few weeks after Inauguration Day, spoke of the basic objective of the program as the enhancement of both the capability and the commitment of local government to respond to the needs of its poorest neighborhoods and its poorest residents.[26]

Still, early experience had persuaded Taylor and Farr that capacity building would have to be given increasing attention. Farr's same memorandum characterized most local governments as inexperienced in program management, poorly staffed, with little or no authority or capability for manpower training, economic development, housing, education, and health. Floyd Hyde, the new As-

---

[26] Walter G. Farr, Jr., memorandum to Assistant Secretary Taylor, et al., "Model Cities Program Management," January 27, 1969.

sistant Secretary in charge of the Model Cities Program, was quick to see this as central to the entire rationale for the program. As a former mayor of Fresno, California, he attached great importance to the strengthening of local government. This was also an attractive way to present the program to the incoming Administration. Other model cities objectives would take years to achieve, and making local government effective was a necessary requirement in any case. During the Nixon Administration, justifications of the program increasingly stressed the strengthening of local government almost as an end in itself rather than as a means for improving conditions in poverty neighborhoods.

Hyde prepared an initial statement on the mission of the Model Cities Program for George Romney, newly appointed as Secretary of HUD. He reworked a draft that the staff had prepared some time earlier but gave it a different emphasis in keeping with President Nixon's "New Federalism." The basic program objective, he argued, was to decentralize government responsibility and promote local initiative by strengthening city government.

For decades the Federal Government has undercut city government's authority by funding programs through independent agencies, special districts or other non-city institutions, thereby sapping city government's capacity and discouraging it from assuming responsibility for most of the physical, social and economic problems of its residents. Model cities can reverse this trend. HUD's grant is to city government; and city government is held responsible for coordinating all necessary local agencies and institutions and for assuring effective citizen participation. Under the Model Cities program, other Federal agencies are also agreeing to give local government a voice in programs which they fund, programs that previously bypassed local governments.[27]

Hyde's conception of the program was mirrored in the long sequence of federal reviews that ensued. A report in April of the Committee on Model Cities of the Council for Urban Affairs adopted much of the same language. Their study team reported from the field that the CDAs were looked on locally as an arm of city hall. They found that Community Action Agencies were still vying with the CDAs for control of federal funds and for support of the poor but noted that

There is a general feeling at the local level that the CDA, with access and accountability to the cities' chief executives is the more powerful arrangement. "The poor" and their spokesmen as well as CAA directors themselves, seem to realize this.[28]

[27] Floyd Hyde, memorandum to George Romney, "The Basic Mission, Goals and Objectives of the Model Cities Program and Its Future," February 8, 1969.
[28] Council for Urban Affairs, Model Cities Study Trip Memorandum, April 8, 1969.

George Romney, in a press conference at the end of April, stated clearly that "Model Cities is intended to be, and will remain, a local government program, centered upon the Mayor's office, with a continued requirement for adequate citizen involvement."[29]

In response to this redefinition of program priorities, HUD's stance on resident participation shifted noticeably. Taylor had also conceived of model cities as a mayor's program, but he was prepared to press city hall to make accommodations with neighborhood groups. Where city government was willing to give resident groups a program veto or other forms of control over the CDA, Taylor went along. Hyde, on the other hand, wanted to define for the mayors the kinds of arrangements that would provide for enough participation and those that would provide for too much. And unlike Taylor, he did not deal with representatives of other agencies who favored a stronger role for citizen groups.

The new policy marked something of a return to the position of the Rafsky Advisory Committee in 1966. Hyde and his deputy Robert Baida wanted to leave no doubt that the citizen role was to be an advisory one only. It was to be a strong advisory role but no more than that. This stand in itself was not very different from that of Taylor and Farr. What soon emerged as a difference, however, was a determination to prevent mayors from compromising their own responsibility for decision making in their negotiations with neighborhood residents. Thus the agreements that individual city halls had struck with citizen groups were subject to closer scrutiny by HUD, and from a new perspective.

The change in HUD's position was passed along informally as it developed in Washington. By May, Hyde took more formal action as well. In a number of cities, administrative arrangements had been made for the CDA director to report to a policy group with mixed city government and citizen representation. In others, the city had promised veto power to the citizen structure. Where either situation held, Hyde wrote to the mayor asking him to reconsider and justify his position. His letter to Mayor Stokes of Cleveland, where the CDA reported directly to a residents' board of trustees, illustrates the nature of this pressure for a reversal of earlier decisions.

We recognize that agreements such as this may be necessary to make individual city programs function successfully. On the other hand, this administrative structure does not make clear how the activities of regular city departments such as fire, police and public works, will be coordinated with the Model Cities Project Director and the overall Model Cities effort.

[29] George Romney, news conference (Policy Statement on Model Cities), April 28, 1969.

We would appreciate having your assessment as to whether this administrative structure will either preclude the City and its chief executive officer from exercising its proper program responsibility or prevent Cleveland's Model Cities Program from moving forward in a timely manner. In particular, we would appreciate knowing what specific mechanism will exist or what steps will be taken to insure close coordination between the Model Cities unit, which is reporting to the Resident's Board of Trustees, and the regular city departments.

We recognize the substantial commitment you have made to this program and hope that we will be able to tender a planning grant contract upon receipt of the requested information.[30]

Stokes's reply did not promise any structural changes but did give assurances that the mayor and the city council held ultimate responsibility—indicating the mayor's role in selecting the project director—and did spell out the involvement of the mayor and of the city department heads in the model cities organization.[31] Similar letters went to the mayors of cities in which residents had been given veto power.

There were still other cities where the CDA had been set up in such a way that only the citizen group had the right to initiate the consideration of projects. The Model Cities Administration rejected this arrangement outright and asked the mayor for assurances that the city would also have this right.[32]

Subsequent policy statements from HUD clarified the role of the chief executive by directing him to "assume early, continuous and ultimate responsibility for the development, implementation, and performance of the Model Cities Program"[33] and by further limiting the administrative authority of citizen groups.[34] Most significant among the new restrictions, the CDAs were not permitted to operate projects under the Model Cities Program, except for minor and temporary projects; and neither the CDAs nor their citizen boards would be permitted to select more than one-third of the board members of any operating agency.[35]

The new strategy outlined by Secretary Romney and Assistant Secretary Hyde was to strengthen city hall against its will, if necessary. Some mayors wanted their City Demonstration Agency to take on operating responsibilities, but the

[30] Floyd H. Hyde, letter to the Honorable Carl B. Stokes, May 5, 1969.
[31] Mayor Carl B. Stokes, letter to Floyd H. Hyde, Assistant Secretary, May 7, 1969.
[32] Walter G. Farr, Jr., memorandum to all regional administrators, "Assuring City Government Responsibility During the Planning Process," May 15, 1969.
[33] HUD, CDA Letter 10A, December 1969.
[34] HUD, CDA Letter 10C, November 1970.
[35] HUD, CDA Letter 10D, November 1970.

decentralization of authority to the cities was not allowed to extend that far. Others, particularly those who had reluctantly given in to resident demands, took steps to remake their agreements with local citizen groups in line with the new HUD policies.[36]

The new position on resident participation represented a change of emphasis from the Johnson Administration but not a drastic shift in orientation. Ralph Taylor, too, had made it clear that elected officials were to have final authority over local programs. But the detailed steps just noted did create a new tone that the mayors were quick to acknowledge. Some exaggerated the extent of change and came to view it as a reversal of earlier policy. For example, John J. Gunther, Executive Director of the U.S. Conference of Mayors, wrote to Floyd Hyde:

> ... the Model Cities program in many cities was launched almost as a continuation of OEO efforts with the ultimate authority and responsibility for the executive vested in a citizens' committee.
>
> We applaud your efforts to turn the program around to place the authority in the hands of the elected executive.[37]

Gunther's interpretation is ironic in view of the earlier conflict between HUD and OEO in which OEO partisans identified even the citizen components of CDAs with city hall, but there could no longer be any doubt about the mayors' central position.

Strengthening the Mayors

The more important component of HUD's strategy for strengthening city hall was its continuing effort, since early 1968, to make the mayor's office the point of entry for all funds, even from other agencies, into the model neighborhood. Federal reviews of the Model Cities Program provided support for this position and found that early interagency agreements were not being honored. An interagency group that studied model cities in the summer of 1969 discovered that in Atlanta, when the CDA raised questions about a grant proposal, the sponsors went directly to the federal agency involved—which gave prompt approval. The study group's first recommendation was that the federal government should establish a common procedure that would require the mayor, or the CDA, to

[36] See Sherry Arnstein (as told to her), "Maximum Feasible Manipulation," *City*, Vol. 4 (October-November 1970), pp. 30-38; and Michelle Osborn, "Postscript: Philadelphia's Model Cities Conflict in Context," *City*, Vol. 4, pp. 39-43.

[37] John J. Gunther, letter to Floyd Hyde, March 20, 1972.

approve all federal funds affecting the model neighborhood. The group did not suggest an absolute mayoral veto but proposed an arbitration procedure similar to that adopted in the agreement signed between HUD and OEO on October 29, 1968.[38]

A memorandum from Robert Mayo, Director of the Budget Bureau, to White House aide John Ehrlichman in November similarly argued that localities could not solve their problems if the federal agencies in model cities "continue to support independent local agencies without regard to the coordinating efforts of the mayor and city council." This memorandum recommended that federal agencies arrange for participation by city government, through the CDA, from the very beginning of the process of applying for federal aid.[39] A White House task force on model cities, reporting in December, endorsed the same goal.

Hyde's revision of the local government strategy to bring it in line with the philosophy of the Nixon Administration, with a reduction of the residents' role and a clearer delegation of authority to local elected officials, did not help much in winning the cooperation of other federal agencies. Through the first year of the new Administration, the bargains that HUD had earlier struck with OEO, HEW, and the Department of Labor were kept with only varying degrees of consistency and vigor. At HEW, Sidney Gardner, Director of the Center for Community Planning, tried hard to implement the agreement and make it work. At the Department of Labor, which had been more reluctant in the first place, officials were waiting for signals from the White House. Assistant Secretary Arnold Weber wrote candidly to Floyd Hyde that "At this point, the CEP-Model Cities question is part of a larger drama and, of course, we would be responsive to an administration policy in this area once such a policy is developed."[40]

The drama to which Weber referred was the long sequence of reviews of the Model Cities Program undertaken by the Nixon Administration prior to making a firm decision on the program's future. These reviews, described more fully in later chapters, came to a head in the winter and the spring of 1970, when the Cabinet-level Urban Affairs Council began a series of meetings at Blair House. This recently created council, where all the domestic executive departments were represented, provided a new setting for policy making on interagency mat-

[38] *Strengthening the Federal Response to Model Cities: An Interagency Report*, September 1969, p. 20.
[39] Director, Bureau of the Budget, memorandum for Mr. John Ehrlichman, "The Model Cities Program," November 4, 1969.
[40] Arnold R. Weber, Assistant Secretary for Manpower, letter to Floyd H. Hyde, August 14, 1969.

ters. During the Johnson Administration, HUD officials negotiated with other agencies one at a time, with White House interest and support applied to each agency separately. The Urban Affairs Council, which involved White House staff as well as Cabinet members, offered better prospects for reaching agreements on uniform policies that all departments would subsequently honor. On the other hand, top HUD officials could face stiffer opposition in negotiating with a series of reluctant agencies at once than their predecessors had in dealing with each one separately. Thus the changing arena for interagency negotiations also influenced the outcome of the partisan mutual adjustment process.

At the first Blair House session, George Romney presented HUD's views on the future conduct of the Model Cities Program, including a proposal that all federal agencies provide the mayors with information on the status of all federal grants and applications that affected the model neighborhood. Further, he recommended that the mayors be given veto power over all grant programs for the model neighborhood, "or at the very least, the right of prior consultation."[41]

The Blair House group quickly decided that only minor improvements in the federal administration of the Model Cities Program as a whole should be worried about, and that effort should be concentrated in those cities selected for a special experiment known as "planned variations." (See Chapter 5.) The Urban Affairs Council subcommittee on model cities at first proposed that the mayor or chief executive in this limited number of cities should have veto power over all federal aid applications affecting the model neighborhood, but as departmental resistance emerged more clearly, they diluted the proposal to call for mayoral review rather than an absolute veto. Thus, when the planned variations were finally established in July 1971, the twenty cities that were selected were given "chief executive review and comment" on federal aid proposals.

This procedure required federal agencies to consult with the mayors on grants for local programs, thus giving them some opportunity to influence the flow of federal dollars. HUD gave the mayors special funds to strengthen their staffs so that they could take advantage of the new procedure. Each federal agency was to specify which of its programs were to be covered, and the major federal agencies did in fact later designate programs to be included and issue instructions to their field staff. From there, the effort to build up the role of the mayor was transferred from Washington to the newly created Federal Regional Councils. These councils, where the major federal domestic agencies were all represented,

[41] George Romney, briefing to the Urban Affairs Council on Model Cities, February 27, 1970.

were supposed to establish workable procedures in the field. By this time HUD was no longer pressing for mayoral or CDA veto power but was looking instead for ways in which it could draw local government into the process of allocating federal aid funds to the model neighborhoods. In August 1972, when President Nixon announced that planned variations would continue in the same twenty cities for a second year, he reminded all federal agencies working with these cities of their responsibility to provide local government with the opportunity to review and comment on federal aid applications.[42]

Local Experience

Experience at the regional and local levels casts further light on the difficulties of carrying out HUD's model cities strategy. HEW, consistently the most cooperative federal agency other than HUD itself, set up a special certification procedure to provide for mayoral and CDA review of aid applications that would affect the model neighborhood. The basic directive went out to the regional staff in November 1969, and a more detailed set of procedures was issued by Sidney Gardner, then Deputy Assistant Secretary for Community Development, in February 1970.

Two years later, in January 1972, a consulting team from Marshall Kaplan, Gans and Kahn conducted interviews in HEW regional offices, city halls, and CDAs in a sample of cities across the country to find out how the certification process was working. At the most basic level, the process was being followed. That is, relatively few grant applications were slipping through the system without the signature of the CDA director on a form certifying that the CDA had been given an opportunity to participate in the development of the project, that there had been adequate citizen participation in this development, and that adequate provision had been made for continued coordination, monitoring, and evaluation by the CDA. A key factor in the enforcement of this certification was the extent to which decisions about individual programs were centralized at the regional level. The Office of Education, which operates primarily at the state level and is not subject to effective control by HEW's regional directors, reported many project "slip-throughs" without certification. Thus the ability to make a review procedure work depended upon the ability of federal agencies to main-

[42] U.S. President, Office of the White House Press Secretary, Statement by the President (Planned Variations), July 29, 1971; HUD, Statement by Secretary Romney: Planned Variations, July 29, 1971; Floyd H. Hyde, Questions and Answers on Planned Variations, November 19, 1971; *Commerce Clearing House*, August 24, 1972, Section 19, 520.

tain a clear point of control over their own funding operations.

A more important question was whether certification meant that the CDAs or mayors had been involved significantly in project development, so that plans could be shaped to meet the objectives of the model neighborhood, or whether their review was perfunctory. In most cases, that review appears to have been perfunctory and last minute. Regional HEW officials seldom checked what lay behind the completed form, citing lack of time and staff and a desire not to jeopardize a proposal's chance for funding. The CDAs seldom used their review authority to gain an active role in project development, partly because they did not recognize their opportunity to do so and partly because they usually did not learn of projects at an early stage of planning. The mayors played no significant part. Most did not even know about the CDA certification, and those who did said they did not have the time or the staff to take advantage of it.

The CDA certification was limited almost entirely to discretionary federal-local grants for projects and services, and excluded from it were the much larger sums involved in federal-state grant programs. Most HEW regional officials understood the procedure to relate principally to federal-local grants and drew on the opinion of HEW's General Counsel that federal-state grant programs, where allocations were made according to state plans and statutory formulas, could not legally be made subject to CDA review. Nevertheless, many tried to persuade state agencies to cooperate voluntarily, and most regional staff believed that it would be desirable to extend the "sign-off" procedure to federal-state grants. However, they were not optimistic that state agencies would cooperate voluntarily.

Underlying the reluctance of HEW staff to press for a more significant involvement of the CDAs in project planning were their commitments to their traditional client groups. In several regional offices, HEW staff members explained that their ties to local school boards, hospitals, or state agencies made them reluctant to question too closely any proposal that had obtained a formal CDA certification. As one Dallas official put it, "You can't ignore past relationships, and you don't change traditional ways of doing things by kicking people in the head. You've got to work with them. They're going to be around long after the sign-off is dead and gone." Only a few staff members saw the certification process as a positive opportunity for HEW to broaden its base in the cities by building relationships with new interest groups.

Federal regional staff saw their job as getting proposals funded. They recognized that many applications fell by the wayside, and as a result they were not likely to raise unnecessary obstacles. Therefore, in the few cases when HEW officials questioned the CDA certification, this was usually in response to local protests such as those from model neighborhood resident groups.

A few proposals were changed as a result of the CDA review, and these changes followed a consistent pattern. Many CDA directors, consulted in the late stages of a grant application, decided not to make a major effort to modify the proposal. Instead they referred the matter to their resident participation group. The residents, usually without adequate staff for a close review, focused their attention on a few issues of immediate interest to them: jobs, service eligibility, and control. Thus the most common changes made related to the number of jobs guaranteed to residents, the number of residents to be served by a project, and the number of residents who would be members of policy boards.

These were not trivial changes, but they fell far short of HUD and HEW intentions. What is more, resident review sometimes had adverse consequences for the model neighborhood. Several regional officials cited examples of "counterplanning," of projects being moved out of model neighborhoods to avoid the CDA certification procedure. This usually occurred in response to what the agency felt was unfair treatment at the hands of citizen groups. In Denver, according to a regional office staff member, the Board of Education had withdrawn from negotiations on subsequent model cities planning because it believed the CDA demanded too much project control as the price of its approval. According to another HEW official, the New Jersey Vocational Rehabilitation Commission refused to "have anything more to do with Trenton and Newark" because of "bad faith and discourtesy" during negotiations over the sign-off. "The residents gave the Commission such a hard time that they've finished with those cities. And there's little we can really do about it," he concluded. Thus the hope of CDA and citizen control over federal funding may well have run counter to the goal of concentrating federal resources in model neighborhoods, as long as state and local agencies had more attractive alternatives elsewhere.

Although they found that the HEW certification process was working to a certain limited extent, the consulting team concluded that it did "not appear to be particularly effective in enabling the CDA director to plan meaningfully the allocations of health, education, and welfare resources in his area of responsibility."[43]

[43] Marshall Kaplan, Gans and Kahn, "Certification of Model Cities Relatedness: CDA and Regional HEW: Use of the CDA Sign-Off in Model Cities for Planning and Coordinating HEW Programs," Report to the Department of Housing and Urban Development, June 27, 1972.

Reform by Negotiation?

In retrospect, the attempt to establish a single point of entry for federal funds through the mayor and CDA seems almost incompatible with the American federal system. Yet to the designers of the Model Cities Program and to a series of HUD officials in two administrations, this appeared to be a modest and reasonable reform. They did not ask for changes in the total flow of federal aid funds into the cities but requested only a waiver of usual procedures for the delivery of aid to 150 neighborhoods across the country. Even this limited goal proved to be unattainable.

No single fact explains the failure to achieve this goal, but a series of obstacles came to light that could not possibly be overcome by HUD's course of action. HUD officials made use of the processes Lindblom described as central direction combined with partisan mutual adjustment. Within HUD itself, but only there, the central direction was strong enough to bring about agreement on urban renewal funds on terms set by the Model Cities Administration. Elsewhere, even with White House intervention on several occasions, protracted interagency negotiations brought about a series of compromises, but these fell far short of accomplishing HUD objectives. Partisan mutual adjustment, of course, was not likely to lead to anything but compromise as long as other participants did not share HUD's purposes and had some power to resist capitulation. When HUD officials during the Johnson Administration were pressed by representatives of other agencies to give citizens a stronger voice in local Model Cities Programs, they, too, responded with a compromise.

Even had other agencies been more accommodating, however, the negotiators in Washington did not have the power to give HUD everything it wanted. The top leadership in HEW was very cooperative, particularly during the Johnson Administration, but it could not alter federal-state grant programs without Congressional action; nor could Washington officials effectively control their highly decentralized field staff. OEO officials could not realistically repudiate the philosophy that provided a rationale for their existence, nor could they turn away from their organized client groups, even in 150 neighborhoods. They were willing to strike a compromise, but once they did, it became evident that they could not follow through in the field. The Department of Labor, on the other hand, was even less interested in compromise and conformed more to Lindblom's description of the decision maker who is reluctant to take an openly partisan position but instead pursues his own purposes under a veneer of cooperation.

The outcome of this effort was a series of compromises that demonstrated above all how deeply rooted were the obstacles to change within the federal aid system. Some progress was made toward unifying control over federal grants in at least a few cities, but it was slow and uneven. Certainly it did not provide the federal reform that was a prerequisite for strengthening city government capability to deal with the problems of the model neighborhoods. The program guide that HUD issued to participating cities called on them to make "marked progress" toward overcoming all critical problems in the model neighborhood within five years. The federal government itself, however, was not operating on a timetable that would permit much progress in a five-year program.

Chapter 5
A Flexible Federal Response: Earmarking and Guideline Revision

Introduction

Very few of the program's early advocates, whether inside or outside the halls of Congress, viewed the monies proposed for model cities as sufficient to achieve the many complex objectives envisaged in the legislation. Participating cities would have to find some way to gain ready access to what was then estimated at $12 billion in categorical aid programs.[1] Clearly, the "complete array of available grants and urban aid . . . to the maximum extent authorized by existing legislation . . . would have to be made available to participating cities."[2] Further, if the new program was to succeed, Congress acknowledged that it would require "far more effective coordination of existing Federal programs than has been achieved in the past."[3] Only in this way would funds be redistributed on a significant scale and concentrated on model neighborhood areas and their populations.

How best to funnel these considerable federal resources into the model cities was thus a relevant question even at the inception of the program. If the funds were to be most effective, they would have to be made available in a manner that fitted in with local model city plans and met the needs of the model neighborhood population—the poor. Traditional, and perhaps understandable, fears of Congressmen and civil servants that they might lose control over the funding process would have to be overcome; planning prerequisites and administrative ground rules associated with particular aid programs would have to be modified, if not abandoned; and funding formulas governing the use of key federal programs would have to be amended to permit recognition of the new priorities. Historical patterns of behavior, reflecting in part national objectives, in part the influence of specific interest groups, and in part administrative rigidity, would have to be radically changed. To achieve such change was a tall order for a pro-

[1] Special Analyses, Budget of the United States, Fiscal Year 1970, Table 0.3, p. 209. James L. Sundquist and David W. Davis indicate in their book, *Making Federalism Work* (Washington, D.C.: Brookings Institution, 1969), that enactment of numerous federal aid programs in the five years prior to the Model Cities Program led to the "transformation of the federal system." These aids covered thirty-nine areas of activity that previously had been the province of state and local government; they generated almost a doubling of the volume of federal grants to states and local governments. Over 219 individual assistance programs were added to the federal inventory between 1963 and 1966, 109 in the year immediately prior to the enactment of the Model Cities Program.

[2] President's Task Force on Urban Problems (Wood task force), report, December 22, 1965, p. 18.

[3] Statement included in Senate Committee on Banking and Currency S. Report 1439, August 1966 (reported in Richard Cherry and Kent Watkins, "History of Congressional Action Relative to Model Cities 1966-1967," HUD, October 3, 1967, p. 28). The House Committee

gram that had yet to test its support in the White House and in Congress and that would require several departments to give way to the legislatively prescribed interests of one department.

Both criticism, and the need for reform, of the categorical program system stood behind the advocacy of the new Model Cities Program. The Wood task force, for example, had stated:

—The administration of the [existing urban] programs has been too much oriented to specific functions. . . .
—The effectiveness of the programs that do exist is impaired by division of authority. . . .
—Inadequate resources, ineffective organization and management arrangements unduly protract the time of execution. . . .
—The goals of major federal programs have often conflicted and been unreconciled. . . .[4]

The proposals were not always specific, but the task force suggested the need for major revisions in the federal aid system. Participating model cities would receive the "complete array of grants and urban aids . . . allocated on a *priority* basis; funds . . . in a common account drawn at the *discretion* of the community in *conformance* to its program requirements."[5] Reform would not be easy, however, as Robert Wood viewed the problems ahead.

Given resistance to change at the federal level, participating Model Cities would have to play a key role in generating a proper federal response. Cities would have the responsibility of pulling it all together; of showing, through their detailed Model Cities proposals, how federal programs could be coordinated and used in an innovative manner. To the feds would fall the task of reacting effectively to city needs and priorities . . . in order for them to do this, they would have to put their own house in order. Thus, basic changes in federal administrative practices would result, at least in part, from city pressure. . . .[6]

Reliance on the participating cities to induce reform of the federal grant-in-aid system had been one of the dominant themes of Secretary Weaver's testimony in support of the legislation before the Congress. Yet intuitively sensing the difficulties he would face in securing an interdepartmental response, the new Secretary shifted the task of coordination onto the participating model cities. Weaver claimed that HUD would not try to mandate the role of other federal departments. Instead, it would tell the cities, "if you want these supplemental funds,

---

used identical language; see Chapter 3.
[4] President's Task Force on Urban Problems, report, p. 4.
[5] Ibid., p. 18 (italics added).
[6] Interview with Robert Wood, January 1969.

you are going to have to coordinate these programs and we are going to *help* you to do it."[7] His optimism about HUD's ability to help would later prove unfounded. Coordination from the bottom up would prove as difficult as coordination generated from above.

Congressmen were aware that a means would have to be found to blend categorical aid programs and model cities funds. They were also aware that this would be difficult, because model city supplemental funds were free of most statutory limitations on their local use, while categorical programs were encumbered with limitations and with additional administrative ground rules. Yet most were unwilling to grant participating model cities any preference in the allocation of categorical funds. Quite the contrary: the legislative history of the program, as noted in Chapter 3, demonstrated the level of Congressional opposition. Most of the members of the House and Senate Committees responsible for the bill were not interested in allowing model neighborhoods any favored treatment, or priority, over existing grant-in-aid programs.[8]

Neither did Congress look with equanimity on the use of model cities funds to provide the local share of other federal aid programs in participating cities. Apparently, many members were worried that this could give model cities an unfair advantage in the competition for federal aid. As it finally passed, the legislation required that the first lien on model city funds would come from totally new, federally unassisted projects identified in local model city plans. Only one categorical program was subjected to a specific legislative amendment, or "set-aside," for model cities. Because many local officials were afraid that the Model Cities Program would divert urban renewal funds from projects that were not in model city areas, or would shun local priorities for renewal, $250 million was specifically provided for urban renewal projects in the model city areas.

Congressional reluctance over the role that categorical programs were to play in the model cities is understandable. Even those legislators who were willing to support the allocation of supplemental funds to a limited number of cities found it difficult to agree to the diversion of categorical programs to model cities on a priority basis, and to selected neighborhoods within those cities. Most Congressmen want to get reelected, and a platform that demonstrates how many federal grants are being received by a neighboring city or an alien constituency rather than their own is not the strongest one to stand on.

[7] Cherry and Watkins, "History . . . Model Cities 1966-1967," p. 17 (italics added).
[8] See Senate Committee on Banking and Currency S. Report 1439 (reported in Cherry and Watkins, "History . . . Model Cities, 1966-1967," p. 29, and in Chapter 3).

HUD's administrative responsibility for the program was established by statute; so, too, was its role in seeking a more flexible, coordinated administration of the categorical programs. As described in Chapter 3, the Secretary of HUD was to ensure, "in conjunction with" other agencies and under the direction of the President, the maximum coordination of federal aid efforts. In carrying out the provisions of the act, including the issuance of regulations, the Secretary was to "*consult* with other Federal departments and agencies administering federal grant-in-aid programs. . . ."[9] This language, taken in conjunction with Weaver's aversion to rule by fiat and Congress's hesitancy to endorse priorities in the flow of grants in aid, suggested that HUD was going to have to rely more on persuasion than dictation in its dealings with other departments.

In essence, HUD would not be able to play the role of Downs's "superman" either easily or for sustained periods of time. The coordination of aid programs when and if it occurred would—because of agency fears, the absence of a consensus over model cities objectives, and the inability of the White House to effect a sustained institutional response—result more from negotiation and chance than from fiat. The anticipated redistribution and concentration of federal aid would become a casualty of the program.

First Efforts: Earmarking and Guideline Revision

While the bill was still under debate in Congress, HUD began to work on building up the administrative capacity to carry out its many mandates. This was no easy task, given the newness of the department itself and the fact that it had inherited from the Housing and Home Finance Agency many programs of quite recent origin. Questions about HUD's role as a model cities agency, particularly its role in securing an interdepartmental response to the program, were understandably set aside at first: there was an immediate need to secure staff; there was a need to debate the very structure of the Model Cities Administration and its relationship to other offices within HUD; and there was a need to develop initial application and planning ground rules. Even the HUD Advisory Committee, which had been created to develop guidelines for program management, and which was reasonably demanding in its requirements for the participating cities, avoided being very specific on the question of interagency cooperation. First efforts in this direction were limited, primarily, to seeking the participation of other departments in the review of early applications.

[9] Demonstration Cities Act of 1966 (Public Law 89-754), Title 1, Comprehensive City Demonstration Programs, Sec. 103b2, Sec. 109 (italics added).

In the spring of 1967, the Assistant Secretary for Model Cities made the first informal attempt to obtain "information" from his counterparts in other agencies about their willingness to commit funds to model cities on a priority basis and simultaneously to relax their administrative guidelines governing the review and use of such funds. He met with only a lukewarm response. "We had trouble gaining reasonable consensus as to the aims and objectives of the program . . . most other agencies had only a general awareness of Model Cities . . . indeed, most senior staff in these agencies were not yet familiar with the intricacies of their own programs. . . ." Clearly, "Model Cities had not yet carved out its turf . . . the degree of Presidential support was not yet evident . . . most agencies were not willing to allocate resources in advance or change then existing practices for what was still seen as a HUD program, particularly when it was still uncertain what city needs were."[10]

Surprisingly, HUD's initial review of applications for model city funds failed to draw attention to the need for flexible administration of categorical programs and priority funding.

Even though few applications were precise, we probably should have sensed the need to gain certain commitments from HUD as well as other agencies concerning . . . the need to set aside funds for Model Cities . . . , the handling of categorical programs and the elimination of onerous administrative criteria. But our staff was small, and our prime effort was directed at getting organized and getting cities underway. We were also very optimistic about what we could do with other agency staff and the possibilities of Presidential and Secretarial support.[11]

The Model Cities Administration Federal Agency Liaison Division was initially assigned responsibility to develop and maintain effective relationships with HUD's sister agencies. Its formal mandate was quite broad; coordination, after all, was not a subject of easy definition. However, because there were no firm ground rules to determine the extent of HUD's role or the precise response wanted from other agencies and because the staff of the new division was unable, or unwilling, to fill the void, it was not able to outline a clear plan of action or convince the Assistant Secretary that it would develop one in the near future. Gradually, and somewhat purposely, responsibility for working with other departments was granted to individual program specialists on the staff. Robbed of

[10] Marshall Kaplan, Gans and Kahn staff interview with H. Ralph Taylor, then Assistant Secretary for Model Cities (HUD), January 9, 1969. Interview undertaken as part of a HUD-funded National Evaluation of Model Cities.
[11] Marshall Kaplan, Gans and Kahn staff interview with Walter Farr as part of National Twenty-One City Evaluation, January 1969.

its mandate, the Federal Liaison Division was abolished in the fall of 1967. Its demise occurred at the same time as the transfer of the Office of Intergovernmental Relations from Assistant Secretary Taylor to Assistant Secretary Haar. This transfer was supported by Secretary Weaver on the grounds that liaison with state and metropolitan governments was more appropriately a function of the Assistant Secretary responsible for metropolitan planning than of the Assistant Secretary responsible for initiating a limited demonstration program such as model cities. Unfortunately, the termination of the one division and the transfer of the other office diffused the organizational focus for intergovernmental relationships. Of necessity, the definition and implementation of a federal strategy toward model cities, already made difficult by the reluctance of sister agencies to give more than lip service to it, were placed directly in the hands of the Assistant Secretary and the Director; there this responsibility faced competition for attention with a wide range of issues and a heavy schedule.

No clear-cut, hard scheme for federal action existed throughout most of 1967. Most of the key staff recognized the need to formalize the informal interagency working groups that had become established. These groups, composed of senior staff from the relevant federal departments, had been meeting occasionally since the inception of the program. In part because there was little general interest in model cities, their tangible accomplishments were minimal; but they had at least provided a forum for the federal players, or would-be players, to get to know one another. They also seemed to offer a forum within which any interagency policy that did emerge could readily be implemented.

In the early summer of 1967, an interagency agreement, stimulated by Assistant Secretary Taylor's desire to "structure the groups already meeting informally," was reached among HUD, HEW, the Department of Labor (DOL), and the Office of Economic Opportunity. This agreement emerged from a series of sessions between Taylor and his counterparts in the other agencies. Involvement in the negotiations of the White House staff and the Secretary was marginal and limited to expressions of support. The agreement called for the creation of *formal* interagency working groups at the Washington, regional, and local levels. Each group was assigned a very general set of responsibilities: The Washington Inter-Agency Committee was to take on policy and coordination; the Regional Inter-Agency Coordinating Committees were to review city submissions and to maintain liaison with the relevant local officials; and the Regional Working Groups[12] were to review and monitor programs and to supply technical assist-

---

[12] The Washington Inter-Agency Committee was to be staffed by top management and policy personnel from each participating federal agency. The Regional Inter-Agency Coordi-

ance to specific cities. Significantly, *no* commitment was made by any of the signatories to the agreement on the question of preferential program funding for model cities. Nor did any agency make definitive promises to amend its categorical program guidelines to simplify the handling of applications or to streamline the review processes. The use of such phrases as "cooperation with HUD" in juxtaposition with statements such as "retain . . . full authority and responsibility for conducting their own programs" symbolized, only too clearly, the hesitancy of most agencies to change existing patterns of behavior.

No significant progress was made by the Model Cities Administration in defining a precise interagency strategy until well after the planning awards were made to cities in December.[13] Serious discussions remained a casualty of agency indifference, and of HUD's, as well as the cities', impreciseness about their needs. Program specialists continued to work selectively with their counterparts in other agencies on a "one-to-one" basis. Areas of opportunity rather than a precise agenda dictated initial "interagency" contacts. Less frequent informal policy discussions continued to be held by the MCA Director and Assistant Secretary with their peers in other agencies. Meetings were, for the most part, generalized and unstructured.

Questions about the use and availability of categorical programs to the cities began to filter through to Washington from the various HUD regional offices by midwinter 1968. Most questions, apart from those about the general availability of funds, concerned either the interpretation of administrative criteria or the timing of the delivery of categorical program funds. For example,

. . . would administrative criteria concerning certain HEW, HUD, DOL, or OEO programs be relaxed to permit us to do what we need to do . . . or would funds from Section . . . be available at the start of our first action year . . . or do we have to submit applications for each separate federal program after our CDP [community development program] is approved . . . or can we fund projects with both categorical and supplemental funds?[14]

---

nating Committees were to contain senior staff from the office of the director or administrator of each federal agency in each region. The Working Groups were to be composed of technicians from each relevant federal agency in each region.

[13] Initially, HUD assumed it would be ready to award planning grants to selected model cities in late summer or early fall. Because of the White House's desire to get Congressional approval of model cities appropriations, the grant awards were held up until late fall, however, and the announcement was not made public until early December. Congressmen from cities that applied for grants and were not awarded them would be less prone to vote for model cities appropriations.

[14] Marshall Kaplan, Gans and Kahn staff interviews with CDA Directors (interviews undertaken as part of National Evaluation efforts throughout 1970).

Neither HUD nor any of the other departments was ready to respond easily to such inquiries from the cities. Certainly, preferential funding by each department to individual model cities remained more of a dream within the Model Cities Administration than a federal reality. Further, because support for model cities remained peripheral in most departments, no one, or agency, was prepared to take a hard look at the detailed guidelines associated with their respective categorical programs. According to Ralph Taylor,

... all that was certain at this time was that Model Cities would have to submit separate applications for categorical program funds. . . . The assumption (hope) held by some that we would be able to offer Model Cities the opportunity to use their CDP as an application or to submit a consolidated application, was just not in the winds. . . . Program prerequisites and review processes were too different . . . further, program managers were not about to give up control. . . .[15]

Defining a Strategy

As the first cities pressed into their first planning year, it became clear that reliance on the voluntary cooperation of other agencies would produce minimal results. Increasingly, the MCA felt the need to present each department with a list of demands. Taylor and Farr thus asked their staff to develop an "in-depth" paper on this problem describing each agency's role. Several working drafts were prepared in midwinter. None, however, was specific in defining what could or should be done, given the statutory and institutional constraints. Each expressed the roles of the federal agencies in general terms only. As one early draft put it, federal agencies were to

—provide affirmative technical assistance to CDA's with respect to program opportunities; . . . urge their constituent state and local counterpart agencies to experiment and cooperate with local Model Cities programs.
—help cities set realistic planning targets by early summer for programs to be funded out of FY [fiscal year] 1969 appropriations;
—earmark, to the extent the relevant statute permits, a substantial portion of available . . . appropriations in every major urban program for Model Cities and keep such funds available for qualifying applications. . . ;
—require city government approval (through its CDA and its Model Cities citizen participation structure) of all Federal program activities that materially affect the Model Neighborhood or its residents, and, where the relevant statute permits, contract for such programs directly with the city as sponsor;
—process applications from Model Cities as first priorities and with flexibility as to administrative requirements; and

[15] Interview with H. Ralph Taylor, July 1972.

—cooperate with HUD and other agencies toward the objective of (a) eliminating duplicative or conflicting program reporting requirements, (b) development of common applications for families or related programs, and (c) standardization of planning requirements.[16]

Obviously, earmarking, or the allocation of categorical program funds in advance of applications for model cities funds, and flexible interpretation of the guidelines were not the only questions that seemed important to HUD. Yet both were viewed initially as the more "important" requests to be made of agencies. As one senior staff member indicated, "if we can't get agencies to set aside their program funds for Model Cities and to permit cities to use these funds in an innovative way . . . we might as well close up shop . . . supplemental funds are not sufficient to meet Congressional objectives, nor city needs."[17]

These early working papers were circulated both within HUD and within other federal agencies. But little came of them. Firm commitments of funds remained elusive. OEO indicated as late as June 1968 that it would "find it extremely difficult, if not impossible, to earmark funds" because the agency did not "control either the specific programs of the CAA or the geographic location of their programs."[18] In late April, HEW began, through its urban task force, to look into the issue of resource commitment, but the complexities associated with its inventory promised little in the way of early help.[19] The earmarking of key HUD programs, such as urban renewal, was the subject of much debate within HUD itself. Until a strong mandate came from Secretary Weaver and Under Secretary Wood, a traditional reliance on the established pipeline, supposed statutory constraints, and a hesitancy on the part of the staff to endorse the partici-

[16] Attachment to memorandum from H. Ralph Taylor, Assistant Secretary, Model Cities, to Robert C. Weaver, Secretary of HUD, March 27, 1968, p. 2.

[17] Marshall Kaplan, Gans and Kahn staff interview with Lawrence Houston, Senior MCA staff, January 19, 1969. Interview undertaken as part of HUD-funded National Evaluation of Model Cities Program.

[18] Memorandum from Donald K. Hess, Associate Director, Office of Program Planning, CAP/OEO, "Federal Response to Model Cities," to Walter Farr, Director, HUD-Model Cities, June 12, 1968, p. 1.

[19] Memorandum from Secretary Wilbur J. Cohen of HEW, "HEW and the Cities," to key HEW officials, April 28, 1968. This memorandum was considered by many in HUD to reflect a significant endorsement of and commitment to the Model Cities Program. It granted to the program "budget priority" and called in the Office of the Comptroller and the Center for Community Change to "determine which financial resources might support Model Cities . . . and to discuss . . . methods for assuring maximum effective programming of funds during the coming fiscal year. . . ." It placed significant authority in the hands of regional directors who were asked to "provide direction for and coordinate agency required activities in contacting, working with, and developing support for Model Cities. . . ."

pation of resident groups as required in the Model Cities Program, all dulled enthusiasm to cooperate. The Department of Labor resisted the very notion of earmarking, preferring instead to rest its participation on the merging of its Concentrated Employment Programs[20] with local model cities plans and also on the recognition of the program in the CAMPS (Comprehensive Area Manpower Planning System)[21] review process.

Both Under Secretary Wood of HUD and Secretary Cohen of HEW responded favorably to pleas from the Model Cities Administration for more flexible reviews of applications and administration of programs by the agencies. Their statements on the subject, however, were quite general and left much discretion to the staff to decide how far each department would go, and when. For example, Under Secretary Wood called for an "examination" of HUD procedures and asked that applications be moved as "quickly as possible."[22] Secretary Cohen called on senior associates to set "objectives" and establish "a Task Force"[23] to facilitate a more appropriate departmental response to the program.

Neither the Department of Labor nor OEO responded at once with intradepartmental mandates to its staff; no examination of program criteria or of review processes was begun within either agency. Negotiations between the Model Cities Administration and these agencies occurred on a program-by-program basis. They varied over time, often depending for even marginal success on the tenacity of the particular member of the MCA staff and the willingness of his counterpart in the other agency to maintain the contact.

Unfortunately, neither the "open-ended" directive to examine the procedures, expressed by Wood and Cohen, nor the program-by-program negotiations with the senior staff of each agency produced many tangible results. Nominal expressions of commitment from top officials were no substitute for serious analysis by their staff or action by individual program managers. Clearly, it would take more than this to rationalize different departmental organizations, varied program funding cycles, diverse regulations governing the management of reviews, and the fears of many program managers over their loss of control, as well as their ability to use often conflicting administrative guidelines to thwart Secre-

[20] The Concentrated Employment Program was an effort initiated in the 1960s to coordinate the then existing manpower programs in selected cities.

[21] The Comprehensive Area Manpower Planning System was a Labor Department term for an effort initiated in the mid-1960s to plan and coordinate manpower programs on a state and metropolitan basis.

[22] Memorandum from Under Secretary Robert C. Wood, "Response to Model Cities," to HUD Assistant Secretaries (May 21, 1968), p. 1.

[23] Memorandum from Secretary Cohen, "HEW and the Cities," April 26, 1968.

tarial admonitions. Similarly, it would take more than the MCA's good intentions to get officials to relinquish some of their control over programs or to eliminate the normal bureaucratic fear of exercising discretion without specific and precise authorization.

White House Intervention

Initially, Farr and Taylor had hoped that they could avoid seeking help from the White House. Until local Model Cities Programs got off the ground, they wanted to keep away from confrontation politics, relying instead on persuasion. As summer approached, however, and the submittal of the first plans seemed only a few months away, intervention by the White House appeared necessary if the first round of participating model cities were to obtain the benefits of the promised coordinated and effective federal response. On April 17, 1968, at the request of Ralph Taylor, Secretary Weaver forwarded to Joseph Califano, Special Assistant to the President, and to Charles Zwick, then director of the Budget Bureau, a memorandum on the federal action required. His covering letter explicitly requested aid in "working out arrangements with other Departments."[24] Califano subsequently made phone calls to the Secretaries of HEW and the Department of Labor and also to the Director of OEO. He expressed the "President's interest in Model Cities and the President's desire that the Departments cooperate with HUD." Those calls were certainly important symbolically, but they made only very general demands. No deadlines were set and no action required.[25]

Califano's calls did little to stimulate performance. Clearly, more would be needed. As Califano later recalled,

Wirtz never liked the Model Cities Program and Labor was very protective of its turf. It had enough problems getting its own programs into shape and fighting off other agencies to agree to give up some control over funds implicit in HUD's request to earmark or amend guidelines. OEO was in a difficult spot having recently been asked by the White House and Congress to delegate many of its manpower programs to DOL. . . . It also was responsible to local CAA's [Community Action Agencies] which were seen in some quarters as competitive to local CDA's [model cities agencies] . Cohen at HEW, while desirous of helping out, sat at the top of an almost impossible agency to administer. . . . Model City requirements imposed on all agencies a different routing system; one that seemed to have statutory as well as political problems.[26]

[24] Letter from Secretary Weaver to Joseph Califano, Special Assistant to President Lyndon Johnson, and to Charles Zwick, Director, Bureau of the Budget, August 17, 1968.
[25] Interview with Joseph Califano, July 26, 1972.

According to Califano, most officials in DOL and OEO felt their own programs deserved to receive priority attention. Mandates from the MCA were not taken too kindly and often treated in a cursory fashion. Senior officials in HEW were more charitable to the program but were hamstrung by the almost ungovernable nature of that large complex agency. All the relevant departments found the requests for speedy and flexible reviews difficult to respond to because of statutory and administrative constraints and also because there often seemed to be differing objectives for their programs and support from differing interest groups.

Califano followed his initial calls with a formal memorandum on model cities to each agency Secretary in midsummer. This time he sought a specific and rapid reply. Each department was to set out its plans for earmarking, technical assistance, application handling, and for the involvement of local chief executives in the categorical programs. All agency heads were to outline

—the steps that the Department will take to assure the success of the Model Cities Program, e.g., including procedural and policy directives which will be issued, staffing and funding allocations, and other actions needed to meet Department's objectives during the current fiscal year. . . .
—the date on which each of these steps will be completed.[27]

The memorandum specifically asked what procedures would be adopted at the federal level to

—speed review of and decisions on applications relating to Model Cities plans?
—assure maximum flexibility in the review of plans and applications so that local needs can be met as efficiently and effectively as possible?[28]

The responses were less than dramatic. No agency appeared enthusiastic; many posed statutory and administrative problems. Their replies varied between general intent and general disinterest. The Department of Health, Education, and Welfare did not identify specific fund reservations but called attention to the fact that a special task force had been created to implement within thirty days a fund reservation plan for the model cities in 1969. Final determination of the amounts to be reserved under the fund reservation plan would apparently be dependent both upon Congressional action and the impact of the reductions that had been required under the Revenue and Expenditure Control Act of 1968. [29] On the subject of guidelines revision and review, the department noted that

[26] Ibid.
[27] Memorandum from Joseph Califano to Secretary Cohen (HEW), July 26, 1968. Similar memoranda were sent to OEO and DOL.
[28] Attachment to Joseph Califano's memorandum to Secretary Cohen, July 26, 1968, p. 3.
[29] Memorandum from James P. Alexander, Director, Center for Community Planning, to Secretary Cohen, July 31, 1968; used to respond to Joseph Califano's initial request.

"general policies and procedures for application review and coordination will be issued by early September. . . ." Apart from promising technical assistance to local model city groups before applications were submitted, the department stated that "A Task Force . . . will develop recommendations concerning further steps to provide uniform and simplified grant policy and procedures. . . ."[30]

The Office of Economic Opportunity expressed support for model cities but acknowledged that it would find it "difficult to answer the question" on fund reservations, because it had neither an appropriation nor an apportionment from the Budget Bureau for the fiscal year 1969. "The combined effort of Congressional reductions, the legislatively mandated rural thrust, earmarking, and the statutory Allotment requirement[31] is to limit severely OEO's flexibility in channeling funds to such high priority programs as Model Cities. Under these circumstances, it would be *foolish* to say that we could make significant new funds available to Model Cities."[32]

OEO promised that it would "take whatever steps are necessary to assure speedy review of and decisions on applications relating to Model Cities plans. . . ." Staff would be made available to "work with HUD and other federal agencies to develop procedures and policies to expedite grant processing and to implement them *after* joint agreement." Differences between the two agencies' programs and their funding cycles for granting aid to the cities could be resolved "through joint discussions."[33]

The Department of Labor did not respond directly to Califano's questions on allocations. It stated, instead, that its Concentrated Employment Program was, and would remain, the main thrust of the department's efforts to support the new program. "Where no CEP exists, funding of manpower programs that will have a major impact on the Model Neighborhood will be determined primarily by CAMPS. . . ." In effect, the Department of Labor made no commitment to earmark funds. As with the other agencies, it suggested the impossibility of determining how much new funding could go into the model cities until Congress had appropriated funds and the department had received an apportionment from the Bureau of the Budget.[34] Only scant reference was made to application handling and review. Basically, the department claimed that the "processing of

[30] Ibid.

[31] The legislation required that each state receive a minimum amount of funding according to a formula spelled out in the act.

[32] Unsigned memorandum from OEO, "The Model Cities Program," to Joseph Califano, August 12, 1968 (italics added).

[33] Ibid. (italics added).

[34] Memorandum from Secretary Willard Wirtz (DOL), "Model Cities Coordination; Plan for Implementation," to Joseph Califano, August 15, 1968.

Model Cities manpower components have been decentralized to the Regional Offices. . . ."[35]

Joseph Califano followed up his original memorandum with further memoranda during the late summer and early fall. Each sought a tougher commitment on funds and a more specific determination of program guidelines and revisions in the review process. Yet continuous monitoring by the White House was not possible. As Califano explained it,

We were not equipped to maintain day-to-day relationship with only one program—no matter how important. . . . White House staff had to accept two or three priorities; priorities dictated by the President. Model Cities, while important, could not compete on a continuous basis with key legislative, domestic and foreign policy crises. . . . Even if staff had more time, it is doubtful whether, given the institutional complexity of most departments, we could have done more than we did. Johnson's becoming a lame duck President made our role all the more difficult. But even if he would have remained a candidate, we could only bang heads at a certain level. The White House couldn't reach out easily to program managers. . . .[36]

Califano could also have added the fact that the ability of the White House or the President to affect the sustained operation of each department is minimal. Successful translation of broad White House policy dictates into specific and continuous department action is difficult, given the bureaucratic, political, and often physical distance between the Chief Executive and his staff and the program personnel in each department. Layers of administrative criteria attached to each federal aid program are used by middle management staff to justify their independence, not only from the President but often from their own Secretary. As important, interest groups associated with categorical programs frequently are able to modify even a determined White House effort to change historical ground rules governing favorite programs through subtle or not so subtle lobbying and pressure. Individual Congressmen, like the occupant of the White House, are political as well as human beings.

Using Califano's memoranda as a wedge, Taylor and Farr continued to petition their peers in other agencies, and the program specialists in the Model Cities Administration did the same with their own counterparts. But no major breakthroughs were recorded during the final days of the Johnson Administration.[37] Only HEW and HUD made any effort to set aside program funds for model cit-

[35] Ibid.
[36] Interview with Joseph Califano, July 26, 1972.
[37] Interview with H. Ralph Taylor, July 1972.

ies. Secretary Weaver wrote a memorandum to the President in early December in support of a budget increase for the Model Cities Program, which aptly summarized the early experience.

As you know, we had anticipated that the categorical grants from the participating agencies would become available to meet in substantial measure the needs of Model Cities. However, this has not occurred to the degree that we had hoped . . . pressing and overriding priorities have prevented funds from coming forth in adequate amounts, either in 1969 or in the form of assurances for 1970. A further complication is caused by the existence of statutory formulas with limited flexibility in allocating funds among States in order to meet the needs of individual cities. . . . The results may be that many Model Cities programs may be seriously underfunded.[38]

A New Ball Game

President Nixon's selection of Floyd Hyde as Assistant Secretary to replace Taylor after the 1968 election was well received among supporters of the still embryonic program. Ralph Taylor viewed Hyde, an ex-Mayor of Fresno and active in the National Conference of Mayors, as "sympathetic to the program, moderately liberal. We were pleased. . . . It was a good signal."[39] Unfortunately for model cities, and indeed for the new Assistant Secretary, the signal was not a strong one.

Hyde's appointment did not symbolize any readiness on the part of the new Administration to endorse the program. Early meetings of the President's Urban Affairs Council, a forum ostensibly created to develop a concerted approach to urban problems, focused primarily on establishing an understanding of the program among the attending Cabinet officers and staff. There followed the establishment of the first of what was to become a seemingly endless series of task forces and working groups to study the program and to examine its benefits and costs. Membership on this first task force was limited to representatives of HUD, HEW, the Department of Labor, and the Department of Transportation, as well as the Urban Affairs Council itself. After a brief study period, which included field trips to three model cities, the task force recommended several proposals to "strengthen" the thrust of the program. Among these it stated that "specific earmarking of funds by the departments is essential. . . . Consideration

[38] Memorandum from Secretary Weaver to President Lyndon Johnson, December 2, 1968.
[39] Interview with H. Ralph Taylor, former Assistant Secretary for Model Cities, mid-June 1972.

should be given to setting aside a portion of the funds available to each Department. . . ."[40]

The task force report was sufficiently favorable that it encouraged, if not permitted, Secretary George Romney to make his first statement on the Model Cities Program since assuming office in January. He spoke at a news conference on April 28, 1969.

. . . my Committee on Model Cities of the Council for Urban Affairs has been intensively examining the program. . . . Its study has shown the program's goals are sound, but there have been critical deficiencies in its admnistration which call for immediate correction.

As to earmarking,

. . . Federal agencies have not been sufficiently responsive to local proposals reflecting specific local conditions . . . in developing their proposals, local authorities have been hindered by uncertainty as to the amounts of funds that would be available from the Federal Government.

To rectify these deficiencies, the President, he said, had approved the following "reforms" in the program:

—The Council for Urban Affairs will assume direct responsibility for inter-departmental policy affecting Model Cities.
—Secretaries of the Departments involved will have personal supervision of their Department's funding of Model Cities proposals and will reserve program funds specifically for that purpose. . . .
—Administration of the program will be fed into the reorganization of the Regional Federal offices, now underway.[41]

Many staff members believed that Romney's statement would finally move the program "off dead center. . . . We finally got our marching orders. . . ." But others were not sure. "What was needed, given the skepticism concerning Republican support of the program was a direct and firm reaffirmation of the faith by the President. . . ."[42] Romney himself was to state, perhaps with clairvoyance, just a few weeks after his press conference that "the Model Cities Program can-

[40] Model Cities Task Force, Council for Urban Affairs, *Model Cities* (White House, April 19, 1969), p. 4. The authors were able to obtain the first draft of this report. Interviews with Assistant Secretary Floyd Hyde (July 25, 1969) indicate that the earmarking recommendation remained in the final draft of the document.

[41] Secretary George Romney, Statement to the Press on Model Cities, April 28, 1969, pp. 1 and 2. The reorganization referred to in the Secretary's statement concerned the drawing up of similar geographic regions for all federal agencies and the decentralization of decision making of some programs to the regional officers.

[42] Interview with John McLean, Senior MCA staff, July 28, 1972.

not possibly succeed unless it has the backing of the President . . . and unless the departments involved are agreed on the policies that are going to be applied and that they are going to comply with its execution. . . ."[43]

Following up on Romney's press conference, Secretary Robert Finch of HEW made a formal decision to implement the fund reservation process initially agreed to by the previous Administration. On May 21, 1969, HEW's Comptroller called on all program heads to let him know which model city projects would be funded and which reserved funds were in danger of lapsing.[44] As a result, approximately $62 million was obligated by the end of the fiscal year.[45]

Other agencies—OEO and HUD, in particular—also began to make good on the minimal commitments of the last days of the previous Administration. Unfortunately, it is difficult to determine how much these funds actually represented new money that would not have been given to the model cities without earmarking, and how much they reflected money for projects already initiated or projects that were connected with the program only because they happened to be located in the model neighborhood. In the rush to get out the money before appropriations lapsed at the end of the fiscal year, most departments were willing to support from the "earmarked funds" projects that had only a tenuous relationship to the model cities.

Fiscal Year 1970 and After

The Urban Affairs Council turned over its responsibility for the program to an Under Secretaries Working Group on Model Cities. In turn, this group asked an Assistant Secretaries Working Group to examine the allocation, earmarking, and commitment processes for fiscal year 1970 and to investigate the overall federal response to model cities. This group met three times in the early summer of 1969. Its mandate from Richard Van Dusen, Under Secretary of HUD, was rather all-encompassing. The Assistant Secretaries were asked to report on

[43] Statement reported in William Lilley III, "Urban Report: Model Cities Program Faces Uncertain Future Despite Romney Overhaul," *National Journal*, Vol. 2 (July 11, 1969), p. 1474.
[44] Section 108 of the Model Cities Act permitted funds appropriated for a federal grant-in-aid program within model cities to remain available until expended. Legal counsel in HEW, HUD, and DOT disagreed over the interpretation of this provision for one-year appropriations, and as a result, earmarking discussions proceeded under the assumption that funds would lapse.
[45] Marshall Kaplan, Gans and Kahn, *The Model Cities Earmarking Process in the Department of Health, Education, and Welfare*, May 21, 1969, p. 35.

(1) the time at which resources are committed (should resources be allocated from various program funds at the time budget is finalized, or should this decision be deferred until after the appropriation is complete?) . . . ;

(2) period for which commitments are made (should resources be allocated to the Model Cities program on a fiscal year basis? On a planning year basis?) . . . ;

(3) control points (to what extent should funds allocated or earmarked to Model Cities programs be controlled from Washington . . . delegated to region) . . . ;

(4) state involvement[46] (at which points should states become involved in the allocation process? What procedures will be most effective to secure allocation of state administered Federal program funds?) . . . .[47]

Floyd Hyde was by now aware that the survival of the program was not assured. There continued to be a gap between HUD expectations and the patterns of response from the agencies, and there was no overt expression of support from the President himself. Hyde drafted a response to Van Dusen's questions and submitted them to Daniel P. Moynihan's special assistant, who was serving as the staff member of the Assistant Secretaries Working Group. He emphasized the "importance of earmarking to the Model Cities effort," and his "continued hope that the White House would involve itself in the program directly."[48] The Assistant Secretary suggested that earmarking for fiscal year 1971 should begin immediately.

. . . commitments should be made to the Model Cities Program on a fiscal year basis as appropriated . . . earmarked amounts are to be floors below which Model Cities funding will not fall . . . control of funds allocated to Model Cities will vary among agencies. . . . Regional offices should control allocations. . . . States should be involved in the allocation process from the beginning of the planning process. . . . State plan guidelines should incorporate meaningful priority expressions from the Federal government which are applicable to state counterpart agencies.[49]

Unfortunately, the Assistant Secretaries Working Group did not directly answer the Under Secretary's questions or review in detail Floyd Hyde's draft response. Instead, the first few rather poorly attended summer meetings were de-

[46] Strategies for state involvement had received slight attention up to this time from the Johnson and Nixon administrations. Despite numerous staff papers urging a more substantial effort, explanatory conferences and the funding of technical assistance contracts were the only visible approaches undertaken by the Model Cities Administration.

[47] Memorandum from Richard C. Van Dusen, Under Secretary (HUD), to Assistant Secretaries Working Group on Model Cities, June 20, 1969.

[48] Interview with Assistant Secretary Floyd Hyde, July 28, 1972.

[49] Memorandum from Assistant Secretary Floyd Hyde, "Van Dusen's Questions," to Christopher DeMuth, Staff Assistant to the President (July 30, 1969). The state plan guidelines referred to here are the numerous planning prerequisites demanded by HEW and DOL of all states before the receipt of federal funds.

voted to the establishment of a framework for a "detailed interagency study of Model Cities management practices, as well as Federal response approaches." Once this study (known as the Chamberlin study)[50] was under way, the group was able to return to the "basic" questions of earmarking and "agency commitment to the program."

In August, Assistant Secretary Hyde, who served as chairman of the Assistant Secretaries group, asked each department to submit its earmarking plans. Once again he sought in advance a commitment of funds from each department and suggested that he had the President's blessing in making this request.[51] A reference to the President's interest may have seemed to be good strategy, but it apparently produced few results. The departments' respective responses to Hyde's requests were noted in the September 2, 1969, meeting of the Assistant Secretaries group:

Broman (DOT)	It is difficult for DOT to earmark without better funding and tie-in with State Highway funds. Attempts will be made to involve State Highway Departments in Model Cities.
Kolberg (DOL)	Memo has been sent by Weber to Hyde stating that most funds have already been earmarked for CEP. Efforts will be made to better coordinate CEP activities with CDA's.
Carlucci (OEO)	OEO will continue to earmark training and technical assistance money but it is difficult for OEO to earmark program money. OEO will look into the possibility of earmarking R&D funds.
Lundley (EDA)	Reorganization has delayed EDA [Economic Development Administration] participation in Model Cities. In addition, by statute only 37 Model Cities are eligible for most EDA funds.
Lyons (Interior)	Interior is still trying to sort out its programs and define its urban objectives.
Butler (HEW)	HEW Task Force is now working on identification of programs for Model Cities earmarks.[52]

Dwight Ink, a senior staff member of the Bureau of the Budget, was asked to monitor the earmarking process by the Director. He felt compelled to express concern to his superior and to the Assistant Secretaries Working Group over the lack of action by all the departments. However, there is no record of direct inter-

[50] Inter-Agency Staff Report, *Strengthening the Federal Response to Model Cities*, September 1969. This study group is discussed in further detail in Chapter 7.
[51] Marshall Kaplan, Gans and Kahn, *The Model Cities Earmarking Process in the Department of Health, Education, and Welfare*, September 1970, p. 35.
[52] Ibid., p. 36.

vention by the Budget Bureau. Indeed, it seemed to Assistant Director Richard Nathan of the Office of Management and Budget (OMB) that the staff of the Bureau, despite a favorable attitude toward the Model Cities Program, were unwilling to "use their muscle with other Federal agencies" over the earmarking process.[53] They could not "go out on a limb for one program. . . . They had to work with all agencies."

Floyd Hyde reported to the Under Secretaries group toward the end of the fall that

Each agency response must be judged on its own merits, but it appears obvious to the Chairman that as a general proposition, there has not been to date a serious inter-agency commitment to the program which is in keeping with the clearly expressed intention of the President and the Urban Affairs Council. . . . Where some improvement over previous years can be noted . . . the kind of clear, priority commitment necessary for success is lacking. . . .[54]

Somewhat surprisingly, considering the disappointing performance of the departments represented, the Assistant Secretaries Working Group adopted without basic changes the strong statement in support of earmarking that was contained in the interagency staff report (the Chamberlin study) that had been initiated during the summer. In effect, this report urged the creation of a formal annual earmarking process that would be closely tied into the model city planning process.[55]

The recommendations of the Assistant Secretaries Working Group were never acted upon. Indeed, neither the Urban Affairs Council nor the Under Secretaries group ever fully involved themselves in the earmarking problem on a sustained basis. The Model Cities Administration was being left primarily on its own. Expressions of support from some senior White House officials, such as Daniel P. Moynihan, no matter how numerous,[56] were not sufficient to make up for the lack of formal statements of support or, more importantly, directives of the agencies from the White House. Seemingly fortuitous meetings between Hyde and other Assistant Secretaries and sporadic sessions between the staff of different agencies were all that was left of a coordinated earmarking strategy

---

[53] Interview with Richard Nathan, former Assistant Director, Office of Management and Budget, and at the time of interview Deputy Under Secretary of HEW, July 26, 1972.
[54] Marshall Kaplan, Gans and Kahn, *Model Cities Earmarking . . .* , September 1970, p. 36.
[55] Inter-Agency Staff Report, *Strengthening the Federal Response . . .* , pp. 12 and 13.
[56] Moynihan is reported to have told each department's Secretary to "give 'til it hurts." (Interview with Sidney Gardner, Director of HEW's Center for Community Planning, August 25, 1972.)

within the Administration. HUD had to depend on agency goodwill, and "honest subversives internal to the administration."[57]

An already difficult situation was made even tougher by a continuous series of White House actions that appeared to undercut Hyde's frequent assertion that the Model Cities Program was central to the President's concerns. The first of these was the appointment of yet another task force, chaired by Edward C. Banfield, to study the Model Cities Program. This task force, like predecessors, discovered that the program was loaded with problems. But also, like its predecessors, it supported its continuation and strongly urged a strengthening of efforts to earmark funds.[58]

The Banfield task force report was not released until completion of yet another analysis of the program, this time by the so-called Blair House group. This group, convened by the White House, included key Administration officials. Its mandate, which stemmed from the newly created Domestic Council, was to review the task force's findings and to make definitive recommendations for the future of the program.[59]

By this time, considerable opposition to the Model Cities Program had come to the surface inside the Administration. The President had not yet committed himself publicly and was not about to do so. Most agencies continued to resist HUD pleas for support. "HUD had not been able to change the program's image. . . . It was seen by most at the White House and an increasing number at OMB as just another categorical program. . . . In this context, even if earmarking were possible administratively, it was not going to succeed."[60]

To Richard Nathan, Assistant Director of OMB, the separate appointment of task forces was the White House way of keeping its options open. "It didn't want to kill the program; the constituency had grown too big and Floyd Hyde was making an impression on some. Yet, it remained suspicious of the program's

---

[57] The classification of honest subversives was given by Sidney Gardner. He was referring to senior staff in each of the federal agencies who supported the Model Cities Program and tried to do something to influence their recalcitrant peers. Moynihan is on record with only one formal memorandum on earmarking (October 17, 1969). It asks for "implementation instructions" from other departments. No significant response to the memorandum is recorded. Moynihan and Assistant Secretary Floyd Hyde both agree that by this time the earmarking drive was stalled partially for lack of White House support. (Interview with Daniel P. Moynihan, November 1972.)

[58] President's Task Force on Model Cities, *Model Cities: A Step Towards the New Federalism* (Washington, D.C.: U.S. Government Printing Office, August 1970), pp. 10-16.

[59] The Domestic Council replaced the Urban Affairs Council and became the policy-planning group for domestic policy in the White House.

[60] Interview with Richard Nathan, July 26, 1972.

intent . . . it was still seen by many as a Great Society effort . . . a poverty program. . . ."

The Blair House study led to the proposal for "planned variations."[61] These were to be, in effect, a "demonstration within a demonstration." By carving out a relatively few model cities for special treatment and by refusing to demonstrate clear support for the entire program, the Blair House study further decreased the importance of model cities to other departments and lessened the incentive to take earmarking seriously. Under-Secretary John Venemen of HEW, in his request to OMB for guidance on the 1971 budget, expressed the ambivalence of an agency that had heretofore been a friend of model cities.

As the Blair House discussion on Model Cities continues, we feel it increasingly important that our posture on Model Cities reflect the closest possible relationship with the President's developing position on the program. . . . We will not be making our Senate submission of the special analysis (earmarking) until approximately May 1. Due to the pending review of Model Cities, we are requesting formal guidance from the Budget Bureau and the White House prior to our submission of FY 71 Model Cities earmarking. Whatever decision is made should, it seems to us, also apply to other Departments involved in the earmarking process.[62]

Most departments, particularly those that did not find the Model Cities Program to be in keeping with their own plans, saw no need to look to the OMB for guidance. They found it easy to turn a deaf ear to HUD's earmarking requests.

Apart from the numerous task forces, several other factors reminded agencies of the nonsupport of the White House and weakened their desire to cooperate with the Model Cities Administration. These included White House efforts to use model cities funds for school desegregation purposes,[63] OMB efforts to "hold back" or slow down the funding of model cities,[64] and HUD's submittal of a

---

[61] See the next section of this chapter for a more detailed discussion of planned variations.
[62] Memorandum from John Venemen, Under Secretary, HEW, to Richard Nathan, OMB, spring of 1970 (undated).
[63] *New York Times*, April 26, 1970. Reports circulated in Washington during the spring of 1970 that the Administration wanted to divert model city funds to support efforts at school desegregation, in effect, to make up for budget cutbacks. In part because of the pressure from mayors around the country (because of Floyd Hyde's efforts, the mayors now represented vocal support for the Model Cities Program), the Administration never really presented the proposal.
[64] In 1970, the Office of Management and Budget placed a limit on HUD's ability to obligate funds. Ostensibly, this was done because cities were spending at a slower rate than projected. This was viewed by the press as an anti-inflationary move as well as being interpreted as one more sign that the Administration was not enamored of the program.

six-month budget for fiscal 1972.[65] John Price of the White House staff summarized agency reactions: "Why give up something when the program was seen as not very central . . . ? Why alienate your own program managers . . . your own client groups . . . ? No incentives to cooperate were present. . . . No sanctions for non-cooperation were available for HUD to apply. . . ."[66]

No definitive figures are available on the budgets for 1970, 1971, and 1972. Piecing together often conflicting memoranda from officials in various agencies, it looks as though the funds announced as earmarked did not exceed $65 million from HEW, $9 million from the Department of Transportation, $4 million from the Economic Development Administration, $20 million from the Department of Labor, and $400 million from HUD during any one year. Although they represent a miniscule portion of each department's budget, even these figures are "soft." According to Floyd Hyde, a good proportion of the supposed earmarked funds never "hit the streets."[67] Equally important, so-called earmarked funds often went to projects that were either initiated prior to the Model Cities Program, only vaguely related to the program, or related to model cities only after the fact; that is, they were held to be consistent with a very tenuous city demonstration plan after a cursory local review.

When Hyde took over from Taylor in early 1969, he made a clear choice of priorities. "Given the lack of White House support and the obvious experiences of Ralph Taylor, we had to make some choices. . . . Earmarking seemed most important. . . . Agencies had to be brought around on funds. . . . The issue of application handling and simplification of criteria was important, but secondary. . . ."[68] This early decision to focus on earmarking meant that efforts to secure more flexible handling of applications and simplified program guidelines were given a lower priority. Basic reform of the categorical program system would have to come from another direction.[69]

---

[65] HUD submitted a six-month budget for most of its programs in anticipation of the enactment of special revenue sharing. Inside HUD the move was seen as a way to pressure cities into supporting special revenue sharing.

[66] Interview with John Price, Special Assistant to the President, July 25, 1972.

[67] Joseph Crane letter to Marshall Kaplan, September 25, 1972. Mr. Crane was director of management for Assistant Secretary Hyde.

[68] Interview with Floyd Hyde, July 1972.

[69] Among the possibilities were the Ash Committee study of agency organization (Presidential Commission on Government Reorganization), the Presidential order creating regional boundaries and regional councils, and OMB's FAR study (Federal Administrative Review). These were no doubt important in their own right, but their relationship to the Model Cities Program was neither purposeful nor direct. For example, the FAR study, begun in March

Numerous task forces and study groups were created during 1969 and 1970 to study the impact of the Model Cities Program. Although none was very prescriptive, each alluded to the need for more effective federal action in the administration of categorical programs. By their tone, as well as their content, each suggested the marginal impact of the efforts made by the Model Cities Administration to induce "priority handling of applications and criteria revision." The staff of the Council for Urban Affairs reported that review and funding procedures remained confused and that there was little confidence that the regional offices would ever receive the fund allocations for model cities from their counterparts in Washington.[70]

Similarly, the Chamberlin report noted that cities still did not know why applications for program funds were rejected and that inflexible interpretation of the administrative guidelines prevented the funding of legitimate projects.[71] The Banfield task force further observed that

Federal laws and regulations not only restrict the purposes for which money can be spent, they also prescribe how the cities are to organize and manage their programs. . . . most of the federal agencies have, until recently, given nothing more than lip service to the Model Cities idea. . . .[72]

Hyde himself accurately summarized the lack of progress in February 1970.

Previous attempts to coordinate the grant-in-aid programs of the various federal agencies have been largely ineffective. . . . The major obstacle to realizing the goal of reduced federal paper-work and processing time must be squarely faced; it is the reluctance at all levels in the Federal Executive Branch and in Congress to allow cities to make mistakes. . . .[73]

Planned Variations

The Blair House meetings in early 1970 resulted in an agreement to choose a limited number of model cities, less than two dozen, to participate in a new "planned variations" program. In those cities the program would permit (1) the extension of planning of the model cities type throughout the city; (2) the pro-

---

1969, "failed to produce any immediate recommendations of relevance to the twin issues of application handling and criteria revision." (Interview with Sidney Gardner, August 1972.) Efforts made within specific departments were "dependent for their substance on agency commitment to change . . . most produced little. . . ."

[70] Staff draft, Council for Urban Affairs, April 19, 1969, pp. 4-6.
[71] Inter-Agency Staff Report, *Strengthening the Federal Response . . .* , p. 11.
[72] President's Task Force on Model Cities, *Model Cities: A Step . . .* , p. 5.
[73] Floyd Hyde, brief to Urban Affairs Council, February 27, 1967, p. 2.

vision to city chief executives of the authority to review and sign off (give final approval to) the array of federal grant-in-aid programs; and (3) the reduction and elimination of federal review requirements, to the extent possible, over grants-in-aid.

The variations were oriented as much toward changing federal behavior in regard to application handling and review as they were toward experimenting with new planning and management approaches at the city level. Richard Nathan saw in the planned variation effort "a way to finally turn the program around . . . to finally go after management reform at the Federal and local level, rather than administer the program like the poverty effort."[74]

Nearly a year passed from the time that the Blair House sessions arrived at an agreement before the President announced the program. Much of the interim was taken up with the selection process, which entailed interagency interviews of prospective cities, the identification of cities, and review and approval by the White House. The potential implications for the budget, together with a residual fear among the White House and OMB staff that by endorsing the planned variations they were implying endorsement of model cities as a whole, and the subjection of some of the proposed cities to "political" scrutiny, further held up approval for over six months.

As cities with "planned variations" went into their second year, the federal response, particularly to the promises of increased discretion in the use of funds and of sign-off powers for the local chief executive, was less than overwhelming. Sign-off practices varied by agency and by region. Often the "privilege" was honored perfunctorily; that is, applicants for funds permitted the chief executive to review their plans only at the last moment and only under the pressure of fast-approaching deadlines. Some programs, because of statutory processes, remained outside the purview of local mayors. Moreover, even before the President's press conference announcing the program, the HUD staff backed away from the initial agreement for reduced federal review. Because the other agencies were reluctant to give up their prerogatives to review their own programs, HUD suggested that only supplemental funds should be freed from review. No agency could or would agree to go beyond what had occurred in the model cities before. Without Presidential support, MCA had trouble obtaining a reaction from other agencies.[75]

[74] Interview with Richard Nathan, July 1972.
[75] Notes of Marshall Kaplan. Kaplan was "on-site" adviser to Assistant Secretary Floyd Hyde, 1970-1971.

Was the Effort Worth the Results?

The earmarking process and the effort to achieve flexible handling of applications produced minimal results under both the Nixon and the Johnson administrations. Supplemental grants allocated to New York and Los Angeles more than equaled the annual average earmark for the whole country. If "new money" alone was considered, the total annual agency earmark for all model cities, in both administrations, fell far short of the supplemental grant offered to two or possibly three medium-sized model cities. At the same time, a recent study indicates that 60 percent[76] of all the supplemental funds used were directed at projects that could have been supported by categorical programs. Because categorical programs were not made available as promised, model city funds were directed away from their intended use for innovative projects. Certainly, a concerted, concentrated, and coordinated federal response to urban ills, as called for in the statute and in the rhetoric of the program's supporters, failed to occur, and the redistribution on a large scale of aid and services to poverty areas did not materialize.

Lack of presidential support for the Model Cities Program during the Nixon Administration certainly weakened HUD's efforts to achieve earmarking and basic administrative reform. It created an environment within which willingness, or unwillingness, to cooperate with the model cities effort became primarily an internal agency decision. HUD was unable to direct or mandate a response from other agencies. Further negotiation or, in Lindblom's terms, partisan mutual adjustment failed to produce much in the way of results.

Unfortunately, White House endorsement of the Model Cities Program during the Johnson years was weakened by the "lame duck" nature of the Presidency. By the time HUD was ready to request White House assistance, the value of such assistance was reduced. Moreover, one should not discount Joseph Califano's comments on the inherent inability of the White House to sustain its advocacy of one program over a long period of time. This, juxtaposed with tough institutional constraints, should at least offer a reasonable counterpoint to the often-heard suggestion that "more or better White House involvement would have made a *significant* difference." Even the most affirmative White House role would not have been able easily to overcome certain significant factors:

[76] Internal HUD study; results related to author by Assistant Secretary Hyde.

—The hesitancy of many Congressmen to approve processes that would apparently result in a loss of Congressional control over the use of categorical programs and, at the same time, provide benefits to only a relatively few cities in a relatively few Congressional districts;

—The existence of statutory criteria governing how, when, and where categorical funds should be used, as well as who should use them and benefit from them;

—The association of strong client groups with individual categorical programs, each such group understandably jealous of efforts to depart from the traditional ways of allocating "their" respective program funds;

—The lack of enthusiasm among departments of equal standing to follow the lead of one of them, and their unwillingness to relinquish even symbolic control over program funds in favor of another department or another department's program;

—The inability of most Secretaries to affect significantly the daily decisions of most program managers and field staff, to overcome the latters' general resistance to policy directions from Washington—a resistance that often succeeded through institutional inertia, weak communication linkages, and "normal" or bureaucratic obstructionism, abetted by the existence and growth of complex administrative and statutory regulations.

Neither the effort to establish earmarking nor the attempt to secure flexibility of applications resulted in more than marginal benefits to the participating model cities. The most enduring conclusion to be drawn is that these efforts present compelling evidence of the continuing need to reform the federal delivery system. We continue to lack an operational definition of coordination at the federal level. Where such coordination will involve efforts to redistribute funds to the poor from the conventional users of federal assistance, the task of definition will be more difficult.

Chapter 6
Defining a Planning and Review Framework: Reform or Reliance

Efforts to define the model cities planning submission and review requirements raised questions about the proper role of the federal government in administering aid. Both within and outside the government there were some who were concerned that cities could not or would not spend federal funds wisely, or with the national interest in mind, in the absence of ground rules. Others, feeling perhaps more charitable toward city government or more critical of federal efforts at rule making in regard to previous categorical programs, were inclined to eliminate or reduce to a minimum any federal involvement.

The dialogue between those two points of view was rarely crisp and clear-cut. Out of it evolved, however, a very rational, orderly, complicated, and by and large unworkable planning process for cities to follow and a complementary federal effort, on the whole successful, to limit federal reviews to a very general set of objectives, or performance criteria, that cities were asked to meet or achieve. Out of it also emerged local Model City Programs that seemed to fit the stated legislative priorities for resource concentration in the model neighborhoods and on their particular problems.

Early Beginnings

Early supporters of the Model Cities Program saw it as a step in the direction of block grants, The President's Task Force on Urban Problems had suggested that the concept of demonstration cities would provide "increased flexibility for local governments to operate outside existing administrative structures and their customary constraints," and would eliminate "substantive standards as to program content."[1] To Wood, chairman of the task force, the program "would not reflect the often overlapping, prescriptive detailed planning and administrative regulations governing the use of most federal programs. . . . The feds would need to rely on cities."

The other objectives of the program, to achieve innovation and the concentration of resources in deteriorating areas of cities, would be secured through the careful selection of cities, the development of very general planning guidelines for cities to follow, and the setting of similar general performance criteria for cities to live by.

Secretary Weaver's testimony before Congress continued some of the same

[1] President's Task Force on Urban Problems (Wood task force), report, December 22, 1965, p. 9.

themes.[2] He noted that "this is a local program; it will be planned, developed and carried out by local people. The character and content of the program will be based on local judgments as to cities' needs." Moreover, in reporting out the legislation, the Senate Committee had stated, "The Committee wishes to stress that the demonstration program is based on local initiative, and local response to local problems."[3]

The Congressional debate over the new program reflected a certain ambivalence about the degree to which participating cities ought to be held to federally defined prescriptions. Some of this ambivalence was generated by habit: the 1960s saw the passage of one categorical program after another, each related to a specific problem area defined by the Congress, and each noted for voluminous and varied planning and project guidelines and federal review processes. However, a good part of the debate resulted from justifiable concern over the cities' capacity to plan and distribute resources effectively, particularly resources aimed at meeting the needs of the poor. Would cities respond to general performance criteria? Would these criteria be enough to get cities to initiate proper planning? What really was the difference between performance and administrative guidelines? Would it not be possible for cities to depart from national commitments if the criteria were too loose? Could you really rely on cities to use the model cities funds wisely? Conversely, would not an open-ended set of criteria generate more, rather than fewer, temptations for federal review?

The Wood task force report, after first taking a negative position on the imposition of "substantive [program] standards" on cities, went on to propose that certain criteria defining the scope, broad character, organizational, financial, and administrative arrangements would be "necessary."[4] In a similar vein, Weaver compromised his earlier expressed belief in home rule and stated, "I don't think that we appropriate federal money with a blank check. . . ." He added, "if any standards had to be set they would be based on performance rather than technical criteria."[5] Noticeably, neither the task force nor Weaver went beyond generalizations.

As finally enacted, Title I, Section 106, provided funds with reduced restrictions but nevertheless some strings attached. Taken as a whole, the legislation

[2] Richard Cherry and Kent Watkins, "History of Congressional Action Relative to Model Cities 1966-1967," HUD, October 3, 1967, p. 4.
[3] Ibid., p. 28.
[4] President's Task Force on Urban Problems, report, p. 9.
[5] Cherry and Watkins, "History . . . Model Cities 1966-1967," p. 5.

seemed to represent a significant departure from categorical programs. Cities would be given more latitude in the use of model cities monies but not complete freedom. For example, although the legislative language restricted the use of funds to projects included in a city demonstration program that had HUD approval, and although program funds had to be directed at improving the quality of life of the disadvantaged residents living in the locally defined model neighborhoods, the legislation did not require cities to focus their expenditures on any one problem area, nor did it limit them in their choice of projects. Further, the participating cities, rather than Congress or any federal departments, could assume responsibility for setting precise criteria for project eligibility and sponsorship. Open-ended performance criteria replaced very precise federal guidelines (of the sort associated with most federal programs) in regard to such factors as resident involvement in model cities planning, the geographic areas in which model cities funds could be spent, the type of local concerns that would justify the use of those funds, the identification of beneficiaries, the need to coordinate and concentrate resources, the need to spend model cities funds in an innovative manner, and the need to improve the delivery of services funded by the new program.

Advisory Committee on Demonstration Program Development

Even prior to passage of the Act, HUD established an Advisory Committee on Demonstration Program Development to recommend policies and procedures for translating the Demonstration Cities Act into an operating program. The group, whose members included leading academicians, private developers, renewal and labor union officials, met frequently during the summer and early fall of 1966. Many recommendations were made relating to federal and local administration of the program. Yet, significantly, the Advisory Committee was unable to decide how far HUD should go in setting planning guidelines. Some members wanted to leave cities free of federal restriction; some wanted to use such guidelines to ensure that cities responded to the program's objectives. The language in its report suggests this uncertainty.

Management of the program should capitalize on the fact that this is a demonstration program. Cities should receive funds *only* as a result of submission of a high quality product, quality being *measured* against the relative performance capacity of different cities.

This meant that HUD "must make *demanding* judgments at the proposal stage; at the mid-planning stage; and at the pre-execution stage"; "the Department must be prepared to *negotiate* program proposals and *impose* firm conditions in order to obtain quality local programs." Yet the Advisory Committee also stated that "Program procedures should be consciously designed to facilitate *flexibility* in program content and scheduling."[6] To the group's credit, it honestly stated the ambiguities in its position and the conflicts between those who believed in relying on cities and those who still wanted to reform them.

> The Committee . . . has had difficulty in resolving the question "How much performance effort is enough?" It has been attracted by two basically *different* approaches to various program components. One approach is to define in performance standard terms the *detailed* characteristics of an "ideal" health, education, employment, etc. system, and ask cities to meet these *high* standards to the extent of their ability to do so. . . .
> The other approach is to leave the initiative completely to the city, letting each city propose its own program goals and how it proposes to achieve those goals.
> The Committee's approach is a *compromise* which hopefully combines these two approaches in a way that will maximize the advantages of both while minimizing the disadvantages. . . . The guidelines outline in very general terms the various functional elements which a comprehensive program *should* contain without stipulating solutions so that innovation is not inhibited.[7]

Members of the Advisory Committee were divided between those who wanted to relax completely the heavy hand of the feds and rely on cities and those who still mistrusted city capacity to meet model city objectives. The committee's report articulated the need for a very rational, comprehensive, often complex, local model city planning process. Words and phrases such as "comprehensive priority determination," linkages between and among problem areas" were frequent throughout the text. Cities were to define problems before goals, goals before objectives, objectives before programs or program approaches. Each aspect of the proposal writing and comprehensive planning was to reflect coordination, citizen participation, and city commitment. At the same time, proposals and program approaches generated by a locality were to be innovative and in keeping with the needs of the neighborhood residents.

---

[6] HUD Advisory Committee on Demonstration Program Development, Report to the Secretary on the proposed City Demonstration Program (HUD, September 1966), pp. 4, 5, 6, and 7 (italics added).
[7] Ibid., pp. 24 and 25 (italics added).

The Advisory Committee left HUD and the cities with a tall order. The report ostensibly emphasized HUD's interest in structuring local planning processes rather than in the specific content of local plans; but the imprecise quality of the proposed federal review criteria still permitted HUD and other federal departments to second-guess the wisdom of city proposals and plans. For example, the committee indicated that a favorable federal review of local efforts should be premised on judgments about a city's capability and on the quality, impact, and innovativeness of a city's proposals; certainly this was not a narrowly prescribed set of standards suggesting only limited federal review.

Apparently, the Advisory Committee did not doubt its proposed planning model or even discuss in a serious manner the benefits and costs of alternative approaches. This is surprising when one considers that urban observers were at that time questioning the relevance of a technically oriented, comprehensive, rational planning process to crisis-ridden city governments. Certainly a more limited inductive and incremental planning approach deserved some consideration. Lindblom's concept of "muddling through" was relevant for examination as a planning alternative, even if only to polarize extremes. As he indicates, "although such an approach [rational, systematic policy formulation] can be described, it cannot be practiced except for relatively simple problems and even then only in a somewhat modified form. It assumes intellectual capacities and sources of information that men simply do not possess, and it is even more absurd as an approach to policy when the time and money that can be allocated to a policy problem is limited. . . ."[8]

Despite the obvious, and perhaps understandable, inconsistencies and unresolved issues implicit in the Advisory Committee's report, the document was viewed almost as sacrosanct by members of the HUD staff—a circumstance that was almost inevitable considering that the committee's staff director became the special assistant to the new Assistant Secretary for the Model Cities Program. Most of the committee's suggestions were converted almost verbatim by the still small staff of Assistant Secretary Taylor into the initial guidelines issued in December 1966. Both the application and the plan submitted by a city would have to be comprehensive; that is, both would have to cover the entire range of social and physical problems in the model neighborhood. The application, to be completed in approximately four months' time, would be required to contain a comprehensive statement of social, economic, and physical problems in the neighbor-

[8] Charles E. Lindblom, "The Science of Muddling Through," *Public Administration Review*, Vol. 19 (Spring, 1959), p. 80.

hood, an initial definition of program approaches and strategies to resolve these problems, and a description of the administrative structure that would be needed to initiate the local Model Cities Program. The comprehensive plan would have to contain similar components. It would be prepared according to a very orderly, rational planning process during the course of a one-year period. The plan would have to provide HUD with a detailed analysis of problems, a definition of its five-year goals, objectives, and program approaches, and a one-year action plan.[9] It would have to involve residents in its preparation, include innovative projects, and demonstrate local willingness to coordinate and concentrate resources in the model neighborhood and commitment to achieve basic improvements in the quality of urban life.

In part because the Assistant Secretary wanted to present Congress and the White House with an estimate of the real costs of responding to urban needs, and thereby justify an increased budget, and in part because the staff wanted to avoid inhibiting local innovation, the guidelines asked cities, implicitly if not explicitly, to assume minimal constraints on resources. Cities were encouraged to raise their level of expectations and to initiate a "high sights" planning process (as it came to be called among the model cities staff).[10]

HUD's initial guidelines presented cities with a difficult set of marching orders, some apparently inconsistent with others. Equally as important, because the guidelines were quite general and contained no precise rules to suggest what would or would not gain approval, they implied the possibility of a very intensive, if not lengthy, federal review process conducted by sophisticated, highly talented personnel.

Early Submittals and Review

Prior to the end of the application period, HUD began to receive informal applications from cities that wanted to be among the first. Many of these applications designated model neighborhoods that included well over 20 percent of the total city population. This raised the specter of too thin a fund spread and minimal impact. Accordingly, HUD's Model Cities Administration asked its regional offices to inform cities that model neighborhood areas were not to exceed 10 percent of the city's population, or 15,000 people, whichever was larger. Some of

[9] HUD, *Program Guide: Model Neighborhoods in Demonstration Cities*, HUD, December 1966.
[10] Interview with former Assistant Secretary H. Ralph Taylor, July 27, 1972.

the staff and some officials in the cities felt that the formula was arbitrary and reflected a retreat from "local definition and local home rule"; to most, however, it was a decision correctly made, given the anticipated constraints on funds and the political pressures on local chief executives to expand their model neighborhood boundaries. Purity is not always a virtue, given budgeting pressures and local imperialism.

Completed formal applications began arriving in HUD by March 1967. Simultaneously, a debate developed between the staffs of Assistant Secretary Taylor of HUD and Assistant Director Ink of the Budget Bureau over the nature and substance of the review process. Taylor's staff proposed essentially subjective reviews based on open-ended criteria similar to those proposed by the Advisory Committee (apparent "city commitment," "administrative capability," seeming "understanding of problems," "clarity and reasonableness of goals and program approaches," "degree of innovation"). Conversely, Ink's staff favored a "more objective and uniform review effort." To achieve this objectivity and uniformity, they proposed (but never fully developed) a rather complex system of numerical ratings for judging city applications.[11] Given the immense job involved in the review of 193 applications and the relatively small staff to do it, subjectivity and judgment won out over the creation and administration of a more complex, rational system.

The application review process took place in Washington, despite official desires to the contrary. HUD's regional MCA offices were not yet equipped to play a significant review role and the other agencies were still essentially "silent" parties at the regional level of the program. The MCA staff carried the brunt of the work load. Other federal agencies often did no more than comment on those portions of the applications that were directly relevant to their own program concerns or make summary judgments on the ability of certain cities to undertake the program successfully.

The judgments on the first submissions were highly qualitative. Many senior staff of the MCA felt that their perceptions about the legitimacy or illegitimacy of individual city documents varied quite considerably, which was to be expected, given the subjective nature of the review.[12] This initial review was not an easy one. In some respects, cities and staff were placed in a more difficult

[11] Marshall Kaplan, Gans and Kahn staff interviews with Assistant Secretary H. Ralph Taylor, John McLean, Director of Program Operations, and George Williams, former Special Assistant, January 1969.
[12] Marshall Kaplan, Gans and Kahn staff interviews with numerous MCA staff, January 1969.

situation than they faced in regard to categorical program applications. The model city review criteria were not precise, and except in very general terms, the cities did not learn of them in advance of their submittals. Opportunities for federal discretion were more numerous. The implicit stress on "capacity building" in the review criteria meant that the urge to reform cities compromised, and at times substituted for, the intention to place reliance on them. Heavy use of consultants to prepare applications, or of a relatively few staff members in local city halls, made an appraisal of city capability and commitment extremely difficult.

The staff review of applications was completed, and final recommendations were made to Secretary Weaver by the end of June. Because of the Administration's desire to obtain Congressional appropriations before it notified the winners, the anticipated August announcements of the planning grants were delayed until November.[13]

The MCA staff put the waiting time to good use. Besides sorting out their roles and responsibilities and initiating some efforts at securing interagency cooperation, Assistant Secretary Taylor and MCA Director Farr directed their staff to "look hard at the quality of the first applications ... to see if there was a need to modify guidelines.." They also asked them to develop more definitive planning requirements for the participating cities.[14]

At an informal conference attended by the MCA staff, staff of other agencies, and a number of consultants in July 1967, the review process and the HUD guidelines were debated. The group agreed that city submittals were generally weak and less than innovative. Many cities substituted shopping lists of projects for hard analysis and meaningful strategy. To remedy supposed defects in local efforts, conference members suggested the redrafting of application guidelines to emphasize problem analysis and strategy definition over the presentation of project proposals and to stress widespread local agency and resident involvement rather than extended reliance on consultants or a limited number of city staff.

Development of More Definitive Guidelines

The initial review of applications led to the development by the MCA staff of a set of new planning requirements. Following the conference, a first draft was prepared for internal comment. Its contents paralleled the general outline pro-

[13] Interview with former Assistant Secretary H. Ralph Taylor, July 27, 1972.
[14] Ibid.

vided in the first program guide. The City Demonstration Agencies were to prepare, in sequential order, a problem analysis, goals, and strategy statement, a first-year action plan, a five-year plan, a continuous planning and evaluation program, and an analysis of their proposed administrative structure. It asked cities to establish linkages between and among planning components and suggested the use of highly skilled techniques of quantitative analysis.

The statement on the problem analysis, goals, and strategy was to be submitted midway through the planning period. As in the first program guide, this draft expected the planning process to reflect how cities met, and would meet, such general performance criteria as the coordination of available resources in the model neighborhood, mobilization and concentration of resources, citizen participation, innovation, and improved local delivery of services. The document posited a very rational, orderly planning process. It retained the flavor of the original guide while elaborating on its contents. Ostensibly, cities were left free to define the way they wanted to spend model cities funds, as long as their plan reflected the very general set of performance criteria defined by HUD and it resulted from a planning process and was presented in a format both of which had been spelled out by HUD.

Distribution of the draft within HUD led to a lengthy, time-consuming staff debate over three issues: first, whether cities should be told to plan against unlimited resources; second, whether the connections should be strengthened between the one-year and five-year plans; and finally, whether HUD should put more detailed requirements into the planning guidelines. As one staff member explained the problems,

If we told cities to set five-year objectives without prejudicing anticipated resource constraints, we would be eliminating their need to define priorities . . . we would also be building up their expectations in an unrealistic manner. . . .
The relation between the one-year and five-year plan in the draft was at best tenuous, and at worst non-existent. . . . We would encourage cities to prepare unrelated short and long-term plans. The action would leave no linkages to the CDP's overall objectives.[15]

Assistant Secretary Taylor continued to support the "high sights" philosophy. This was therefore kept in the draft of the planning guidelines. His reasoning reflected part hypothesis and part political instinct. To be innovative, he argued, cities could not have federal fund limits imposed on them. Cities' estimates of

[15] Marshall Kaplan, Gans and Kahn staff interview with Ammi Kohn, then a member of the MCA planning and evaluation staff, January 1969.

their real needs would support appropriations two years hence and would provide an agenda for Congressional action.[16] The linkages between the five-year and one-year plans that were called for in the original draft were strengthened in the final version. In addition, significant expansion was given to the discussion of the planning process to make it more substantive.

Publication of the draft in November as CDA Letter No. 1 did not end discussion of the planning guidelines either inside or outside HUD. Most participating cities accepted CDA Letter No. 1 without complaint, but several expressed dissatisfaction with the complexity of the proposed planning process and the regulations imposed on them in a supposed block grant program. They were supported in their protestations by many members of HUD's regional staff who believed that "systematic planning was beyond the capacity of most cities."[17] On the other hand, many of the MCA staff still thought that CDA No. 1 needed more substantive content. They argued that it did not really provide a discussion of the contents of the midyear plan, that it did not specify what was meant by program approaches, and that it was not at all clear on how the program analyses, five-year plan, and one-year action plan were to be linked.[18]

After much soul searching, the rationalists won out. The somewhat systematic, obviously very rational and idealized planning process of CDA No. 1 remained intact. A new set of guidelines was prepared, however, to clarify obscure portions of the early guidelines and to relax somewhat the artificial deadlines, particularly those for the submittal of interim planning documents.

It took the MCA nearly four months to complete CDA Letter No. 4, the amended planning guidelines.[19] The product remained consistent with the tone of CDA No. 1. Changes were for the most part ones of degree, not of kind; they were cosmetic, not basic. Instead of a midyear planning product, cities were asked to submit their problem analyses, goals, and program approach statements some two-thirds of the way through the planning period. Considerable wording was added to emphasize the "linkages" between various components of the plan, to strengthen the concept that planning was a continuous process, and to seek from cities an analysis of the basic causes of their problems.

In general, CDA No. 4, in line with the preceding documents, asked cities to respond to four different types of planning requirements. The first defined

[16] Interview with H. Ralph Taylor, July 1972.
[17] Interview with Melvin Mogulof, former Assistant Regional Administrator for Model Cities, San Francisco Regional Office, October 1972.
[18] Marshall Kaplan, Gans and Kahn staff interview with Ammi Kohn, January 1969.
[19] CDA Letters Nos. 2 and 3 were not related to planning.

HUD's criteria for the local planning organization. Cities were asked to create a new structure, a City Demonstration Agency responsible to the chief executive, that would initiate planning activities. Resident participation was to occur through "some form of organization structure" that had a leadership acceptable to the neighborhood. The second type of requirements defined HUD's criteria for the appropriate local planning processes; that is, not only did HUD seek submittal of a comprehensive development plan, but it required that the internal components of the plan be completed in a certain order, within a certain time frame, and through the use of certain techniques. The third type of requirement related to the specific products of the planning process. These products were to include, first, a description and analysis of problems, the causes of problems, and the goals of the program and the program approaches; second, a statement of five-year objectives and the subsequent costs anticipated to achieve those objectives; and third, a precise statement of first-year action plans and programs as well as their intended administrative arrangements.

In common with earlier HUD application and planning regulations, CDA No. 4 predicated a favorable review of local model city efforts on the achievement of general performance criteria. As in CDA No. 1, cities would have to demonstrate in their efforts such requirements as coordination and concentration of resources in the model neighborhood, the definition of innovative projects, and resident involvement in model cities planning. These criteria constituted the fourth type of planning requirement. Once its efforts met with approval from HUD, a city would be provided with its model city funds and the "wide array of categorical programs." Supposedly, the building up of city capability through HUD's planning requirements and the resultant appropriateness of the local model city plans and programs, when combined with substantial federal resources, would result in improvements in the quality of life in the model neighborhood.[20]

CDA Letter No. 4 illustrated a very structured, highly rational set of planning guidelines. It was destined to remain HUD's basic planning model until the change of administrations and represented a victory for the planner-rationalists and reformers inside HUD. The victory was neither sudden nor unexpected. Every guideline or memorandum published by HUD since the inception of the program had reflected the strong influence of the planning advocates, who be-

---

[20] See "Comprehensive Program Submission Requirements" (CDA Letter No. 4, July 1968). Analysis of the planning "model and impact" is contained in the Marshall Kaplan, Gans and Kahn studies for HUD, *The Model Cities Program: A Comparative Analysis of the Planning Process in Eleven Cities* (Washington, D.C.: U.S. Government Printing Office, 1970), and HUD, *The Model Cities Program: A History and Analysis of the Planning Process in Three Cities* (Washington, D.C.: U.S. Government Printing Office, 1969).

lieved that comprehensive planning provided the means to improve the decision-making ability of cities and to lead cities to allocate scarce resources effectively.[21]

Although the rhetoric of CDA No. 4 did not specify the content of city proposals, its numerous requirements and the impreciseness of the federal review criteria allowed the MCA staff to intervene in local efforts if they wanted to. However, even among the reformers there remained a strong desire to avoid federal reviews of projects. One staff member stated, "We saw our ability to build capacity in terms of our ability to initiate and review local planning processes . . . and monitor performance. Hopefully, our reviews would be limited to the overall quality of a city's performance. Did they coordinate . . . Were residents involved . . . Were funds used in the MNA? Control over project content was not consistent with the block grant character of the act. . . ."[22]

Taylor pushed for an interagency review structure because he wanted to co-opt other agencies to secure their involvement and their funds in the program.[23] A somewhat hierarchical review process was created by interagency agreement (see Chapter 5) to assure adequate federal reviews of local plans. Central to the review process were the Regional Inter-Agency Coordinating Committees (RICCs). These committees, composed of at least one representative from the regional office of each federal department involved in the program, were asked, together with the MCA's regional staff, to review each city's submittal. Comments from the regional review group were to be sent to the Washington Inter-Agency Committee (WIC). The latter group would resolve any "policy" differences among federal departments. It would also allow for one more "court of appeal" for individual offices within departments. The WIC's recommendations would be forwarded to the Assistant Secretary of Model Cities and Governmental Relations, who, in turn, would make recommendations to the Secretary of HUD.

HUD staff, both in the regions and in Washington, chaired the respective interagency groups. Although it generally sought a consensus on the various city submittals, HUD retained responsibility for final approval or disapproval. "Only one or possibly two RICCs used a vote to make decisions. Generally, diverse agency reviews were recorded where agreement on positions could not be reached. . . . At the WIC level it was always clear that HUD was in the driver's seat. . . ."[24]

Unfortunately, Taylor's perceptions of the benefits of an interagency review

[21] Marshall Kaplan, Gans and Kahn staff interview with Richard Langendorf, January 1969.
[22] Ibid.
[23] Interview with H. Ralph Taylor, July 27, 1972.
[24] Marshall Kaplan, Gans and Kahn staff interview with selected Assistant Regional Administrators, Model Cities (HUD), September 1969-June 1969.

process failed to come to pass. The RICC reviews were, with some exceptions, of marginal importance. Indeed, formal reviews of the city submittals were apparently infrequent.[25] Many of the committee members were not knowledgeable about the participating cities. And at times they were also very concerned with protecting their own departments and the interests of their clients.

Product reviews seemed devoid of contextual understanding and were often perfunctory in nature. Equal time was certainly not given to a review by RICC members of structure, process, and performance components of HUD's requirements. . . . Many members concentrated primarily on the review of their "department's" section of the report.[26]

It was not uncommon for departmental representatives on the RICC to seek modifications of local plans when the local groups funded by their respective departments expressed disapproval of a City Demonstration Agency's proposals.

Despite often valiant efforts, reviews by the WIC, other federal agencies, and at times the MCA were only slightly more rewarding than those of the RICCs. According to MCA Director Walter Farr, meetings of the WIC were often attended by "sincere but clearly junior staff representatives of their respective Departments. . . . Time was short . . . all that was possible were perfunctory reviews of key policy issues and remaining agency complaints."[27] John McLean, a senior staff member of the MCA, was compelled to state, in reference to the reviews by HUD and, to some extent, other agencies' staff,

. . . there is a striking discrepancy between the three critical elements—policy, submission requirements, review. Submission requirements and review procedures bear little relationship to each other.
   The review carried on at the Regional and early Washington levels bears too little relationship to the final policy considerations debated at the Assistant Secretary and higher levels.
   The review process . . . sought a way of early and repeated involvement of the other agencies in the hope that this would lead to more coordinated funding from them as the cities' plans come in. This has not happened. Instead, the formal review process tends to be a set of hurdles through which our staff has to put the programs—hearing out OEO on CAP involvement, HEW on its specialized concerns, Labor on its worry that everything go through CAMPS, etc. With some notable exceptions, it isn't perceived as a way of deciding the value of a program or of getting more resources in support of a program.[28]

[25] HUD, *The Model Cities Program: A Comparative Analysis . . .* , p. 37.
[26] Ibid., p. 37.
[27] Marshall Kaplan, Gans and Kahn staff interview with Walter Farr, Director, Model Cities Program, January 1969.
[28] Memorandum from John McLean, MCA, "Some Concerns on Submission and Review," to Assistant Secretary Floyd Hyde, June 26, 1969.

There were several reasons for the obvious gap between initial expectations for the review process and the reality. In the first place, cities found the early HUD planning guidelines difficult to understand. The language of these guidelines (CDA Letter No. 4) was more appropriate to a college classroom than a mayor's office or a residents' meeting. Most local participants had difficulty in separating "problems" from "causes of problems," "program approaches" from "strategies." Moreover, few cities were able to come close to meeting HUD's orderly logical process. Given the unreality of the guidelines, it was not easy to judge city performance fairly on a comparative or individual basis.

All [the] cities had trouble . . . in meeting HUD's rational planning approach. This is quite understandable. . . . CDA's had to get organized, had to hire staff, and had to define appropriate relationships both with City Hall and with resident groups. HUD's first year planning calendar did not anticipate that these functions would consume as much time as they did. When each CDA finally initiated substantive planning efforts, the tasks, more often than not, were carried out in a frenetic atmosphere. . . . *Order* and sequence often fell by the wayside. Resident needs were so great and problems so large that priority determination was more an art than a science. . . .[29]

A second problem was that staff shortages did not permit most federal agencies and most interagency review groups to look behind a city's paper plans or submittals. On-site monitoring was limited to infrequent visits, which were made primarily by leadmen, overextended HUD staff who had been assigned to the cities, and by program specialists from other agencies. Bimonthly progress reports were treated in Washington as summarily as they were prepared by the cities. Reviews, prior to federal approval of local plans, were based more on claims of capability and commitment than on hard data or informed judgments.

Third, there was no consensus among the many agencies over the planning review criteria. Irrespective of MCA's initial hopes, many RICC personnel and many staff from the involved departments undertook reviews that seemed to be directed at second-guessing the wisdom of city plans. As already suggested, protectionism on behalf of local clients or constituencies was expressed in many of these reviews; the perspectives of local Community Action Agencies, school boards, and Concentrated Employment Program groups were often assured more than a fair hearing when they differed from the CDA. Members of OEO would represent recalcitrant Community Action Agencies; HUD's urban renewal personnel would represent the local renewal agency; and HEW would represent the

[29] HUD, *The Model Cities Program: A History* . . . , p. 90 (italics added).

errant school board. Fears that they might have to continue programs after the termination of the supplemental funds, or that they might have to combine categorical efforts with supplementally funded efforts, led many agencies to take a close look at projects and to attempt to veto or amend project descriptions when these were not consistent with their own guidelines.

Although the basic structure of the review process remained intact throughout the review of the "first-round" cities, two political factors affected the speed with which some cities were helped through the system. These were, first, the desire of the outgoing Democratic Administration to protect the program by approving and funding a few cities prior to the new President's inauguration; and, second, the effort of the new Administration to "push a number of cities through the review process before the end of FY 1969 . . . in order to recapture the program's momentum; illustrate HUD's efficiency; and avoid lapsing $200 million of Model City funds."[30]

Efforts at Simplification

By the late spring of 1969, HUD and its Model Cities Administration, by this time under the direction of a new Assistant Secretary and a new Administration, began looking again at their planning guidelines and the entire review process. They were joined in this effort by the staff of other federal agencies, particularly HEW's Center for Community Planning and the Chamberlin task force (specifically created to study ways for improving the management of the model cities program). Surprisingly, because there was a general belief that neither the guidelines nor the review process had been particularly successful in aiding cities, no one challenged HUD's basic approach to planning. Most of the staff analysts devoted their primary attention to shortening and simplifying the guidelines and to reducing the number and size of submittal requirements from the cities. Comprehensive planning was still "in" at HUD; the rational, orderly planning process was still sacrosanct.

The new guidelines retained the basic format of the original CDA Letter No. 4. Cities were relieved of much paperwork and of numerous submittal requirements contained in CDA No. 4, such as the statement of goals, program approaches, and five-year tables, but they were still to follow a prescribed planning process and turn in a plan with components prescribed by HUD.

---

[30] Interview with John McLean, July 1972.

The purpose of this memorandum is to simplify the requirements of CDA Letter No. 4. It makes *clear* what the first-year comprehensive plans submitted by second-round cities *should* contain and where cities *should* place their first year planning emphasis.[31]

Second-round cities, those receiving their model cities grant later than the first group that had been selected in the fall of 1967, would have to submit a midplanning statement no later, as the term suggests, than midway through the planning period. This statement would be required to contain a description of the planning process, a summary of conditions and problems in the model neighborhood, and a set of program objectives and strategies. Following their submittal of the midplanning document, and no later than two months before the end of the planning period, the cities would be asked to transmit their first-year plan. This plan would have to contain an updated or revised midplanning statement, a definition of projects included and their respective funding sources, a proposed administrative structure, a work program for continuous planning and evaluation, a relocation plan, a listing of nonfederal contributions, and an employment plan for residents of the neighborhood.

Requirements for the submittal of first-year action plans were prepared and distributed to first-round cities almost simultaneously with the development of the "simplified" second-round document. First-round cities were asked to develop and submit their program for continuous planning and evaluation in the same format, essentially, as that established for the initial plan prepared by second-round cities. No midplanning statement, however, was required of first-round cities.[32]

Increasingly, it became clear that many cities would seek amendments or changes in their plans already approved.

While we take a longer look at all aspects of the submission and review process, the problem of handling amendments to approved comprehensive plans is immediately upon us. . . . They are already coming in. It is critical that we be able to react promptly to the cities. On the *other hand*, some of the proposed amendments are so substantial that they deserve as full review as the original submission of a comprehensive plan.[33]

[31] Assistant Secretary Hyde, "Submission Requirements for First Year Comprehensive Plans," memorandum to second-round CDA directors, August 22, 1969 (italics added).

[32] The statute indicates the need for an approved plan. It is at least debatable whether a second-, third-, or fourth-year plan was legally required—debatable except among those who viewed HUD's planning requirements as helpful in building up city capability (reform) and as useful in permitting the agency to monitor city performance.

[33] Memorandum from John McLean, "Review of Amendments to Comprehensive Program," to Assistant Secretary Floyd Hyde, July 9, 1969 (italics added).

Beyond the problem of staffing shortages, the continued juxtaposition of both reform and reliance objectives within the MCA made it difficult to develop an adequate approval procedure for amendments. How could a review process be devised that would grant cities flexibility to change their proposed projects without at the same time seeming to minimize the importance of the prescribed planning process? If HUD readily allowed amendments to local plans, would this not indicate to the cities that HUD did not really place great stock in its planning process—a process that supposedly led to a city's original project proposals? In effect, how much flexibility could the cities be granted without destroying the rationale for planning? Some of the staff argued that cities ought to be able to modify their plans and projects at will; conversely, a few proposed relatively stringent criteria for amendments. Through the direct intervention of the Assistant Secretary and his Special Assistant at that time, Warren Butler, the problem was resolved in favor of a compromise. Butler decided that

Only significant amendments would be subject to review . . . the test of significance being essentially the dollar impact on the budget . . . or the impact of the proposed change on initially described and approved city objectives, strategies, and projects.[34]

Although the submission requirements, as proposed by Butler, reduced the potential paperwork, the review process still entailed a heavy workload. The need to respond continually to amendments, at the same time that they were receiving submissions of completed five-year plans from some cities and first-year action plans from the other cities, kept the relatively small staff quite busy. Neither did simplification of the planning guidelines reduce the complexity of the review process. The MCA's staff continued in general to avoid a detailed review of individual project proposals, but they did attempt to assure themselves that the planning documents submitted did reflect, at least in form, the rational planning process and the performance criteria. On the other hand, several other federal agencies and most of the RICCs and WICs were less concerned with process and performance criteria than with the "legitimacy" of project proposals. The test of legitimacy ranged from an appearance of viability to consistency with their respective departmental priorities. Formal federal approval, although often a perfunctory matter, remained necessary for initial and continuous funding as well as for "major amendments."

Many critics continued to point to the submission and review requirements as

[34] Interview with Assistant Secretary Floyd Hyde, July 1972.

a problem. The Banfield task force, for example, after correctly paying tribute to Secretary Hyde's effort to cut red tape, had this to say:

We must add, however, that in our judgment, the cities are still nowhere as free as they should be. They are still required to prepare too many documents according to specifications from Washington, and they are still required to run too long a gauntlet of review bodies before their proposals are approved and funded. . . .[35]

The report of the HUD Task Force on Simplification and Consolidation, published in 1971, suggests that hope may spring eternal, but that ambiguity and ambivalence prevail.

The present submission requirements are more burdensome than they need to be. Each year's submission tends to be self-contained and to stand on its own, rather than building on submissions and focusing on change and evaluation results. The length of the submissions could be substantially reduced and a great deal of paperwork eliminated without changing the elements of the planning, programming, evaluation process and without eliminating basic information needed by HUD for program approval.[36]

The interagency review efforts were also subject to continuing negative criticism. Hyde's customarily candid memorandum briefing the Urban Affairs Council in midwinter 1970 reported that the "WIC members lack authority to make firm decisions or to represent the entire views of their departments. WIC members are generally at least three or four echelons below the Secretary." Hyde added,

The performance of the RICC's has been rather uneven among Regions . . . a problem associated with the RICC process is that agency representatives, often three or four echelons below the level of the Regional Administrator, tend to reflect the views of a segment of the agency or identify with a particular program, rather than bringing a more comprehensive view of their agency's mission to the table. Consequently, there is too often a tendency for the RICC reviews to become parochial, and in the end, to be lacking in authority. Also, there is little continuity in representation—agencies tend to send whoever is available at the time.[37]

Hyde's pejorative comments about agency parochialism reflected his increasing frustration with the de facto veto powers that were constantly sought by HUD's

[35] President's Task Force on Model Cities, *Model Cities: A Step Toward the New Federalism*, The White House, August 1970, p. 9.
[36] Unpublished report of HUD Task Force on Simplification and Consolidation, June 1971, p. 277.
[37] Memorandum from Assistant Secretary Floyd Hyde, "Briefing to the Urban Affairs Council on Model Cities," February 27, 1970, pp. 8 and 9.

sister agencies over their own areas of interest. Yet the sustained pressure from the agencies to assume a veto power over local plans, particularly those sections within their respective departmental domains, arose from their legitimate fears about their future funding obligations and also from their hurt feelings at not receiving the right of "last" refusal over matters that were ostensibly within their areas of expertise. HUD's funding of projects appeared to lock these other agencies into the support of future local projects. Some people thought it was going to create competitive and duplicating sets of local services. John McLean's pleading memorandum to Sidney Gardner in April 1970 accurately reflected the somewhat normative character of the sustained debate.

HEW's reviews have been less decisive with us when they appear to be enforcing categorical program requirements on the supplemental funds without convincing reasons. . . . I suspect that we haven't always wanted to accept the remote possibility of funding way down the pike by HEW as a convincing reason to turn down what cities want to do today. But where HEW funding seems likely to come fairly promptly, I hope we have leaned on cities to get right with HEW now.

. . . this should shift the emphasis in review from the traditional one of preventing that which some Federal reviewer thinks may not work, to the more challenging one of letting things happen. . . . The task will not be to make sure there never is a weed in the hothouse, but to know what flowers are there, in what soil, and whether they should or will grow anywhere else.[38]

Apart from the demise of the WIC in 1970 as a significant group owing to its impotence and the addition of specific requirements calling for a detailed explanation of citizen participation, minority employment, and relocation strategies, the planning guidelines and the review processes remained basically intact after the efforts at simplification in mid-1969. Numerous pleas since then for additional review staff in the RICCs and at HUD were not met by the Administration, and no precise set of review criteria was established. The monitoring of programs remained subject to the vagaries of a staff whose extended span of attention often appeared to eliminate substantive knowledge of any one city.

HUD's recent attempt to decentralize administrative responsibility to new area offices has confused the role of that agency in the RICCs. According to one HUD Regional Administrator, "Most other agencies remain organized around regional boundaries. . . . The role of HUD's regional staff is not clear . . . neither is the role of HUD's Area Office personnel assigned Model Cities responsibilities as part of their other functions."[39]

[38] Memorandum from John McLean, "HEW Reviewing," to Sidney Gardner, Deputy Assistant Secretary for Community Development, April 13, 1970.
[39] Interview with Robert Baida, HUD Regional Administrator, July 1972. Secretary Rom-

In Retrospect

By and large the model cities submission and planning process requirements seemed to provide most participants with an obstacle to overcome rather than a welcome component of the program. The initial thrust toward relying on the cities, toward viewing model cities funds as a "block grant," was compromised by the desire of some to use the program to reform local institutions and the desire of others to protect their historical control, or that of their client groups, over the disbursement of federal funds. Much of the paperwork mandated by the program guidelines appears, in retrospect, to have brought more direct benefits to the many consultants who prepared them than to the cities that were asked to submit them.[40] Certainly, relatively few pages of the encyclopedic local submissions documents ever became key factors in the deliberations of the federal agencies that were responsible for funding the projects.

The Model Cities Administration's highly rational planning approach did not win many converts at the federal or local level. For most agencies, the comprehensive requirements were unreal, required too much time to monitor, and were antithetical to their own more functional or programmatic outlook. For most cities, the incentives were not equal to the task of converting their Model Cities Agencies into the type of planning organization that HUD wanted. Further, the politics of running a city government, the limited capacity and resources of the city staff, and the daily operational priorities and crises of city government did not permit easy acceptance of HUD's complicated dictates.

On the positive side, HUD's agreement on ground rules did permit cities more flexibility in the selection of projects and in decisions on project expenditures than had been true with categorical programs. Because of staff agreement on the correctness of having a veto-proof system, very few city projects were rejected. Only about two dozen out of the nearly 2,000 submitted were cast aside, and these were rejected because they did not conform with the statute. HUD's ability to substitute performance for detailed administrative criteria also allowed cit-

---

ney decided in 1971 to create a large number of area offices. These offices would have administrative authority for HUD's many programs. Romney wanted to get HUD's "program" people closer to the cities. In choosing to decentralize its administration to a level below the region, HUD was creating an organization that differed from that of most of its sister agencies. It also left the regional offices in doubt about their role.

[40] It can be argued with some justification that the process of developing the plan often "sensitized" various groups in the city to one another and to the problems of the model neighborhood. Yet it can also be argued with perhaps similar justification that brevity of presentation would have sharpened the local dialogue and helped pinpoint local issues for both participant and reviewer alike.

ies the freedom to determine the use of funds as long as they maintained the broad purposes of the program. This they generally did. Interviews with staff and a reconnaissance of the HUD files suggest that almost without exception model city funds were spent in the model neighborhoods and on the sorts of problems defined in the act.

Where Do We Go from Here?

No one planning model will respond to the varied conditions of many different cities. The model cities experience suggests the need for an eclectic approach to planning. The values inherent in orderly comprehensive planning are probably no more and no less compelling than those found in a less synoptic, more limited, and even chaotic approach. "Muddling through" probably contains a similar number of problems to a rational planning process. A technical analysis of problems and solutions is neither more nor less compelling than the analyses of politicians or residents.

If the comprehensive planning model is discarded, the federal government should be able to get out of the business of reviewing a city's planning process or the results of that process. From an analysis of the Model Cities Program, we would suggest that the federal role might be limited to recording or monitoring a city's performance in terms of a broad set of objectives. These objectives, as in model cities, would outline where federal funds were to be spent, who would benefit from such expenditures, and who would participate in the allocation process. Their articulation and use in a simplified review process could provide cities with maximum flexibility in determining the precise use of federal funds, and it could provide the federal government with the assurance that legislative commitments were being met.

Chapter 7
Supplying Technical Assistance

Even before the Model Cities Program's enactment by Congress, its supporters were apparently worried about a lack of sufficient local expertise to meet its objectives. The Wood task force, for example, speaking of the need for a new program, stated that a "dramatic new approach is required built on three principles," among them "the coordination of all available talent. . . ." The task force further suggested that a city's capacity to "bring to bear all the techniques and talents of which our technology is capable" would determine in part whether they would qualify for the program or not.[1]

No clear-cut definition of the types of techniques or the kinds of talents that were needed emerged from the task force report. Its language was as broad as it was general. Implicit in this plea, however, was apparently a residual fear that cities might not have the capacity to plan, manage, and carry out the program's quest for innovative, bold new approaches. In effect, although the task force had articulated the need for new and flexible funding, as discussed in Chapter 5, it apparently was not quite sure that most cities would or could spend the money wisely unless they had some help.

The HUD Advisory Committee on Demonstration Program Development, created just before the enactment of the program to develop initial guidelines, was understandably more urgent in its concern over the talent gap. Only if the federal government provided expertise in a coordinated manner, its members believed, could cities build the type of skills required to meet the objectives of the program. According to the group's report, HUD would have to

. . . vigorously implement the provision authorizing technical assistance activities. This will require staffing commitments of a different order from the past. Highly skilled "urban generalists" supported by appropriate specialists, will be required by the Department to counsel cities and to properly review and assess applicants. . . .

. . . [HUD] should not attempt to duplicate expertise in non-HUD substantive fields, but *should draw on resources* of other Federal agencies.[2]

The Advisory Committee's rhetoric was direct, but it, too, failed to provide HUD with a reasonably specific guide to follow. Questions about the delicate relationships between federal, state, and local governments were not asked, let alone answered. Similarly, no detailed thought was given to the type of assistance the federal government could provide or its capacity to provide any meaningful as-

---

[1] President's Task Force on Urban Problems, report, December 22, 1965, pp. 5 and 6.
[2] Report of HUD Advisory Committee on Demonstration Program Development, September 1966, pp. 4 and 5 (italics added).

sistance, and no thought was given to the local capacity to receive outside help if it was offered.

Seemingly, no one on the Advisory Committee was concerned over HUD's ability to get other departments to provide aid, despite the fact that technical assistance could well be viewed as a threat to these other agencies. If the technical assistance granted was at least partially consistent with the program's objectives, it could well generate criticism of the way the client groups of most federal agencies handled their urban aid programs and lead those groups to protest and withhold their political support. Moreover, if the assistance produced new applicants, or "nontraditional" applicants, for existing scarce federal aids, it could weaken and upset the relationship between federal program managers and their traditional client groups, leading to unrest and uncertainty over federal funds and federal-local relationships.

Despite its weaknesses, the report was sufficiently blunt, at least, to make HUD realize that there were many serious questions to be asked and answered about technical assistance. Its tone was also sufficiently alarmist to provide a mild antidote to the more conservative view of HUD's role that had been advocated by some of the key staff right after the Congressional hearings on the legislation.

... the legislative history is saturated with legislative intent emphasizing local initiative. *Caution should be exercised* in rendering technical assistance lest it be construed as dictating. Complaints by Mayors to Congress or to the press about Federal meddling would be most unfortunate for the program's future.[3]

The tasks of getting organized, defining roles, and developing initial application and planning guidelines took precedence over all else immediately after passage of the legislation. Taylor and his staff gave very little attention to technical assistance strategies, even though the guidelines being developed would ultimately place severe planning demands on participating cities. No one could define with any preciseness at this early stage what the cities' technical needs would be or, even in a general way, how the federal government could respond to them.[4]

[3] Richard Cherry and Kent Watkins, "History of Congressional Action Relative to Model Cities 1966-1967." HUD, October 3, 1967, p. 44 (italics added). The staff's view seems in part to have been premised on Congressional hesitancy to approve federal coordinators in local areas. These individuals would have played an activist role in matching existing federal aids to city needs.
[4] Interview with former Assistant Secretary H. Ralph Taylor, June 1972.

Initial Organization—Locating Technical Assistance

When HUD set up the Model Cities Administration in January 1967, one of its three sections, the Operations and Technical Services Division, was given responsibility for technical assistance. No specific details were laid down, however, as to how the group would function or how many staff it would have. Nor was it clear whether the group would give assistance directly or merely propose or manage appropriate strategies.

Initially, Assistant Secretary Taylor believed that technical assistance, along with the rest of the program, should be "run from Washington." Taylor's views were intuitive. Apart from the normal bureaucratic desire to maintain control, he felt that because of salary and staffing limitations, management at the regional level would mean management by less qualified people. He also believed that regional management would subject the program to the more traditional federal restrictions on cities. He argued that "innovative and experimental programs could best be handled out of Washington. . . . Regionalization at the outset would have robbed the program of its uniqueness; would have failed to separate it from categorical programs . . . , and would have deprived it of the priority attention of top-notch staff."[5]

But most of his senior staff aides disagreed. In their opinion, "Model Cities, if run out of the capital, would have limited support even from HUD, given HUD's efforts to decentralize . . . ; would have become buffeted by political pressures." They felt that technical assistance would fall by the wayside. "Not enough talent could be mobilized . . . we needed to rely on the Regions. It would be easier for HUD people in the field to get action from their peers in other Agencies than we in Washington. Further, proximity breeds knowledge. . . . Most of us in D.C. knew little about participating Model Cities. We didn't have the time, numbers, or skills to offer real continuous help."[6]

Ultimately, both sides compromised their positions a bit: HUD's Model Cities Administration in Washington would retain the primary role in policy making for the still fledgling program. HUD's regional offices, however, would be given the responsibility for operations and technical assistance. Staff generalists, both in Washington and in the regions, would be supported by a "swing team" of specialists (for health, employment, citizen participation, etc.) based in Washing-

[5] Interview with former Assistant Secretary H. Ralph Taylor, June 1972.
[6] Interview with former Special Assistant George Williams, June 1972.

ton. This team, as indicated by its name, would be able to swing into position whenever requests for technical assistance were made from the region. It would serve to buttress the regional staff when and as needed.

Expectations about the efficiency of the new organization were not borne out. Staff shortages had created significant work overloads, and requests from participating cities for help in planning and preparing grant applications were not receiving attention. By mid-March 1967, a change seemed necessary. Walter Farr, the new director of the program, borrowing perhaps on his State Department experience, suggested that "desk officers" in Washington should be given responsibility for coordinating HUD's model cities operations in specific geographic areas. He further proposed that "leadmen" for individual cities be designated in HUD's regional offices. These leadmen would be generalists. They would provide HUD with its eyes and ears, and they would provide the cities with a "federal coordinator of sorts" as well as a modest amount of technical assistance.

The functions of the leadmen would be complemented by city and regional teams composed of program specialists, some of whom would come from HUD, some from other federal agencies. Each team, assuming the availability of staff, would be capable of providing technical assistance to the individual Model Cities Programs. Farr's recommendations were accepted by Taylor and instituted in March. Only the Washington-based program specialists, who obviously feared that the contemplated reorganization would eliminate or reduce their own roles, opposed the new emphasis on decentralization.[7]

Clearly Farr's amendments to the organization reflected his belief that the federal capacity to deliver sustained, meaningful technical assistance, particularly in program development and management, was minimal. Essentially, his changes de-emphasized the role of the specialist in Washington and placed direct responsibility for responding to anticipated needs for technical assistance in the hands of generalist managers. To the extent that program specialists could be found and regional teams put together, federal technical assistance would, or could, become more than nominal help with grantsmanship. But Farr saw this as no more than a possibility.

Organizational change did not, however, create a capacity for providing technical assistance. No one knew what city needs were or would be. The new staff hired were only vaguely familiar with the program and were in no position to offer meaningful help. Moreover, other departments were as yet only informally

---

[7] These program specialists were ultimately transferred to the MCA's evaluation section.

involved with the program. For the most part, their staff were unwilling or unable to do more than provide information. Fortunately, announcements of the first model cities grants were delayed.

The interagency agreement to establish formal working groups in Washington and the regions, which was developed in early summer (see Chapter 5), was not publicly announced until December 1967; the delay, as has been indicated earlier, was due to the late announcements of the planning grant awards. The agreement reflected HUD's still soft position on technical assistance. Questions were still not resolved about the choice of local recipients of technical assistance, the wisdom of alternative approaches for coordinating the provision of technical assistance, and the capacity of federal staff to provide any technical assistance. Neither was the still marginal involvement of the other departments fully recognized. Understandably, the resolution of these issues would involve a tough reappraisal of traditional federal behavior patterns and federal-client relationships. The agreement itself said almost nothing specific on these points. For example, the responsibilities of the regional working groups were defined as follows:

Discussion with the Mayor and his City Demonstration Agency and continuing review of Model Neighborhood planning efforts *with a view to facilitating* such planning efforts and development of programs consistent with the overall strategy for the Model Neighborhood. . . . Providing for obtaining *technical assistance as needed and requested* for the Model City.

The required Model Cities Coordinating Group . . . has overall responsibility for creating and maintaining the relationship and technical services in connection with broad program matters. . . .

Each Regional Model Cities Working Group will be assigned a particular Model City and will focus on day-to-day activities relating to specific program matters. . . .[8]

In effect, the agreement provided HUD with the language, the moral underpinning as it were, to go shopping for interagency support. However, it clearly did not generate the necessary support to make it work.

Developing an Agenda

During the early months of 1968 the Model Cities Administration developed and distributed several "technical assistance bulletins" touching on problems that it assumed would be significant for the City Demonstration Agencies. These documents contained, essentially, illustrative "how to" material on planning for the

[8] Interagency Agreement, December 1967, pp. 4 and 5 (italics added).

cities to follow.[9] The staff also prepared various draft papers on the federal role in general and its role in regard to technical assistance in particular.

By early spring, the MCA staff had apparently achieved a consensus on the meaning, at least, of technical assistance. It was limited to the following kinds of activities performed by federal and state officials: the provision of initial information about grants and the methods of applying for funds; assistance in making long- and short-term projections of goals; and assistance in matching local model cities projects to grant availability, and to statutes and administrative guidelines.[10]

HUD's conception of technical assistance was considerably more specific and limited by this time; but it still lacked detail about staff needs or about strategies for providing this aid. Departmental reactions to HUD's pleas for increased cooperation were, at best, lukewarm. Most departments claimed, with some justification, that their staff capacity limited the roles that their Washington and regional offices could play in any technical assistance system. All referred participating model cities, at one time or another, to the local groups funded by them as possible sources of help—in effect, to the very groups that many local CDAs were ostensibly trying to change or reform. For example, the Office of Economic Opportunity suggested that the CDAs should look to, indeed rely on, Community Action Agencies to train residents and initiate citizen participation. Similarly, HEW suggested that HUD should look to the state and county agencies that provided the social services traditionally funded by them. The Department of Labor and HUD's own offices proposed reliance on their respective friends in the community: in the former case, the beneficiaries of the Comprehensive Area Manpower Planning System and the Concentrated Employment Programs; in HUD's own case, organizations such as the local planning agencies and public housing authorities. No agency was willing (it would say able) to make a major and firm commitment on the assignment of funds or, in most instances, of staff to meet the assumed needs of cities.

Help from the White House

By late spring 1968, the Model Cities Administration had decided that interven-

[9] For example, TAB (Technical Assistance Bulletin) 1 described the appropriate uses of planning funds and discussed the professional qualifications of the CDA staff.
[10] This definition of technical assistance is taken from numerous MCA staff papers on the federal response which were prepared during the spring of 1968.

tion by the White House would be necessary to obtain the cooperation of other agencies for all aspects of the program. This led to a memorandum from Special Assistant Joseph Califano. This document, which has already been discussed (see Chapter 5), requested a plan from each department, a plan that among other things specifically provided for "effective technical assistance." An attachment also asked departments to indicate specific staffing patterns, consultant strategies, and assignments of agency field groups.[11]

The responses to Califano's request were not significantly different from earlier reactions to the MCA's petitions. The Department of Health, Education, and Welfare called attention to the existing network of staff and client groups in the regions and in participating cities.[12] The Office of Economic Opportunity noted that "priority consideration will be given . . . to the Model Cities program requests in the use of OEO specialty emphasis programs." The agency also said that "consultants would be made available to meet Model Cities-OEO related requirements." However, "*no specifics can be given* . . . until we know the magnitude of this demand by technical area. . . . Competing demands between our ongoing efforts and any new requirements will have to be reconciled within the context of available resources. . . ." OEO stated that its "staffing objective in our Regional Offices is to have one CAP Analyst assigned for each Model City served by a CAA who can work with the local agencies as well as the interagency Model Cities team." The office went on to illustrate how Budget Bureau restrictions on hiring impaired its participation.[13] The Department of Labor proposed a reliance on existing and contract personnel who would be available through their network of regional manpower administrators. It suggested that state employment security agencies would "make staff available to the Regional Manpower Administrators as needed to provide technical assistance to Model Cities." The DOL estimated that the "equivalent of two additional full-time staff or consultants are required in each of the eight Regional Manpower Offices. . . ."[14]

None of these responses met Califano's request for a reasonably comprehensive and specific technical assistance plan. Real staff constraints, the historical ties to traditional client groups in cities, the still-marginal commitment to "HUD's pro-

[11] Memorandum from Joseph Califano to the Secretaries of HEW, DOL, and the Director of OEO, July 26, 1968.
[12] Memorandum from James P. Alexander, Director, Center for Community Planning, "Plans for Model Cities Program," to Secretary Cohen, July 31, 1968. Memorandum used in response to Califano's of July 26.
[13] Memorandum from OEO to Joseph Califano, "Model Cities Program," August 12, 1968, pp. 4 and 5 (italics added).
[14] Memorandum from Secretary Wirtz (DOL) to Joseph Califano, August 15, 1968, p. 4.

gram," and a continued lack of understanding of city needs had led to departmental submittals that "were not particularly assuring." Yet the MCA was itself partly to blame, because its call for technical assistance though extensive remained imprecise on specific approaches and costs.

Despite obvious interest and pressure from the White House, technical assistance plans did not improve significantly during the late summer and fall. In response to a second memorandum from Califano, HEW was more specific in defining the staffing network that would be assigned to the model cities. It also noted that it had "designated 75 community liaison representatives for first-round Model Cities and will designate additional representatives as soon as second-round cities are announced."[15] This commitment was not entirely satisfactory to the MCA, however, as HEW itself stated, "Most . . . representatives were Social Security district managers, who live in or near the Model Cities and [could only] spend up to a third of their time working with the demonstration program. . . ."[16] Not only was their time limited, but their background and interests were only vaguely appropriate to the interests of the program.

HEW sought more staff positions, as did OEO, to meet the anticipated but unknown level of technical assistance required. The Department of Labor continued to express minimal commitment with maximum rhetoric.

The Department of Labor will continue to cooperate fully in placing highest priority on successful structuring of the Model Cities program. . . .

On September 13, I initiated action to appoint two professional staff members in each of our eight Regional Manpower Administration offices. These new staff members will devote full time to the Model Cities program. The positions will be filled at the *earliest possible feasible date within the framework of the Department's merit staffing procedures and Civil Service regulations.* . . .

The executive staff of the Manpower Administration was directed to increase technical assistance in manpower and employment programs to city officials and city demonstration agencies. . . .[17]

Complementary Efforts

While the Model Cities Administration was attempting to get help from the White House, it was also considering alternatives to the regional teams, working on an appropriate interagency federal and state strategy for providing technical

[15] Memorandum from Secretary Cohen to Califano, August 10, 1968, p. 2.
[16] Ibid., p. 2. Staff of the Social Security Administration were not thought to be a particularly relevant choice to solve model city problems.
[17] Untitled memorandum from Secretary Willard Wirtz to Joseph Califano, Jr., October 7, 1968, p. 1 (italics added).

assistance, and attempting to bring to fruition a promise from OEO of $4 million for technical assistance.

The Regional and Local Teams

By early summer, it was already apparent that the newly established interagency teams were not working well.

RICC members, with some notable exceptions, spent little time in most of the studied cities. Their lack of knowledge of the context within which cities were initiating planning processes, combined with their generalist skills, limited their usefulness.

City teams showed up as events in only two cities. . . . In both instances, their role was primarily ceremonial. Their members could not, primarily because of their background, really help cities with respect to planning process problems.[18]

In effect, most federal staff were unprepared. Competing demands on their time did not permit them to learn much about individual cities. Because of this, many of the cities resented their involvement. The MCA's response, at this early stage, was to seek a reaffirmation, through informal meetings with senior staff of other agencies, of the functions prescribed for the RICC and the city teams. Beyond this, at the suggestion of Farr, it developed a proposal to train six teams to provide concentrated technical assistance in six cities. The idea was to test the effectiveness of such teams under optimal conditions. Although most of HUD's sister agencies expressed passing interest in the new proposal, it nonetheless died of inertia. No one had time to pick up the cudgels, given the need to write planning guidelines, respond to unscheduled city requests, and just keep the program going.

State Strategies

Most funds from HEW and DOL flow through the states to urban areas; yet despite this, only minimal efforts were made through the summer of 1968 to obtain direct state involvement. According to John McLean, chief of the MCA Operations and Technical Services Division, "Everyone talked about involving state agencies, but no one really knew how or knew precisely what states would do or could do. . . . Traditionally, states had not been involved in responding to city needs. Only HEW really dealt on a regular basis with the states and we had not yet been able to win their commitment to the basic program. . . ."[19]

[18] HUD, *The Model Cities Program: A Comparative Analysis of Eleven Cities* (Washington, D.C.: U.S. Government Printing Office, 1970), p. 35. This study was prepared by the firm of Marshall Kaplan, Gans and Kahn.
[19] Marshall Kaplan, Gans and Kahn staff interview with John McLean, January 1969.

James Alexander, in a candid memorandum to Secretary Cohen of HEW, corroborated this view.

One of the major problems in connection with the development of the Model Cities program has been the almost complete lack of attention in interdepartmental efforts to developing a logical federal-wide approach to states in the Model Cities effort. In the first place, the law itself did not indicate any fixed role for state government in this operation. Secondly, early groundrules and guidelines produced by MCA definitely failed to discuss the subject or to give any impetus to a concerted federal effort to work with the states in the development of the Model Cities program.[20]

A first stab at involving the states was attempted in mid-July. Nine states were invited by Secretary Robert Weaver to participate more fully with the Model Cities Administration in developing policy, reviewing applications, and in providing technical assistance to CDAs on a demonstration basis. Close association between the MCA and the staff from these nine states would, it was thought, provide HUD with a sense of the states' role in the program and would offer sufficient insight to develop alternate strategies for further state involvement.

Unfortunately—and perhaps understandably, considering the weak incentive for states to participate at all, the absence of an urban constituency, and the traditional lack of state interest in city problems[21] the anticipated close association between the staffs of the nine states and the MCA staff did not materialize. Only a few summer meetings were held, and these were very ineffective. None of the nine states was able to suggest the immediate availability of funding or personnel for technical assistance. Conversely, most felt, given the statutory and administrative criteria then governing federal assistance to the states, that specific directives from Washington would be necessary. All of the states agreed only to *consider* arrangements that would facilitate coordination of the Model Cities Program and the provision of technical assistance at the state level. Many urged use of existing metropolitan councils of government to provide technical help. But none was optimistic or specific about how HUD could move such groups.

Although only modest achievements were recorded, HUD interest in state in-

---

[20] Memorandum from James Alexander, Director, Center for Community Planning, "Plans for Model Cities Program," to Secretary Cohen, July 31, 1968, p. 2.
[21] HUD could offer only 701 and 701(b) planning assistance to the nine states, and even these funds were limited. More important than fund constraints, however, in limiting state participation was the fact that most state governments did not view urban populations, particularly poor urban populations, as part of their constituency.

volvement remained reasonably high. Toward the end of August, the MCA asked all regional administrators to write to the governors of those states in which there were approved Model Cities Programs to ask for their individual participation and the participation of their state agencies. Included among the very general kinds of state action asked for were

... the provision of technical assistance required by CDA's to perform comprehensive planning and to launch action programs. ... This includes staff members who, upon request, can authoritatively explain relevant programs to CDA staff and residents, provide information on current activities affecting the area, assist in the planning process, assist in the preparation of applicants, and provide current advice regarding the amounts of state funds available and the rules governing their allocation and commitment. . . .[22]

However, there was still no discussion of precise needs and priorities.

HUD was curiously silent on the possible funds available for states that agreed to cooperate. A staff progress report that was circulated within the MCA in December showed that there had been only a nominal response to HUD's plea for help.

An Agreement with OEO

The Office of Economic Opportunity, in its response to Califano's request of midsummer 1968, had promised to earmark $4 million for technical assistance purposes. Most of this money would be directed toward neighborhood groups that wanted to receive independent assistance. Cities that were awarded model cities funds would be required to contribute a limited amount of those funds toward the same objective. A number of months passed, however, between the time of OEO's promise to deliver technical assistance money and their agreement with HUD on ground rules governing its use in the cities. The reasons for the delay illustrates some of the major obstacles to the creation of a technical assistance strategy at the federal level.

OEO's willingness to develop a resident-oriented technical assistance program, in keeping with what it believed to be its mandate, became known to HUD's MCA staff early in 1968. OEO initially insisted that its client group, the local Community Action Agencies, should review and approve local applicants for technical assistance. Conversely, the MCA insisted, at least at the outset, that its local counterpart, the City Demonstration Agencies, should have a veto power

[22] Letter attached to memorandum from Walter Farr, Jr., to HUD Assistant Regional Administrator for Model Cities, September 17, 1968, p. 2.

over the contents of proposals and over the potential applicants for funds.

The agreement of October 1968 to create a conciliation process for local CAAs and CDAs (described in Chapter 4) did not touch on the use of funds other than those of the Community Action Program; yet these were the funds to be set aside for technical assistance. OEO and HUD reached a specific agreement on the issue late in 1968 and made this known to their respective client groups in January 1969. This second agreement asked for the concurrence of the CAAs, the CDAs, and local chief executives before any one of them approached selected resident groups to ask whether they were interested in the program. A final proposal had to be submitted by the neighborhood group to the local executive, and to the CAAs and the CDAs, at the same time that it was submitted to HUD and OEO. Because the later agreement referred to the one made between HUD and OEO in October 1968, which had created a conciliation process should local disputes arise about the dispersal of CAP funds, any visible disagreement between the CDAs and CAAs over the use of the technical assistance funds would presumably be subject to conciliation by the regional and Washington offices of HUD and OEO.

Implicit if not explicit in the year-long hassle between HUD and OEO was a disagreement over the shape that technical assistance activities should take. Most of the OEO staff would have granted the neighborhood groups and their consultants considerable freedom to define what they wanted from the grant: for example, funds could have been used to prepare resident plans as alternatives to local model city agency plans and to build local resident organizations. Conversely, most of the model cities staff would have preferred to confine technical assistance activities to the specific planning requirements of the program, and they would have directed funds only to the local model cities agencies and their related groups. Because there were some objections from the City Demonstration Agencies and from its own regional offices, the MCA was hesitant to endorse what it thought was the ideological approach of many of OEO's favored consultants and the environment of contention that seemed to have been fostered by previous OEO efforts at providing technical assistance. The final agreement was noticeably vague and a compromise. It permitted funds to be used for a wide variety of endeavors so long as they had the concurrence of CAAs, and the local mayors. In effect, each party had a veto.

A Change of Administration

No clear-cut technical assistance strategy had emerged by the end of the Johnson

Administration. The Model Cities Administration was still not able to make a precise estimate of the cities' technical assistance needs. Moreover, the federal agencies were either not able, or willing, to make more than nominal commitments in this area.

A thorough reevaluation of HUD's efforts to mount an effective strategy for providing technical assistance ranked low on the initial agenda of the new Administration. Yet, according to Robert Baida, the new Deputy Assistant Secretary for Model Cities, "given the new Administration's early perception that Model Cities was a 'capacity-building' program, the subject was always just below the surface . . . and frequently became a legitimate item for discussion." [23] A published analysis of program experiences in three cities gave support to the belief that something had to be done. The federal staff were not making a dent; their backgrounds were often not appropriate for responding to city needs. In Atlanta, for example,

Neither the HUD Regional team, the federal city team, nor the RICC was able to provide sustained technical assistance. Staff shortages and commitments to other Model Cities communities limited their impact. Federal people would have been most helpful if they could have given the city precise knowledge of federal funding flowing into Atlanta and detailed information about availability of federal program money.[24]

And in Seattle, the CDA

. . . sought minimal technical assistance from the HUD team. Most visits from HUD's Regional staff occurred at their own instigation. . . . Distance, as well as limited sign-off abilities, obviated participation by the RICC. It played a rather peripheral role in Seattle.[25]

Some staff members believed that increased use of consultants through the development of national technical assistance contracts would offer a solution, because this would substitute for absent or limited federal staff. HUD signed five contracts with consulting firms by the close of fiscal 1969. They totaled close to $2 million.[26] These contracts provided for the provision of assistance in such

[23] Interview with Robert Baida, HUD's Regional Administrator, San Francisco, July 1972. Robert Baida was Deputy Assistant Secretary for Model Cities, 1969 to 1970.
[24] HUD, *The Model Cities Program: A History and Analysis of the Planning Process in Three Cities* (Washington, D.C.: U.S. Government Printing Office, 1969), p. 34. This study was prepared by the firm of Marshall Kaplan, Gans and Kahn.
[25] Ibid., p. 58.
[26] Several other contracts were signed by HUD during fiscal 1969. Their scope of services clearly involved the provision of technical assistance, but because they were not granted by the program development division of MCA, they were not listed in budget summaries as technical assistance contracts. In total, close to $2,500,000 were allocated for technical assistance purposes during fiscal 1969.

diverse areas as planning and management, health, civil service, and employment needs. They generally called for direct consultant visits to cities. Most of the consultants were from nationally recognized firms; they were given resources to provide help to only a limited number of cities. No consistent set of criteria, however, was used in selecting these cities. Some cities were chosen on the basis of an analysis of their ability to receive technical assistance, some on the basis of general appraisal of city needs, some on a judgment of overall city capacity, and some were chosen on the basis of their specific requests for assistance.

Unfortunately, the consultants did not noticeably add to the substance of federal efforts. Reports from HUD's field staff, as well as many of the local and federal evaluation studies, pointed to the difficulties. "In and out" consultants rarely provided the City Demonstration Agencies with significant and sustained help. The infrequency of their visits, owing to budget and staff constraints, limited the consultants' understanding of the cities; the CDA staff were not able to plan effectively for their use; most of the consultants, because of their technical background, were not able to relate easily to residents of the neighborhood; and consultants were often substituted for local staff.[27] When consultants attempted to criticize the administration of old-line agencies, they were resented, often kept in the dark, and asked to limit their assistance.

Assistant Secretary Hyde acknowledged the difficulties with technical assistance in his memorandum to Secretary Romney on February, 1969.

> Localities have neither the time nor the experience to develop as high a quality of programs as hoped, and the federal government has *not* been able to mount as effective a technical assistance and program development effort as is needed.[28]

Comments by Walter Farr, written around the same time, were more direct.

> The Federal government has made only a nominal contribution to development of quality programs. . . . Personnel restrictions have made it impossible for the MCA personnel to provide significant direct technical assistance to cities in specific program areas. Functional specialists in regional offices had to be transformed into generalist leadmen. One man can't be responsible for East St. Louis, Gary, and Chicago and also give technical assistance in employment and economic development programs through HUD's Region IV. . . . Other agencies couldn't or didn't staff up to do the job; and regular regional HEW and Labor staff are tied to their own categorical programs, their own guidelines, their own

[27] These conclusions are drawn from Marshall Kaplan, Gans and Kahn field interviews with HUD staff, September 1968-June 1969. They are corroborated by findings reported in HUD, *The Model Cities Program: A Comparative Analysis* . . . , p. 34.
[28] Memorandum from Floyd Hyde, "Basic Mission, Goals and Objectives of the Model Cities Program and its Future," to Secretary Romney, February 8, 1969, p. 10 (italics added).

constituent local agencies, and their own paperwork. . . . This lack of Federal capacity to provide comprehensive technical assistance in specific program areas means HUD also lacks the capacity to review specific proposed programs. . . .[29]

To the extent that their competing assignments permitted them, some of the MCA staff, particularly those in the Office of Program Development, once again began to outline alternate technical assistance strategies. There were two factors that apparently limited their freedom to suggest more than modest amendments. First, most of the staff directly concerned with technical assistance were also directly involved in the contract consultant process—that is, they functioned as contract monitors—so their positions were very much tied in with the existing system. Second, and perhaps more important, a conscious decision was made by the Assistant Secretary to continue to "push for increased agency involvement, for a more effective federal response." Unfortunately, technical assistance was only one element in this federal response and by this time not the most important element. So it remained a residual concern. Certainly in Hyde's mind it was not on the same level as the need to obtain agency commitments on funding and reforms in their handling of applications.

Apart from the continued extensive use of consultants, and various short-term training efforts directed at the RICC's and at HUD's regional staff, no major amendments were made to the technical assistance system in 1969. OEO's own technical assistance program, which had been initiated prior to the beginning of the new Administration, continued in a limited number of cities. HEW's regional offices, primarily at the urging of the young and aggressive director of the Center for Community Planning, were prodded into providing more technical assistance. But even here, meager staff resources and the variable commitments of office and program managers limited the general effectiveness of the effort. The Department of Labor remained noticeably cool, the availability of its staff depending more on the good feeling of the regional staff of the Office of Manpower Training than on prodding from Washington. Other offices within HUD itself were willing or able to provide only sporadic technical assistance to a relatively few cities.

The Chamberlin study prepared for the Assistant Secretaries Working Group on the model cities in the fall of 1970 called attention to the inept performance of the federal government.

Federal agencies are not staffed in D.C. or in Regional Offices to provide the

[29] Draft memorandum from Walter Farr, Jr., "Model Cities Program Management," to staff, January 27, 1969, pp. 4 and 5.

quantity and quality of technical assistance required by cities to make effective use of available resources. . . .

Federal agencies have not established a priority system which would give Model Cities an appropriate amount of staff time which does exist. . . .

No system for projecting the quantity of technical assistance required by cities to make effective use of available resources has yet been devised by MCA.

A comprehensive technical assistance program in urban management has not been provided by the federal government.

Interdepartmental systems have not been established to assure that technical assistance reaches the cities.

HUD has concentrated on getting funds from other agencies instead of providing technical assistance to help cities overcome the complexities of the program. . . .

Conceptions of what is meant by technical assistance vary from expert help in how to do things, to reminders to local applicants of every rule they must comply with to get funds. . . .[30]

There is no evidence that either the Assistant Secretaries Working Group or its parent body, the Under Secretaries Working Group, responded to the analysis of the Chamberlin task force. Hyde's own attention, in the coming months, as well as that of his key staff, was diverted to several more important endeavors including "constantly having to respond to new White House Task Forces set up to study the program."[31]

The Model Cities Administration continued to rely heavily on consultants through the fall of 1970. They were asked to concentrate primarily on building up the management abilities of cities and on installing "information systems" in participating cities. Both requests emphasized the new Administration's attempt to emphasize administrative reform or capacity building. The provision of technical assistance by the agencies continued to be sporadic and uneven.

The fiscal 1972 budget requests for technical assistance contracts were subjected to more than the normal scrutiny by the Under Secretary. This reflected an increasingly lukewarm attitude toward model cities and also the obvious lack of hard data on the impact of such assistance. The tone of the Under Secretary's memorandum of August 28, 1970, suggests that the end of the consulting strategy was close. He questioned the duplication of contracts, their clarity, objectives, and viability.

How close [does this one contract relate] to the $650,000 we have already paid [another contractor] for technical assistance in evaluating project and pro-

[30] *Strengthening the Federal Response to Model Cities: An Interagency Report*, September 1969, Attachment 1, pp. 1-2.
[31] Interview with Floyd Hyde, July 1972.

gram performance and to the $400,000 we have just agreed to pay [yet another contractor] to train CDA staff in evaluation techniques. . . .

The description of the [proposal] for a CDA management assistance program, to put it as gently as I can, leaves something to be desired. . . . Aside from the inadequacy of the description of the contract, which makes it difficult to understand what [the contractor] is to do, I am disturbed by that portion of the description which I think I do understand. You have impressed upon me the fact that the Model Cities program is supposed to strengthen general city government and the mayor in particular. This description suggests that one of the mayor's new problems is how to get along with the CDAs. If [the contractor] is supposed to tell 148 mayors how to run their cities, he can't do it for $425,000 and in one year. If what [the contractor] is doing adds up to revising the city charter of Winooski, Vermont, it isn't worth $425,000. . . .[32]

Assistant Secretary Hyde asked each of his office directors to prepare a reply. The Director of the Office of Program Development, in his defense, considerably extended HUD's earlier rationale for technical assistance contracts.

Technical assistance contracts with national organizations have provided entree into local and state organizations. Contracts are and have served as levers to get organizations involved after the contract has formed the interests; the interest will be sustained after the contract is continued. . . .

Agencies have begun recognizing the need for assistance and, in many of our existing contracts, have committed funds for joint assistance; and have committed funds for grant assistance ventures. In some instances, this has been used to get commitments out of agencies. . . .[33]

In retrospect, the attribution of such powers of co-option to HUD's contracts seems to be more an expression of fond hopes than a reality; yet both this argument and Hyde's persuasiveness managed to prevent significant cuts in the 1971 budget for technical assistance. The 1972 budget, however, would be a different story. In effect, the Assistant Secretary was by now convinced that HUD's technical assistance contract activities had produced little and were in need of thorough evaluation, and he initiated a massive cutback. The cutback was readily accepted by the Under Secretary.

The MCA's technical assistance contract authority for fiscal 1972 was reduced from $3,837,000 to $2,300,000. Numerous contracts were brought to a close; very few new ones would be added during the next two years. Of the projected $2,300,000, a sum of $700,000 was set aside to induce other agencies, through joint or shared funding, to provide contract technical assistance. Similarly, $500,000 was allocated to federal technical assistance, or the development

[32] Memorandum from Under Secretary Van Dusen to Floyd Hyde, August 28, 1970.
[33] Donald Dodge, strategy paper on technical assistance contracts, October 10, 1970, p. 3.

through contracts or the direct transfer of HUD funds of an increased capacity by other federal agencies to supply technical assistance.

Hyde's final justification of the proposed budget illustrates the gradual turnaround in HUD's attitude. Federal agencies would now have to be "bribed" to participate in a meaningful way. The MCA could no longer count on persuasion and voluntary action. Other priorities, taken in conjunction with the prevailing negative view of past assistance efforts, would not permit the MCA to make further appeals for help to senior HUD officials or to make a direct approach to either the interdepartmental groups or the White House. Doubts about the Model Cities Program, fears about the impact of technical assistance on other agency programs, and doubts about its value, given resource constraints, could not be assuaged without direct financial incentives—or so Hyde thought.

The Assistant Secretary's assertions that the increasing capability of the city agencies would allow for further reductions in later budgets were obviously directed at convincing staff in the Secretary's office of the virtue of his budget. But they did not represent any hard projections. In effect, if he wanted to secure approval even for his reduced budget, it was necessary for the Assistant Secretary to demonstrate the possible impact—even if the projection was a bit illusory. Floyd Hyde made his point in a memorandum addressed to the Under Secretary and to OMB.

Our technical assistance package is primarily directed at: (1) securing commitments of other federal departments relative to funding and providing technical assistance; (2) securing increased state and city participation in funding technical assistance contacts; (3) using technical assistance to "lock in" categorical programs. We will *also* use funds on a limited basis to provide cities with assistance from otherwise unavailable nationally proven public and private groups. It is anticipated that: (1) increased interagency provision and funding of technical assistance; and (2) increased capacity of cities to meet their seen needs will significantly reduce the contract budget of FY 1972.[34]

Soon after submission and approval of the budget, Assistant Secretary Hyde initiated a highly innovative pilot program aimed at recruiting and training young people to be placed in cities as "staff" to chief executives and public agencies. He also contracted with the National Conference of Mayors-National League of Cities to screen and recruit unemployed aerospace engineers to fill vacant city positions. These two programs totaled only a small portion of HUD's technical assistance budget, but they reflected the Assistant Secretary's growing

[34] Memorandum from Floyd Hyde, "Fiscal Year 1972 Contract Activity," October 19, 1970 (italics added).

belief that "the best way to help increase the capacity of cities is to help them get adequate staff.... We have come full circle ... complete reliance on Feds and consultants won't do. I know we may need more ... but rather than permitting or forcing cities to rely on outsiders we should develop strategies to help strengthen their staffs."[35]

Renewed State Effort

Considering the problems that HUD faced in defining and initiating a relevant role for the states in the Model Cities Program during the Johnson Administration, the efforts made by the MCA after 1968 seem quite significant. Stimulated in part by a report of the Urban Affairs Council, which commented on the failure to engage the states, and in part by his own background as a state governor, Secretary Romney made a statement in support of state involvement, albeit a general one, at his April 1969 news conference.

Hyde responded quickly to Romney's directive and asked his staff to develop alternative strategies. Explicit in the diverse papers prepared during early and mid-1969 was the need to gain a handle on the federal funds that flow to the states and the complementary need to obtain state and metropolitan resources for the participating cities. How this could be accomplished without infringing on the sensitivities either of the cities themselves, jealous as they were of their limited funds and their primary role in the program, or of the many diverse national interest groups, all jealous of their own respective prerogatives for "coordinating" the role of the states, became a major problem.

Ultimately, Hyde, with Secretarial concurrence, decided to expand use of the 701 planning assistance program. In effect, 701 funds would be given to the states and/or metropolitan planning groups to increase their staff capacity to help the participating model cities. Model city support units could be created, responsible to the governor. The MCA staff hoped that state assistance would be provided to help cities meet the planning prerequisites for the use of state funds and of federal funds flowing through the state agencies. HUD's staff also hoped the councils of government and metropolitan planning agencies could be induced to provide technical assistance, particularly with planning and grant requirements.

By mid-1971, over thirty states had used 701 funds to establish staff resources

[35] Interview with Floyd Hyde, July 1972.

for the model cities. Yet more encouraging to HUD, governors of at least forty-five states had designated model city representatives. Many had allocated their own funds to provide staffing to respond to local requests for technical assistance. HUD was able to use 111(b) demonstration funds to initiate a demonstration effort that concentrated specifically on developing and testing alternate assistance approaches in four states: Connecticut, North Carolina, Pennsylvania, and California.

No comprehensive evaluation of the impact of state involvement has been undertaken by HUD. One recent study suggested that a promising beginning had been made but that state technical assistance had not been particularly helpful in securing additional state funds for the model cities.[36] A second analysis suggested that less than half of those states studied put emphasis on a continuing program of technical assistance.[37] Obvious problems impeding the effectiveness of this approach were the diverse, and conflicting, views of the role of state technical assistance, the lack of an urban or poverty focus of most state governments, the marginal ability of many new model cities staff, tenuously linked to the governor's office, to get commitments from other state agencies; and the limited availability of resources, both of staff and money. Very little response was recorded from the metropolitan groups. Like the states, they were apparently short on resources. Similarly, they found it difficult to merge their own constituencies with those of the model cities.

In Retrospect

Technical assistance, despite the recognition given to it by the original Wood task force and the implicit promises expressed in the early guidelines, never became a significant element of the Model Cities Program. Certainly, no coherent technical assistance strategy was ever developed by the Model Cities Administration. And even if it had been, most departments would not have been able or willing to provide continuous help. For the most part, they were immobilized by budget problems and limited staff capacity, as well as the competing claims on their attention. For similar reasons, HUD's staff in the regions found themselves coping with various cities' technical assistance needs in an ad hoc, haphazard

[36] Marshall Kaplan, Gans and Kahn, *Model Cities Supplemental Funds Study*, February 1971, Phase 1.
[37] Arthur D. Little, Inc., *The State Role in the Model Cities Program*, prepared for the U.S. Department of Housing and Urban Development, September 1971, p. 17.

manner. Ultimately, most of the technical assistance was provided by consultant firms under national contract. Their efforts were limited to a relatively few cities and were generally confined to brief visits. Their impact was, with some exceptions, quite marginal. The few bright spots seem to have resulted more from the heroics or idiosyncrasies of particular individuals than from conscious and sustained attention of the federal government.

Several significant obstacles stood in the way of a flexible and effective federal response to the technical assistance needs of model cities.

1. *The varying commitment of most departments to the program.* Each federal agency was, and remained, linked to one or more state and/or local groups. These groups were either conduits or recipients of agency funds. As a result, they provided each agency with a political constituency, and each agency staff member with a job justification. It was not easy in this environment for HUD to obtain or "coordinate" agency commitments on technical assistance or anything else. Its role as a lead agency merely placed it first among equals and granted it no real clout. To most agencies, survival dictated primary attention to their own programs and their own local connections. Even those agencies whose senior officials were willing to play HUD's tune found it difficult to influence lower-echelon staff, in view of the prescriptive nature of traditional bureaucratic behavior and ground rules.

2. *Sensitivity about the appropriate federal role in dealing with city problems.* Fear of being charged with encroachment on the turf of local government made many federal personnel and agencies wary of offering assistance. Similarly, fear of being accused of being "dictated to" caused many local officials to avoid seeking available federal help.

3. *The all-encompassing objectives of the Model Cities Program.* Neither the model cities legislation nor later HUD guidelines provided the cities or the federal departments with a distinct and precise work program. To the contrary, as has been indicated in previous chapters, the objectives were both comprehensive and open-ended. Relevant planning regulations were similarly opaque and less than definitive about content. Given this frame of reference, it was quite difficult for participants in the program to measure and state their agenda for technical assistance.

4. *The questionable capacity of the federal government to deliver sustained and meaningful technical assistance.* Although there were exceptions, federal staff attempting to provide technical assistance found themselves woefully unprepared to cope with or comprehend specific city problems, city politics, and

city institutions. This was understandable. Most federal personnel going into the cities were generalists rather than specialists. Even those who were prepared were not able to provide substantive help because of the limitations on their time and their subsequent span of attention.

5. *The lack of desire on the part of traditional local agencies to receive technical assistance.* Most agencies were glad to receive assistance in the filing of applications. Yet only a few welcomed assistance in making changes in their staffing patterns, work program, planning processes, or resource allocation priorities. This, too, was understandable: the former type of assistance was seen as supportive, but the latter type offered a threat to their institutional well-being.

Where Do We Go from Here?
Unfortunately, the model cities experience offers little in the way of firm guidelines to those interested in developing a "coordinated" federal technical assistance role in the cities. The impediments standing in the way of a direct, sustained, major effort by federal staff to help cities will not be easy to remove. Clearly, one agency is not in a position to commandeer attention or a response from other agencies. Further, the more assistance is directed at reform and redistribution objectives, the more such assistance will be resisted both in Washington and locally.

Expectations about the possibilities for federal assistance ought to be reevaluated. Simplification of the federal aid structure will go a long way toward defining technical assistance in terms of substantive issues and thus reduce the need for advice on grantsmanship or the use (and threat) of technical assistance to create favored treatment for the flow of federal funds. The provision of federal funds for the direct hiring of staff or locally selected consultants should be considered as a possible substitute for placing reliance on visits by federal staff or on help from federally selected consulting firms. Just as important, the ability of the federal government to convey information, given its central position, ought to be viewed as favorably, at least initially, as its ability to supply advice. Indeed, just as the federal government serves a redistributive function in regard to income, it might be assigned a similar function in regard to the transmission of ideas and talent.

Chapter 8
Defining a Relevant Evaluation Program

Implied Understanding and Commitment

The Model Cities Program distributed a large amount of resources to a limited number of cities. Selecting a few cities for benefits was a difficult political feat for Congress and the Administration. It could be justified only if it generated programs that could be repeated in other cities and if it led to future legislation directed at improving the quality of life for all Americans. If the program was to lead to these wider benefits, however, one would suppose that a sustained and continuous evaluation would be required of its impact.

Yet, somewhat surprisingly, evaluation was not given major emphasis in the Wood task force report. References to it were brief, often oblique. Perhaps naively, considering that evaluation was often seen by both federal and local agencies as a threatening activity, it was assumed that "no one would object to evaluation . . . that it would be accepted as a major part of the administration of a limited demonstration program."[1] Even more surprising, given the influence of academia on the task force, no apparent thought was given to the modest state of evaluation research methods and the massive problems of evaluating such a comprehensive program as model cities.

Everyone seemed to assume that evaluation would be a part of the program, but little more than passing reference was made to it during the Congressional hearings. Secretary Weaver, both in his testimony at the hearings and in other speeches, implied that he had already given some thought to measuring the effect of the program. Yet he was quite unspecific about the form, content, timing, and methodology of the evaluation. For example, Weaver, before the Congress, noted the need for a purposeful selection of cities and the wisdom of a wide sample. Yet he said nothing about anticipated evaluation processes or who would undertake the evaluation.[2]

The HUD Advisory Committee charged with developing program guidelines (Rafsky committee) was more direct in its statements.

. . . the Department: must make demanding judgments at the proposal stage, at the mid-planning stage and at the pre-execution . . . must place greater emphasis on program evaluation than has been the case in the past. . . . Management of the program should . . . capitalize on the potential to evaluate local programs against

[1] Observations of Bernard Frieden, staff member, President's Task Force on Urban Problems.
[2] Richard Cherry and Kent Watkins, "History of Congressional Action Relative to Model Cities, 1966-1967," HUD, October 3, 1967, p. 2.

general performance standards rather than detailed specification standards. . . .

Program success must be measured in terms of social gains: the number of people better housed, the number of students better educated, the number of unemployed made employable and employed, and the creation of a modern, livable environment with the strength to endure. . . .[3]

Despite its clear support for evaluation, however, the Advisory Committee did not offer HUD any indication of how it should initiate such an effort; nor did it raise the possibility of problems if HUD assumed responsibility for evaluating itself or if it tried to induce other federal agencies to evaluate their own efforts. Nowhere in the report is there a precise description of alternate, or preferred, approaches to evaluation. Who would do what, when, and how was still left unanswered. According to George Williams, staff director of the Rafsky committee,

We assumed that continuous evaluation would be done at the local CDA level. . . . What HUD's and a possible inter-agency role would be was up for grabs. . . . No thought was raised that Model Cities' objectives relative to reform or the poor would threaten Federal or local participation. We felt that we would have to measure impact and that we would be required to engage in some sort of monitoring of city performance. . . . Yet we did not have a good handle on how to do it. . . . Organization specifics and techniques would have to develop over time. . . .[4]

The bill, as finally enacted in November, was thought by HUD's staff to provide a mandate for national as well as local efforts at evaluation. Richard Langendorf, a senior member of the MCA evaluation staff, explained, "Statutory language suggesting performance criteria hinted at the need for monitoring and evaluation. . . . How else could the nation record improvements sought by Congress concerning the quality of life; how else could we attest to the fact of program 'magnitude' . . . 'impact' . . . in Congressionally defined areas?"[5]

Local evaluation rested on more certain statutory mandates. Section 103(c) of the act stated

. . . the preparation of demonstration city programs should include to the maximum extent feasible: (1) the performance of analyses that provide explicit and systematic comparisons of the costs and benefits, financial and otherwise, of alternative possible actions designed to fulfill urban needs; and (2) the establish-

[3] Report of HUD Advisory Committee on Demonstration Program Development, pp. 4-7.
[4] Interview with George Williams, December 1968.
[5] Marshall Kaplan, Gans and Kahn staff interview with Dr. Richard Langendorf, January 1969.

ment of programmed systems designed to assure effective use of such analyses by city demonstration agencies and by other government bodies. . . .[6]

Attempts at Implementation

Nothing much was done to implement a comprehensive evaluation program until the spring and summer of 1967. The first priority for the new Model Cities Administration was to put its own house in order, to get the program started. Perfunctory and summary evaluation guidelines were sent out to cities as part of the initial program criteria and in later documents. Most of the guidelines were quite general and rather vague about what should be done.

CDA . . . should have the capacity and authority to evaluate. . . .
Local programs should include measures designed to develop the capability to evaluate on a continuing basis the relative costs and benefits of alternative program directions.[7]

By the spring of 1967, a small staff had been hired for the program development and evaluation office, one of three offices set up within the Model Cities Administration. Assistant Secretary Taylor and the MCA Director Farr asked the office to develop an initial draft of an evaluation program. The outcome, "Evaluation of the Model Cities Program With Issues for Decision," assumed three types of program effect: (1) changes in the attitudes and behavior or neighborhood residents; (2) changes in the physical, social, and economic character of the model neighborhood; and (3) changes in the public and private institutions serving the neighborhood. For their evaluation, the staff proposed three "output" and two "impact" studies. The output evaluation would include a study of resident attitudes, an institutional change study, and a statistical survey of physical, economic, and social changes in the model neighborhood. The impact evaluation would include a study of the planning process, and a study of financial experiences. The difference between output and impact studies was not defined clearly by the HUD staff. Generally, output analyses were viewed as studies of the long-term effect of the program on people and institutions. Conversely, impact studies were seen as descriptive analyses of selected events initiated by the program or as analyses of related strategies.

Somewhat surprisingly, given the brief history of categorical programs aimed

[6] Demonstration Cities Act of 1966 (Public Law 89-754), Title 1, Comprehensive City Demonstration Programs, Sec. 103(c).
[7] HUD, "Improving the Quality of Urban Life," December 1966, pp. 11, 19.

at urban areas, the draft assumed without challenge the sustained availability of significant federal funds. Clearly, without such funds there would be no rationale for an extensive evaluation effort, because it would be difficult to assume that there was anything of significance to evaluate.

More surprisingly, the draft made little mention of the serious gaps in knowledge about the appropriate evaluation techniques. For example, the paper only hinted at the difficulties of treating model neighborhoods as if they were a scientific laboratory. The creation of controlled environments and experiments in crisis-prone, politically sensitive cities would at the best be hard to do and at the worst impossible.

In a similar vein, the draft did not dwell on the methodological problems involved in developing measurable performance criteria. How could standards be defined that would be free of cultural bias? Would evaluation be able to trace the impact of the model city funds, considering the often overwhelming effect on local neighborhood problems of such factors as the national economy or interest rates?

Almost totally absent from the paper was any awareness of the political risks implicit in first defining standards and then measuring the performance of public institutions. To most of the evaluation staff, the new demonstration program provided an opportunity to test and demonstrate still undetermined approaches to evaluation. They strongly recommended that HUD should take immediate action, and they proposed that many of the studies be conducted by outside consultants.[8]

No funds were specifically set aside for evaluation in the budget for fiscal year 1967-68. Circulation of the MCA staff draft in the early summer thus raised the issue of funding for the first time. William Ross, then the Deputy Under Secretary, believed that evaluation should not be given priority until the cities had already begun implementing their model cities activities. He and others on his staff questioned the soundness of the proposed plan, particularly its emphasis on subjective evaluation indices. A memo written to Ross from a key staff member argued that "HUD should not rely on outside contractors for evaluation studies . . . ; Cities should carry on most of the evaluation; The Deputy Under Secretary's Office, rather than the MCA, should have responsibility for the Model City

[8] MCA staff draft, "Evaluation of the Model Cities Program with Issues for Decision," Spring 1967. (Contents reviewed in internal draft history of MCA prepared by Marshall Kaplan, Gans and Kahn, February 1969, p. 78.)

program evaluation; Evaluation efforts should be much more management-oriented."[9]

Clearly, Ross and his people wanted to have control over HUD's evaluation efforts at the same time that they disputed the relevance of qualitative evaluation and judged the methodological problems inherent in the MCA's holistic, comprehensive approach as difficult to overcome.

Needless to say, the staff of the MCA rejected most of Ross's criticism. They argued that consultant help would be needed because HUD's resources devoted to evaluation were minimal. They agreed that local evaluation was important, but the City Demonstration Agencies could not meet national evaluation requirements. Also, the MCA was closer to the program and could better define and establish a relevant program than the Deputy Under Secretary's Office—and management-oriented evaluation, while important, was only one part of a much larger work program. As Richard Langendorf of the MCA evaluation staff put it, "To miss an opportunity to go beyond the conventional analysis of services provided and the cost of such services overall, and not measure real impact on people, would be a mistake—even if we had to experiment on approaches."

Neither Under Secretary Wood nor Secretary Weaver was apparently willing to give firm support to either the MCA's or to Ross's position. The RAND Corporation was asked to arbitrate and was given a small contract to evaluate the proposed draft design. At a meeting of staff from Deputy Under Secretary Ross's office and the MCA on August 23, 1967, the RAND consultants offered support for the MCA on most of the key issues. Agreement was still not reached, however, within HUD. The MCA staff prepared a second draft evaluation plan in early fall. This differed only in degree from the first paper. This time eight, not five, studies were proposed: (1) a study to develop adequate statistical indicators for measuring program impact; (2) a program information study to suggest the kind of information system to be implemented by the CDAs; (3) a study of neighborhood resident attitudes toward the program; (4) a study involving a panel of community leaders; (5) an observation study conducted by community residents; (6) a study of institutional change; (7) an analysis of the planning process; and (8) a study (undefined) of program impact.[10]

[9] Staff memorandum, "Planning for the Evaluation and Successful Expansion of the Model Cities Program," July 20, 1967.
[10] Staff memorandum, "Plan for Departmental Evaluation of Model Cities Program," November 20, 1967. (Contents of memorandum described in MCA history prepared by Marshall Kaplan, Gans and Kahn, p. 82.)

The Model Cities Administration meant to send the "revised" draft as budget justification to the Budget Bureau. Their hopes were dashed, however, when the paper was held up en route by the Deputy Under Secretary's office. Again, the primary substantive and public issues separating the two staffs concerned the timing, control, and content of the evaluation efforts. A November 5 memorandum to the Deputy Under Secretary from one of his staff illustrated how little either side had moved since late summer. This memo stressed that evaluation was not needed until mid-1970; that the directors of the City Demonstration Agencies should have much of the responsibility for it; that HUD itself should develop a series of objective program indicators; that the evaluation should be oriented toward program management or direct indices of services; and that overall responsibility should rest with the Deputy Under Secretary's Office, with the Model Cities Administration only providing some technical assistance and serving as the information link between the cities and the Deputy Under Secretary. [11] The MCA staff had obviously not made headway with Ross's office.

A "summit" meeting was called on December 12, 1967, to resolve "once and for all" the problem between the two offices. This was attended by Under Secretary Wood, Assistant Secretary Taylor, Deputy Under Secretary William Ross, David Carlson, Deputy Assistant Secretary to Ralph Taylor, and Walter Farr. The outcome represented a victory of sorts for the MCA. The decision was made to allocate $2.5 million for evaluation in fiscal year 1969 and give direct responsibility to the MCA for conducting in-depth studies. The Deputy Under Secretary's Office would monitor all of HUD's evaluation efforts.

Spurred on by the December 12 meeting, the MCA staff planned a conference at which they hoped to define a work program and resolve methodological problems. They invited academicians and professionals who had obvious expertise in evaluation. Most approved the directions established in the MCA's plan. They agreed that it would be necessary to study institutional change, to solicit information direct from community residents, and to use existing data sources. They recommended that evaluation be concerned not only with quantifiable measures of impact but with other program and community processes that would help to give a greater understanding of urban problems. Time constraints did not permit the discussion to become specific about technique or methodology. Even the question of who does evaluation was left unanswered. Many conference participants, particularly those from universities whose regulations prevented competitive bidding, felt that contractors should be chosen on the basis of background

[11] Memorandum from George Wright, "Model Cities Evaluation," to Deputy Under Secretary William Ross, November 5, 1967.

and capability and not competition among written proposals. Yet many of the HUD staff felt that competition was necessary to show that their selection process was free of bias.

Armed with what they felt was a general endorsement of their approach from their peers in the academic world, the model cities staff held its own position on the selection of contractors and developed a series of draft "RFPs" (the federal acronym for study proposals used to solicit competitive or selective bidding). Nonetheless, HUD's Office of Research and Technology still insisted on a cumbersome and detailed review process that delayed their release.[12]

Because of continued internal office bickering, many of the studies proposed by the MCA never became "acceptable" RFPs. For example, the MCA had to substitute proposals asking for study designs in place of proposals actually to initiate national survey and institutional change studies.[13] The early RFPs were limited to a study of the local planning process, the development and testing of a prototype information system for CDAs, and a resident observer study of changes in the life-styles and organization of the model neighborhood as a result of the program. Taken together, these early evaluation efforts reflected the MCA's desire at least to initiate national studies of program impact. Yet at the same time they illustrated the MCA's willingness to use evaluation to build local management capacity and define "qualitative" indices.

Many public and private groups expressed interest in these first RFPs and submitted proposals. These were reviewed by the staff—a review focusing on the qualifications of the bidder and the content of the proposal—after which the bidder was interviewed by a jury, which included representatives of other agencies. Awards were finally made in June 1968 to Marshall Kaplan, Gans and Kahn for the planning process study, to Urban Systems for information systems development, and to A. L. Nellum and Associates/Training Corporation of America for the resident observer study.

The signing of these contracts did not put an end to the MCA's internal problems. It did, however, grant the staff a brief respite from what had been frequent criticism and questions from the Deputy Under Secretary's office. Farr, in a memorandum of August 7, 1968, sent to the CDA directors, summarized the ostensible accomplishments and anticipated the next steps.[14] He placed much of the responsibility for evaluation in the hands of local model cities agencies.

[12] Marshall Kaplan, Gans and Kahn staff interview with Dr. Richard Langendorf, January 1969.
[13] Ibid.
[14] Memorandum from Walter Farr, "Model Cities Program Evaluation," to CDA directors, August 7, 1968.

Yet he acknowledged the MCA's view that national studies of program impact were necessary and noted that a number of such studies were already under way.

Local Evaluation

By the summer of 1968, participating cities were beginning to ask "what HUD wanted from them in terms of evaluation." HUD's first set of planning requirements, issued in CDA Letter No. 1, did not provide much help. It contained nothing that enlarged on HUD's initial open-ended guidelines. Much of the language was quite normative in nature.

> Program evaluation will be particularly important. The nature of a demonstration program such as the Model Cities Program requires a probing for new solutions. . . .
> Because of the importance of accurate and consistent data for planning and evaluation, the city should describe any existing data system which can be used or modified to insure valid and comparable statistics for the model neighborhood and should describe any existing machinery in the city to improve the quality of and to standardize statistical data. If existing machinery or procedures are inadequate, the city should indicate how it plans to establish or improve its system of statistical standards. . . .
> . . . rigorous cost benefit analysis is not expected where appropriate data cannot be obtained or where the nature of the problem defies measurement. However, procedures should be developed for evaluating program decisions in a systematic manner even where costs and benefits cannot be translated into dollars or other quantitative measures. . . .[15]

Preparation of a first-draft Technical Assistance Bulletin had actually begun before the first evaluation contracts were signed in June. This TAB described HUD's assumptions about the local data needs. It suggested alternate ways that the CDAs could collect data, and it set out varied evaluation approaches. The document also stressed the needs to solicit neighborhood opinion and to involve residents in local work programs.

General acceptance of the initial draft by the MCA staff permitted development of a "final" product during the summer. This document provided the City Demonstration Agencies with HUD's general expectations about the form of their local evaluation plans. It generally did not prescribe either technique or content. Rather, because many of the MCA staff felt the cities had a marginal commitment to evaluation, the document was intended primarily to encourage local efforts.

[15] HUD, CDA Letter No. 1, pp. 15, 16.

Some basic evaluation focuses might be on five and one-year objectives, on the strategy of projects and program approaches, and on the administration and management of the CDA. With limited funds, each city will have to decide those evaluative approaches it feels are most important, and how to distribute money and other resources among the different approaches which must be covered.

In their evaluation statement, CDAs are required to indicate:

—What evaluation activities are planned for the first action year

—How these activities relate to the Five Year Forecast and the One Year Program

—What part of the administrative budget reflects the cost of evaluation

—How the CDA is organized to carry out evaluation and ensure that the results of evaluation will affect the planning and programming of the CDA.[16]

Although the MCA staff had agreed on the wisdom of the proposed TAB, this agreement did not extend to the Deputy Under Secretary's office and the Office of Research and Technology. For somewhat obscure reasons, both offices held up department approval of the document. Apparently, their objections stemmed from the legacy of early arguments over alternate evaluation approaches. These arguments focused on whether it was worth initiating large-scale evaluation prior to implementation; whether evaluation should place equal stress on indices of management, process, and impact; and whether it should include subjective or judgmental measures. Of course, on a deeper level, the conflict was also concerned with which part of HUD should have control over evaluation and whether evaluation processes and objectives should be precise, as desired by non-evaluation staff, or more open-ended, as favored by MCA evaluation personnel. Apparently, to most in the Under Secretary's office, evaluation without specific bounds could raise internal and external political problems for HUD. No mayor likes a negative appraisal of his role, and no HUD official likes conclusions suggesting inept administration.

Assistant Secretary Taylor and MCA Director Walter Farr continued publicly to support evaluation inside and outside HUD, but they did so more out of loyalty to their own office staff than out of any conviction of the merits of the design proposed. Increasing numbers of the MCA staff began to express doubts about the wisdom, relevance, and technical appropriateness of national studies; a few questioned the merging emphasis on prescriptive criteria for local evaluation plans. Other offices inside HUD were not so charitable. They seemed to view the continuous stream of drafts and memoranda issuing from the Model Cities Ad-

[16] Staff draft TAB (undated), pp. 7, 33.

ministration more as reports from a competing organization than from an office within the same department. Often intelligent criticism of substance was lost in bureaucratic nit-picking and personal feuds. MCA staff had not been able to convince their peers that HUD ought to get involved in developing the art of evaluation. Apart from MCA staff, no one inside HUD appeared eager to tackle the job of measuring the program's impact on the numerous objectives set for it by Congress. Methodological uncertainties, normal bureaucratic in-fighting over the placement of new functions, the fear that evaluation would possibly uncover administrative shortcomings and limit future funding seemed to weaken the willingness of HUD to go out in front.

Despite the expenditure of much time and effort, the MCA was not able to establish a coherent national program of evaluation or even a locally relevant one. The few contracts for national studies and study designs that were signed in June remained the only ones extant at the end of 1968; no local Technical Assistance Bulletin was issued by HUD, and the local CDAs were increasingly confused about what was expected of them.

A New Administration

The advent of the new Administration did not change the environment for evaluation. The MCA's evaluation staff continued doggedly and somewhat obstinately to advocate their basic approach. Although the faces changed, the offices of the Under Secretary and Deputy Under Secretary continued to question the relevance and impact of that approach. The new Assistant Secretary, Floyd Hyde, obviously not wedded to the previous Administration, was not inclined to accept without question the perceptions of his inherited staff.

In January 1969, the evaluation staff prepared a forty-page defense of their design. The document, "A Plan for Evaluating the Model Cities Program," updated from a draft prepared in September, was used to brief the new Assistant Secretary and other newcomers to the MCA. It was also utilized to support budget requests for fiscal 1969—which included the studies already outlined earlier, and among them the controversial survey and institutional change analyses.

... MCA has responsibility for comparative analyses, and for purposes of such analyses, it is important that trends within Model Neighborhoods be compared with trends elsewhere. ...

Studies of institutional change, occurring within the same cities as the surveys and resident observer studies can provide the bases for relating resident perceptions of institutional change, actual institutional change, and changes in the lives of residents that result from institutional change.[17]

Although Assistant Secretary Hyde sat on the proposals for surveys and analyses of institutional change, he gave tacit approval to the general thrust of the staff's efforts. As he explained later, however, "his approval was not based on a careful reading of the benefits and costs of MCA's approach . . . only the planning process study was under way and producing real policy relevant results . . . all the others were still proposals and not at a stage where a judgment could be made . . . it was not possible to make a hard decision at this early time."[18] The Assistant Secretary was committed to neither the overall design nor its details.

Not even tacit approval, however, was granted by the "10th Floor" (the Secretary's office). The proposed study of institutional change, which Hyde finally agreed to send forward for approval, was the subject of a particularly heated memorandum from William Ross, still functioning as the Deputy Under Secretary and still opposed to the basic thrust of MCA's approach to evaluation. His memorandum apparently reflected the views of an increasing number of HUD officials who were concerned over the "loosely structured purposes and methodology associated with the proposed study."[19] Hyde could not convince the Deputy Under Secretary or the Under Secretary to release funds either for the institutional change study or for the survey of neighborhood attitudes.

I had difficulty because both studies seemed to have limited early pay-off . . . both were difficult to explain because they might uncover problems in agency methods of *operation* . . . both relied on techniques and measurements which were unproven . . . both would have been politically threatening. . . .[20]

HUD's failure to get these basic studies under way demoralized the evaluation staff. Several wondered how hard the Assistant Secretary really fought for the program. Just as important, many wondered out loud whether a line agency such as HUD really could mount a sustained long-term in-depth evaluation effort. Curiously, considering the obvious reluctance of the Deputy Under Secretary to endorse its approach and the hesitant attitude, at best, of the Assistant Secretary, the evaluation staff continued to submit, almost without change, the same evaluation design.

Two types of evaluation efforts have been formulated in order to accomplish the general purposes and meet the needs of the various users of evaluation:

[17] Staff draft, "A Plan for Evaluating the Model Cities Program," January 1969, p. 31.

[18] Interview with Assistant Secretary Floyd Hyde, July 1972.

[19] Interview with Assistant Secretary Floyd Hyde, July 1972; interview with Deputy Under Secretary Charles Orlebeke, September 1970.

[20] Interview with Assistant Secretary Floyd Hyde, July 1972 (italics added).

—A set of large scale national studies will be undertaken in a sample of cities in order to determine the overall *impact*. . . .
—Special studies of relatively short duration will focus on specific MCA policy and decision-making issues. . . .
—A related set of tasks performed by MCA evaluation division is the development of information systems to support program planning, management, and evaluation.

National studies . . . include . . . a study of institutional behavior . . . survey studies.[21]

The staff's obstinacy, while perhaps intellectually meritorious, was politically devastating for them. Certainly the articulated shift in program objectives from improvements in the quality of life to the building up of local capacity, which has been described in early chapters—a shift made necessary by the Administration's ambivalence toward the Model Cities Program and one that reflected perhaps a realistic appraisal of the program's possible achievements—marked the end of Hyde's willingness to support, even nominally, the proposed extensive national impact studies. Continued promotion of such studies led the Assistant Secretary to question the entire thrust of all evaluation schemes. No longer was overt criticism limited to the Deputy Under Secretary and the Under Secretary. Increasingly, the phrases "policy relevance" and "operational relevance" were used by the Assistant Secretary to describe what he wanted from evaluation and, by implication, what he felt he was not getting.

Hyde wanted insights into how his program was running. While long-term critical analyses that would generate an understanding of impact and institutional behavior patterns were accepted as important, Hyde could not wait for the conclusions of lengthy studies. He also did not care much whether evaluative techniques were "pure," "academically" acceptable, or complete. Analyses, to be useful to him, needed to be converted, almost while in process, into amended strategies. The clock was running; Hyde needed quick feedback even if only to protect himself from outside critics.

Significantly, those RFPs that dealt with specific areas of immediate policy concern, such as the analysis of the role of state government in the Model Cities Program, were approved by Hyde and the Deputy Under Secretary during 1969 and early 1970. More significantly, perhaps, all other RFPs were held up, even though funds were available in the budgets for both 1970 and 1971.

In the fall of 1970, Warren Butler, then Special Assistant and later Deputy

[21] Staff Draft Plan on Evaluation, August 19, 1969, pp. 2 and 3 (italics added).

Assistant Secretary, and Marshall Kaplan, then a consultant to HUD, were asked by Floyd Hyde to develop a more systematic approach to evaluation. They were commissioned to work on building up staff capacity at HUD to undertake "quick and dirty" analyses of problem areas and to redirect contract efforts toward key policy and operational issues; among those were to be analyses of special city responses to the MCA guidelines, of interagency efforts to administer program applications in a flexible manner, of the local use of supplemental funds, and of local efforts to stimulate citizen participation.[22] Butler and Kaplan, working with the evaluation staff and under pressure from the Under Secretary to reduce the budget, placed narrow boundaries on the requirements of the institutional change and survey studies and significantly reduced their project costs. In addition, they provided more budgetary flexibility for "special studies," the euphemism for specific policy studies. Most important, perhaps, staff in each office of the MCA were asked to serve on short-term evaluation teams. Such teams would be asked to go into the field on specific assignments; the products of these could then, if necessary, be used to meet rising Congressional and outside demands for "data" about the effects of the program.

Once these changes had been made, Hyde wrote to an official in the Office of Management and Budget about the 1972 budget. Obviously pleased at the "turnaround," he made the assertion that "Our evaluation program has been restructured to (a) clearly provide policy relevant and strategic information . . . ; (b) secure appropriate, but selective national data relative to the program's impact; (c) provide relevant comparison of local government's progress in planning and implementation activities."[23]

Hyde's optimism may or may not have been warranted. To the evaluation staff at the MCA, however, the events of the fall signified the demise of any opportunity to establish a coherent set of national studies on the program's impact on the quality of life, on visible social pathologies, or on agency behavior. From then on, the MCA's efforts—both its own and those handled through contracts— would be clearly directed toward specific short-term policy and operational issues. Only the study of planning processes would survive as a symbol to the staff or what could have been.

[22] Interview with Assistant Secretary Floyd Hyde, July 1972; Marshall Kaplan's notes taken during "on site" tenure as adviser to Hyde, September 1970, an assignment referred to in Hyde's memorandum to Under Secretary Van Dusen of September 11, 1970, "Review of Model Cities Contract Activities."

[23] Memorandum from Assistant Secretary Floyd Hyde, "Fiscal Year, 1972, Contract Activity," to Thomas Ubois, OMB, October 20, 1970, p. 3.

Local Evaluation

Efforts to induce the City Demonstration Agencies to develop local evaluation programs fared only marginally better than the efforts to establish a comprehensive national study program. Most City Demonstration Agencies felt that HUD's requirements generated perfunctory and peripheral activities, which were necessary to win HUD approval but had little relevance to local needs. A memorandum of May 19, 1969, from Farr to the directors of the first-round model cities agencies implicitly recognized this and admonished the cities to do better.

... most cities did not consider continued planning and evaluation until late in the initial planning period with the result that many of them submitted hastily prepared inadequate programs.... [To assure a better effort] CDA's that have already submitted or will submit their plans before July 31, 1969 and have not met the Continuing Planning and Evaluation requirements ... must submit amended work programs and budgets to MCA no later than 60 days after contract execution. CDA's submitting their plans after July 31, 1969 will need to meet these planning and evaluation requirements within their CDP [Community Development Program] submissions as a condition of comprehensive plan approval.[24]

But no real change occurred either in the quality of local submittals or in the local commitment to evaluation. During the winter months, the MCA staff prepared a working paper to illustrate the desired evaluation approaches. This paper described various techniques for collecting data and provided examples of questions that local agencies should ask to evaluate this program's impact.

Many local CDA directors accepted the paper as a set of prescriptions, which, if followed, would permit a favorable response from HUD. As a result, HUD began to receive evaluation plans that mirrored the form of the working paper but not necessarily its obvious substantive intent; that is, the plans did not necessarily reflect a real commitment to evaluate the results of local efforts and use evaluation in structuring future actions in the model cities areas. The MCA staff felt that most evaluation plans were quite weak. In March 1970, they drafted a circular and transmitted it to all the CDAs. The circular was tough in tone and promised retribution if the cities did not improve. For all first-round cities:

(1) Failure to submit an approvable evaluation plan by June 30, 1970 will result in suspension or termination of funds.
(2) No second year CDP will be approved until there is an evaluation staff in place.

[24] Memorandum from Walter Farr to First-Round CDA Directors May 19, 1969, pp. 1 and 2.

(3) No new second year action projects may be implemented until there is an approved evaluation plan (see MC Circular 3180.0) which contains specific reference to evaluation of second year projects.

For all second-round cities:

(1) No CDP will be approved unless it contains an adequate evaluation budget and administrative structure which provide for an acceptable level of evaluation staffing and appropriate relationships between this staff and other Model City activities.
(2) No action projects may be implemented until an evaluation plan submitted by the city has been approved by HUD.[25]

There was no readily apparent response. HUD continued to receive "paper plans" from participating cities. In many instances, these plans came close to matching in form and language what the cities thought HUD wanted; but, for the most part, they did not reflect any careful thought about what were relevant evaluation processes. For the most part, also, they did not suggest any ability to carry out submitted proposals or any willingness to use the results of such proposals. HUD's skepticism was warranted. Lack of funding for city staff, the pressure of numerous other tasks to be accomplished in regard to the Model City Program, and the fact that evaluation was threatening to many local public officials led, at best, to only a modest local commitment to evaluation and to a similarly modest achievement.

Evaluation—in Retrospect

Except for critical studies of the planning and management processes, HUD was not able to mount a nationally relevant, coordinated, and sustained evaluation effort. Neither was it able to induce a relevant local response to evaluation. Why did the MCA's efforts produce so few results?

With the shift in the program's objectives from neighborhood rebuilding to local capacity came an obvious weakening in the rationale for a comprehensive national evaluation effort based on the output of the program or its effect on people, the physical area, and local institutions. It is clear that the staff did not realize this until quite late. And therefore they were unable to recast the evaluation program to meet the direct operational needs of the Assistant Secretary or the needs and capabilities of the participating cities.

Judgments on the effectiveness of the evaluation staff should be tempered,

[25] Circular MC 3180.2, "CDA Evaluation Requirements," March 1970, pp. 1 and 2.

however. Clearly, their objectives were unique, and their game plan was, if anything, more consistent with the statutory intent of the program than were the
objectives implied by their constant critics. Even if the program had generated a
significant and "measurable" impact on the quality of life, a reading of the
model cities experience suggests that the contraints on establishing meaningful
federal and local evaluation efforts would have been severe. There were several
reasons:

1. *The absence of any consensus on program legitimacy.* Very few people even
within HUD could agree on precise goals and objectives, let alone priorities. The
absence of such a consensus resulted in a synoptic approach to evaluation; in
effect, coverage took the place of focus. More relevant, a lack of specificity and
preciseness permitted bureaucratic in-fighting within HUD to get out of hand.
Organizational questions about the appropriate role of an administering office
such as the MCA in evaluating its own program were never clearly debated.
Often "turfing" between offices substituted for dialogue about alternative approaches to evaluation and organization imperialism for the resolution of technical issues.

2. *The lack of any definitive consensus on the appropriate methodology.* Structuring a worthy evaluation program, given the broad, open-ended, and
imprecise purposes of the legislation, would be difficult under ideal conditions.
No ready technique existed for sorting out and recording measurable performance indices. Similarly, there was no easy means available to isolate what causes
and effects could be attributed to model cities activities and what ones to unrelated events in the same neighborhood. The model city neighborhood did not
provide a ready, well-defined laboratory. And there were no well-defined control
populations within which to test alternative approaches.

In this context, the MCA evaluation staff struck out in favor of a wide-ranging,
and in retrospect all too encompassing and complex, evaluation program. They
sought to demonstrate technique as well as produce a product. Only the descriptive nonimpact studies survived reasonably unscathed; this was in part because of
the legitimacy of the methodology and the policy relevance and immediacy of
the results. Similarly, others in HUD, particularly those in the Under Secretary's
office, tried to narrow the boundaries of the evaluation effort to include practices that were known and accepted and that could prove valuable in providing
readily usable benefits and costs.

3. *The need to produce immediate visible results.* Administrators, such as
Floyd Hyde and Ralph Taylor before him, and Congressmen need immediate,

often hard, quantifiable results—results not readily provided, at least initially, by a highly structured and extended evaluation program. No matter how important the theoretical need to obtain a tough and legitimate analysis of the ultimate impact of model cities, officials and politicians alike who were associated with the program could not afford the uncertainty inherent in the testing of methodology or the speculation inherent in the long-term effort that had no short-term alternatives. Both seem to require, at least in the short run, "success stories" and anecdotal evidence to build up program support. Similarly, in order to be sheltered or protected from gross error, both require early feedback on the impact of program support. In this context, "dirty" and less systemic research is appropriate.

4. *The fear of evaluation.* Lurking behind the arguments over evaluation within both the halls of HUD and the city halls of the participating cities was the "threat of exposure" implicit in an evaluation design that had no precise limits. Proposed studies of institutional change did not easily win a constituency: the phrase "institutional change" connoted a criticism of existing institutions, and the described evaluation on standards implied the need for organizational reform. Similarly, it understandably bothered many federal and local providers of services to be asked to go beyond measuring direct services and assess the satisfaction of those being served by local and federal institutions. It would be noted not only what was being delivered in terms of services but how it was delivered. No agency readily creates a potential problem for itself.

5. *The absence of a realistic and consistent local perspective.* HUD's efforts to induce local evaluation were subject to at least two contrary objectives: first, to achieve data that would be relevant for the national measurement of impact; second, to build up capacity at the local level to make effective decisions and change established patterns of behavior. The former demands a structured attempt at creating and initiating a sustained evaluation effort; the latter, an effort at producing immediate policy-oriented results. The output of one (quantitative data) may not always agree with the output of the other (qualitative judgments).

Beyond these competing objectives, HUD was not able to surmount the absence of adequate funding and adequate rewards. Why should local Model Cities Programs with only limited staff spend time on evaluation? What benefits would they gain from such evaluation? Would not local institutions react negatively to public criticism? What Model Cities Program, conversely, was cut off by HUD, despite threats, because it had a poor evaluation plan?

Unfortunately, HUD's guidelines were generic. They called for a similar response from all cities, irrespective of their needs and capacity. In effect, coverage and form substituted for substance and direct relevance.

Where Do We Go from Here?

As indicated, the activities of the beleagured, often seemingly heroic, model cities evaluation staff bore little fruit. In essence, the reasons why they failed to mount their program are of more value to us than the tangible results of their efforts. Certainly, we should be aware of these reasons as we proceed to look at the next generation of urban programs. In this context, there is need for a thorough examination of the still-marginal nature of evaluation technology. Except where program objectives are well defined or limited and where program impact is directly and specifically related to the services supplied, analyses of program output or effect on individuals and areas are at best methodologically risky and at worst a technically spurious and expensive endeavor. Except where there is a reasonably shared consensus about the precise, anticipated results of an administered program or a strong departmental commitment to undertake such a program, bureaucratic behavior will resist comprehensive evaluation efforts and experimentation. It will also impede substantive debate over the appropriate organizational assignment for such experimentation.

Further, where, as in model cities, evaluation is linked in part to programs that are directed at reforming federal or local institutions or at redistributing funds from one group to another, it will be necessary to have more than nominal incentives to induce agencies to participate. One agency is in no position to commandeer a "coordinated" evaluation effort or mandate the participation of other agencies in evaluation. Operational priorities are apt to be viewed as more important than evaluation. As a result, adaptation and negotiation rather than fiat are likely to govern interagency and federal-local relations in regard to coordinated evaluation efforts for future urban aid programs. Clearly, the superman syndrome, given competing interests and limited budgets, will be too costly.

Part III
Model Cities and the Future of Federal Urban Policy

Chapter 9
The National Commitment

The series of frustrations described in the preceding chapters demonstrated that what the Model Cities Program set out to do was indeed very difficult to achieve. There were two themes winding through the entire effort: Model cities was an attempt to respond to the crisis of the cities and at the same time to improve the management of the federal grant-in-aid system. These twin purposes led to an emphasis on concentrating federal resources in selected poverty neighborhoods across the country and to a further emphasis on making the full range of federal categorical aids readily available to the participating city governments. Both purposes ran counter to deeply ingrained ways of managing programs in Washington. As a result, the attempt to establish local model cities agencies as a single point of entry for federal aid, to earmark categorical funds, to simplify federal reviews, to provide effective technical assistance, to make the categorical programs more flexible, and to undertake systematic evaluations of the results all fell far short of early expectations.

To say, however, that the effort failed because of the difficulties of reversing administrative practices of the federal bureaucracies may not be a sufficient explanation. Both the legislative history of the Model Cities Program and some of its subsequent experience suggest that a more fundamental question also needs to be addressed: Was there ever a national commitment to the purposes of this program? By the late 1960s, when many of the Great Society programs were losing favor, numerous critics, including Presidential commissions, found reason to question the seriousness of the nation's commitment to solve the problems of the cities, the poor, and minority groups. The issue of commitment is appropriate to raise in connection with model cities, as well. If the necessary commitment was lacking, then no federal program aiming at the same goals could have had very promising prospects, regardless of how it was organized.

One qualification is in order. Commitment can mean many things. Programs such as model cities can succeed with something less than overriding national interest and public acclaim. Other programs, such as the building of the federal aid highway system, were quite successful without the need for White House rhetoric, frequent declarations of support by prominent figures, favorable showings in the opinion polls, and grass-roots letters to Congress. What these programs required was an organized constituency satisfied with the benefits it was receiving, a bureaucracy functioning with reasonable smoothness, enough support in Congress to ensure sources of funding, and a delegation of administrative authority sufficient to get the job done. If model cities achieved these things, the national will to improve living conditions in urban poverty areas would have been as clear as the national will to build highways, support farm prices, or send aid to elementary and secondary schools.

A minimum commitment to make the Model Cities Program work required steady support over time from something like the following series of actors: federal agency heads and key officials in several departments as well as HUD, a significant number of Congressmen, the mayors and city councils of the communities included in the program, residents of the model neighborhoods, and officials of city and state agencies that had a major impact on the neighborhoods. Others were needed who could influence the government—the urban interest groups who keep in touch with Congress, the elusive public at large.

Because of the special nature of the Model Cities Program, leadership from the White House was particularly important. At the outset, the program was too new to have an organized constituency that could protect it and press for adequate support. Its main beneficiaries—residents of poverty neighborhoods in the cities—were not usually an effective force in either local or national politics. In focusing on these neighborhoods, the program would inevitably be seen to help primarily the blacks and other urban minorities. While these groups could make a strong claim on the nation's conscience, past history led many to assert that the society was racist at heart and would not respond adequately. The Kerner Commission, two years after the Model Cities Program began, unequivocally held white racism to blame for the conditions of life in the black ghetto: "White institutions created it, white institutions maintain it, and white society condones it."[1] Legislative progress in civil rights had been possible in the 1960s only with strong Presidential leadership. More of the same was needed to channel substantial federal aid into black and Spanish-speaking communities.

Further, the basic conception of the program as a device for bringing the resources of many federal agencies to bear on the problems of slum neighborhoods meant that the politics of the typical single-agency programs would not suffice. A way had to be found to bring several cabinet departments and independent agencies into line, and where necessary to override prior commitments to other constituencies. Apart from the White House and its administrative arms such as the Bureau of the Budget, there was no federal mechanism able to perform such a task. Thus the administrative demands of the Model Cities Program, as well as the lack of a potent constituency to support it, made the response of the White House a key indicator of the federal will to make it succeed. In assessing the

[1] U.S. National Advisory Commission on Civil Disorders, *Report* (Washington, D.C.: U.S. Government Printing Office, 1968), p. 1.

national commitment, this chapter will thus concentrate initially on the actions of the White House, viewing other participants from the perspective of their interaction with the President and his staff.

The initial conception of the program called for a concentration of resources in the poverty areas of selected cities to make possible wide-ranging improvements in the living conditions of low-income residents. Therefore the national will to achieve the purposes of the Model Cities Program must be measured in dollars as well as in administrative reforms, in terms of the adequacy of the budget that was made available. The issue of commitment requires an appraisal of the federal will to appropriate the necessary funds and then to concentrate them in limited target areas. The poverty neighborhoods of cities, however, have traditionally suffered from municipal as well as federal neglect. Thus a secondary issue is the will of city governments to reverse the pattern of the past and to use new federal resources to mount ambitious programs focusing on the needs of low-income residents. Although the actual conduct of Model Cities Programs in the field is beyond the scope of this study, the question of city government commitment is of such clear relevance that we shall make use of limited evidence available to evaluate the extent to which participating cities shared a commitment to the goals of the program.

No single branch of government could be decisive in itself, but taken together, the network of actors involved in implementing the Model Cities Program ultimately determined what it could achieve.

The White House gave considerable support to the Model Cities Program. During the Johnson Administration, it was responsible for the origin and legislative passage of the program, for getting the first appropriations from a reluctant Congress, and for pressing federal agencies to cooperate with the Department of Housing and Urban Development. During the Nixon Administration, the White House kept up this pressure on the federal agencies. Further, President Nixon created new administrative machinery for interagency decision making and used it to resolve policy questions concerning the Model Cities Program. Despite the President's personal reservations, the White House kept the basic commitments that had been made earlier and took the necessary action to maintain this program.

During the entire period covered by this study, however, the President and his staff had only limited power over federal domestic agencies. Although the Model Cities Program had more direct White House support than most programs, neither the Johnson nor the Nixon Administration treated it as a matter of utmost urgency. The attempts of two Administrations to bring federal agencies into line behind the program confirmed a principle that Anthony Downs terms the Law of Counter-Control: The greater the effort made by a top-level official to control the behavior of subordinate officials, the greater the efforts made by those subordinates to evade or counteract such control.[2] White House pressure plus interagency negotiations led to a series of compromises on issues affecting model cities, but the program needed more than these compromises in order to succeed.

In Congress, a majority never was committed to the Model Cities Program as the White House had originally conceived of it. Congress redefined the program to make it another grant-in-aid to the cities, not the unifier of all other federal aid programs. Having redefined it in this way, Congress was willing to support it over the years and kept its promises on appropriations.

Those cities that made use of the program responded positively to its main purposes, although they resisted some of the federal requirements on specific procedures. Nevertheless, they tried to make it work according to the original intentions, and they rallied to protect the national program on several occasions when future appropriations were in jeopardy.

The Presidential politics that started model cities gave the program impetus for a few years. During this time, interest groups began to appear around it. Their political activities kept it alive, but in the face of mounting coolness in Washington they were not able to create the climate of acceptance and continuity needed to make it work well.

This combination of commitments limited the possibilities for successful implementation in several important ways:

1. The nation was unwilling to concentrate substantial funding in a few cities, but the participating cities were willing to concentrate funds in designated poverty neighborhoods. This mix of national spread plus local concentration permitted a moderate increase in aid for poverty neighborhoods—in comparison with what the cities were then spending out of local budgets, in comparison with earlier antipoverty programs, and in comparison with revenue-sharing proposals. The level of support that emerged was sufficient to make possible improvements in public services to the model neighborhoods, but it was not sufficient to fund programs that would add substantially to the incomes of the residents. To achieve a much higher level of support would have required far more massive federal aid to the cities overall, as well as the local concentration of funds that was in fact achieved.

[2] Anthony Downs, *Inside Bureaucracy* (Boston: Little, Brown, 1967), p. 147.

2. The ideal of comprehensive local programs, drawing on flexible federal aid to cope with the wide variety of problems affecting the urban poor, was unattainable through this program. Such comprehensiveness and flexibility required interagency cooperation, which was never achieved through the grant-in-aid reform that model cities attempted to bring about. As a result, the cities had great difficulties coping with the maze of federal agencies whose cooperation was needed for comprehensive local programs. These difficulties arose in part from limited city capacities, which neither the strategy of establishing a single point of entry for federal funds nor federal planning reviews nor federally funded technical assistance did much to strengthen. In the end, the cities were not able to spend even the limited model cities funds made available to them.

3. Through the Model Cities Program, the nation demonstrated a greater willingness to redistribute resources to the poor than was evident in most other federal programs for the cities. This redistribution, however, was blunted by political pressures to spread the funds to many localities and by both bureaucratic and political resistance to interagency support. The model cities experience thus suggests there is a degree of tacit recognition that the urban poor have a special claim to federal resources and therefore that political support may be found for other channels of redistribution in the future.

White House Support

The First Steps
Commitment from the White House was decisive in formulating the Model Cities Program and enacting it into law. Lyndon Johnson appointed the task force that recommended the program; he assigned Harry McPherson, his Special Counsel, to keep in touch with the task force during its deliberations; and he accepted the task force report as the basis for his legislative proposal. McPherson was then asked to draft a Presidential message on the cities, which was circulated among the White House staff and to the Budget Bureau and the Council of Economic Advisers. McPherson discussed the draft at length with the President.

He made many changes in language, crossing out and writing in the margins, and many more in substance—"I don't want to say that on page 8; I want to tell 'em to give me a supplemental appropriation right now." He had designed the task force, and had given it its charter. He was aware of what it was doing throughout. His staff was deeply involved, as were his counselors on the budget. There were no last-minute surprises. Altogether, the process was a model for the writing of Presidential messages. It was also atypical.[3]

[3] Harry McPherson, *A Political Education* (Boston: Atlantic-Little, Brown, 1972), p. 298.

White House commitment to the program was evident in the initial battle for enactment and again in the struggle over appropriations. President Johnson and his political aides worked long and hard for Congressional passage. When the prospects seemed dim after several months of effort, Postmaster General Lawrence O'Brien rallied the Department of Housing and Urban Development and White House officials by his refusal to give up an important part of the President's legislative program without a more determined fight. White House staff members played a decisive role in working out the substantive compromises that won the support of Senator Muskie and other key Congressional leaders, and White House phone calls and contacts were an integral part of the strategy that led eventually to enactment.[4]

When a personal statement was called for, President Johnson supplied it. Just before the critical House vote, a reporter asked a hostile question about the pending bill at the October 6 press conference. Johnson replied,

I am glad of the opportunity that you have given me to state that I believe there is no domestic problem that is more critical than the problem of rebuilding our cities and giving our people who live in the cities opportunities to develop as healthy, educated, productive citizens of our society—citizens who have the ability to get and to hold jobs, and to take pride in the place in which they live. . . . As I said in the beginning, and as I would repeat again, I think it is one of the most important pieces of legislation for the good of all American mankind that we can act upon this session.

White House action on behalf of the program was evident once again in the late summer of 1967 when the appropriations were at stake. During the contest over initial passage of the bill, the Administration fought off Congressional attempts to limit the funding authorizations to first-year planning grants. In 1967, the Administration asked for the full amount authorized for supplemental grants, administrative expenses, special urban renewal funds earmarked for use in model cities areas and for planning funds for a second round of cities. Congress was reluctant once again. By this time, in mid-July 1967, HUD's screening and review of city applications had been completed, and Assistant Secretary Taylor had forwarded to Under Secretary Wood and Secretary Weaver a list of cities that were considered acceptable.

The White House intervened at this point to delay final selection of the first

[4] See Edward C. Banfield, "Making a New Federal Program: Model Cities, 1964-68," in Allan P. Sindler, ed., *Policy and Politics in America* (Boston: Little, Brown, 1973), pp. 137-140; and Robert B. Semple, Jr., "Signing of Model Cities Bill Ends a Long Struggle to Keep It Alive," *New York Times*, November 4, 1966, p. 1.

round of cities until the decision on appropriations had been made. The delay was strategic, giving the Administration leverage to use on wavering Congressmen. That members of Congress were subject to such influence was clear enough. Some invited it openly. One prominent Democratic Senator wrote to Weaver to ask about the prospects for two cities in his home state if the Senate-House conference committee was to act favorably on funding for the Model Cities Program. Apparently those prospects were very good indeed, because both communities were added to the program a few months after the first selections were announced. Smithville, Tennessee, the home of Chairman Joe L. Evins of the House Appropriations Subcommittee responsible for HUD funding, represented another obvious political choice. (Later, when Under Secretary Wood was questioned why Smithville had been selected for the program, he replied, "Smithville is a small city, but there are those who love it.") These political choices did not seriously compromise the quality of the program. Most, in fact, had reasonable applications to start with. But they did represent direct White House intervention to protect the new program by helping key Congressmen take care of the voters back home.

Despite strong opposition, especially in the House, Congress appropriated $300 million in supplemental funds and special urban renewal funds out of a requested total of $650 million. They also appropriated another $12 million in planning funds for a second round of cities. Congressional commitment was obviously weak at this time, and White House pressure was essential to pry the funds loose. Secretary Weaver was then free to proceed, and he announced the awards to the first-round cities two weeks later on November 16, 1967.

Pressing hard for Congressional action was entirely consistent with Lyndon Johnson's style as a builder of new programs who attached prime importance to his legislative record and knew how to get what he wanted out of Congress. The design of the Model Cities Program, however, meant that the White House would have to give it continuing, if intermittent, attention in order to bring the various federal agencies into line behind it. This requirement was a less familiar demand on the Johnson White House, which was not normally attuned to the management of operating programs. Harry McPherson had other messages to draft, the President had a war in Vietnam that demanded his attention, and the support for Great Society social programs was evaporating rapidly. As McPherson saw it from his perspective as a speech writer, promises of social reform drew a rapidly diminishing response.

Democratic politicians traditionally broke the bonds, struck the shackles, lifted up, gave new hope, made possible. . . . We had not come this far to quit in sight of our goal. Answer the following rhetorical question: Shall we quit trying to feed the poor, train the uneducated, heal the sick, just because it is hard and costly? (One hoped for a chorus of "No's," but usually there was only silence. By 1967, one was satisfied if no one yelled, "Yes!")[5]

In late 1967 and early 1968, HUD pressed forward with its efforts to get other federal departments involved in the Model Cities Program. The national climate reinforced the urgency of these efforts, with riots widespread in the summer of 1967 and again after Martin Luther King's assassination in the spring of 1968. The problems of urban black communities obviously demanded attention. But increasingly the country's attention was focused on the Vietnam War, where the peak buildup of American forces, the Tet offensive, and the military request for more troops created the overriding crisis of 1968. In February and March of 1968, the White House was tied up in a reconsideration of Vietnam policy. At the end of March, President Johnson announced a halt in the bombing of North Vietnam and his decision not to run again.

This was not an auspicious time for HUD to count on White House support. Presidents have, at most, an important but limited influence on the federal bureaucracies. Their directives compete with those of the Congress, with the wishes of constituencies that support particular programs, and with the bureaucracies' own traditional styles of operation. President Johnson's imminent departure from the White House was bound to dilute his influence still further. But HUD's own efforts were bringing only token cooperation, and there was no better alternative available than to ask for White House help.

Joseph Califano and Budget Director Charles Zwick quickly promised their support. Califano's help was more than perfunctory, as Chapters 4 and 5 have already noted. When agency responses were not persuasive and their commitments remained elusive, he worked closely with Assistant Secretary Taylor and MCA Director Farr to prepare a series of memoranda for Secretaries Cohen and Wirtz of HEW and Labor, and Director Bertrand Harding of OEO. Exchanges between Califano and the agency heads continued for several months. Further, President Johnson, together with Califano, took a direct hand in negotiations with OEO.

The results in all cases left much to be desired, but the efforts made by the White House showed a clear, continuing commitment to the program. Conceivably, a greater effort could have brought the other agencies more fully into line.

[5] McPherson, *A Political Education*, p. 331.

President Johnson himself might have dealt more firmly with recalcitrant agencies, or Califano could have given more time. But the failure to obtain full cooperation of the federal agencies seems to have resulted more from the limits of Presidential power and the built-in rigidities of federal aid programs than from a wavering will at the White House.

In the waning days of the Johnson Administration, the White House also took a few steps to improve the prospects for the program's survival through the transition to a new Administration. First, the Presidential team did what it could to strengthen the financial base for the future. Its Housing and Urban Development Act of 1968, enacted on August 1, added a new authorization of $1 billion for supplemental grants in fiscal 1970, twice the level authorized for 1969. Then it managed to extract more generous appropriations for the 1969 fiscal year than it had obtained for 1968: $312.5 million for supplemental grants, plus another $312.5 million in urban renewal funds for use in the Model Cities Program (compared with $200 million and $100 million, respectively, for fiscal 1968). These higher authorizations and appropriations also represented a sign of increasing Congressional commitment, at a time of tight budgets for most urban programs.

As a last-ditch measure, the White House worked out a strategy, together with HUD officials, for committing certain fiscal 1969 funds to the cities before the Nixon Administration took office, in the belief that the new Administration would then find it more difficult to drop the program, if they were so inclined.[6] The HUD regional office staff were told in October to hurry along those cities that were close to submitting their first-year action plans for funding. Cities judged to be close to finishing were offered funding at 175 percent of the levels they had earlier been advised to anticipate—if they submitted their plans by December. (The offer was based on the increased appropriations for fiscal 1969 that had just been secured; later all cities would be told of the higher expected level of support.) Sixteen cities got their plans in by the end of December; nine were approved and announced before Inauguration Day.[7]

In early December, Wood and Weaver asked the President to help the program's future prospects in still another way. The White House was preparing a final budget message for fiscal 1970. This would not bind the Nixon Administration, but it might help to set the sights for future appropriations. In a memorandum on December 2, Wood and Weaver informed the President that the categori-

---

[6] Marshall Kaplan, Gans and Kahn, *The Development of the Model Cities Program: The M.C.A. Perspective*, Spring 1969 (unpublished), pp. 147, 153.
[7] Ibid., pp. 148, 153.

cal funds they had expected from other federal agencies were not forthcoming. As a result, the Model Cities Program could be seriously underfunded, compromising the promises made to the cities and discrediting the administration of the program. They asked for a budget allocation of $1 billion in supplemental funds, the full amount authorized. The final budget message in January requested $750 million, but it offset this cut by asking for advance authorization of $1.25 billion for fiscal 1971.

Surviving the Transition
There was little reason for anyone to expect President Nixon to support the Model Cities Program. It was closely identified with the Johnson Administration and had been touted as the keystone of the Great Society, as the program that would tie together all others to solve the problems of the cities. The Nixon Administration would surely want to develop its own urban strategies—later to emerge as welfare reform, decentralization of programs, and revenue sharing with state and local government.[8] Still, there were certain aspects of the program that might well appeal to the philosophy of the incoming Administration, particularly those features that approached the concept of revenue sharing. And perhaps the same bureaucratic inertia that had made it difficult for Lyndon Johnson to get new programs operating would make it difficult for Richard Nixon to dismantle those that existed.

There were a few hopeful portents of support within the new Administration. The appointment of Floyd Hyde as Assistant Secretary was the most important of these. In addition, shortly after Inauguration Day, Secretary Robert Finch of HEW called for more effective administration of the programs for the poor and focused on model cities as the way to do it.

We've tried to call for a more practical application of this in the model cities concept which will probably be the most single important decision in terms of

[8] Revenue sharing was later proposed in two different forms, both of which are discussed in this chapter. *General* revenue sharing was to consist of federal aid allocated to state and local governments on a formula basis, with very few restrictions on the purposes for which it could be used. *Special* revenue sharing for community development would consist of federal funds allocated to local governments on a formula basis, to be used flexibly for any combination of activities previously eligible for support under urban development categorical grants, such as urban renewal, public works construction, and housing code enforcement. *General* revenue sharing approximated an unrestricted federal grant to state and local government. *Special* revenue sharing was essentially a consolidation of previous categorical grant programs, with fewer administrative regulations.

its implementation that this Administration will make. It offers us the vehicle to provide this consolidation and coordination I'm talking about—the melding together in more meaningful packages that deliver the services we're trying to get to the disadvantaged.[9]

Omimously, however, Secretary Finch made these remarks at a meeting of the American Gas Association!

During the first year of the Nixon Administration, HUD Secretary George Romney and Assistant Secretary Floyd Hyde made strenuous attempts to win White House support for the program. Their efforts to make model cities a part of the Nixon program got under way shortly after the inauguration. With a few deft changes of emphasis, they redefined model cities as a reform of the federal aid system in conformity with the Nixon philosophy. The differences of emphasis come through clearly in a comparison of program purposes as defined by Walter Farr, Director of the Model Cities Administration under the Johnson Administration, and Floyd Hyde, newly appointed as Assistant Secretary in charge of model cities. Farr remained with HUD for several months into the Nixon Administration. On January 27, 1969, he circulated a memorandum to his HUD colleagues on the objectives of the program.

The priority overall objective of the Model Cities program is to enhance the capability and commitment of local government to respond to the needs of its poorest neighborhoods and poorest residents. By concentrating resources in selected neighborhoods and concentrating authority in local government, the Model Cities program hopes to demonstrate that local government can solve the problems of poverty and frustration.

By February 8, Hyde had begun to shift the focus in his own memorandum to Secretary Romney on "The Basic Mission, Goals and Objectives of the Model Cities Program and Its Future."

Inasmuch as there is some misconception about the role and future of the Model Cities Program (which I believe is, unfortunately, misnamed), I feel it is necessary to go into some detail to explain its mission and its future and the philosophy underlying the program as I view it. The basic mission of the Model Cities program is not to "add on" another Federal program, but to enhance the capability and commitment of local government, working with neighborhood residents, to marshall the public and private resources needed to solve the problems underlying blight and poverty—with the objective of improving the quality of life of all its citizens.

Hyde went on to argue that the Model Cities Program was the only existing fed-

[9] Simpson Lawson, "Programs," *City*, February 1969, p. 38.

eral program capable of carrying out five of the eight charges given to the Council for Urban Affairs by President Nixon through Executive Order. These five charges were the coordination of federal programs in urban areas, the creation of intergovernmental cooperation with special emphasis on local decision making, improvement in the delivery of services to citizens, decentralization of government responsibility, and encouragement of voluntary organizations to deal with urban concerns.

Poverty neighborhoods and the urban poor were displaced from a central position in the rhetoric of the program; greater emphasis would now go toward reforming the grant-in-aid system, decentralizing authority to local governments, and improving conditions and services for all citizens. The goal of innovation remained only by inference within the need for change in the delivery of traditional city services. Instead of the earlier goal of concentrating additional resources in problem areas, the program would "increase the efficiency of use of existing resources." As an aide to Under Secretary Richard Van Dusen put it, "What we have done to model cities is to scrape away the Johnsonian rhetoric and show that there's a lot of Republicanism in the program—such as good planning, coordination and strengthening of local government."[10]

While Hyde and Romney were defining their own positions and starting their campaign for Presidential backing, the White House had already sponsored the first of numerous reviews of the program—all of which turned out to be favorable. As each study group turned in a positive endorsement (usually calling for some modifications), another was sent out to have a fresh look at it. A preinauguration task force on intergovernmental fiscal relations, chaired by Richard P. Nathan, had looked at model cities and found it a very promising instrument for achieving several goals that President-elect Nixon had already emphasized: decentralization of decision making to local government, simplification of the federal aid system, and improved local coordination of federal programs. Newly appointed as Assistant Director of the Bureau of the Budget, Nathan wrote another strong endorsement of model cities in a staff paper of February 5. He proposed nothing less than that "the new Administration adopt the Model Cities Program as its central strategy for dealing with the problems of the cities." The program would require basic modifications if it was to be used in this way, however. Cities would have to be permitted to include all their poverty areas; additional cities would have to come into the program; state government would have to be en-

---

[10] William Lilley, III, "Urban Report: Model Cities Program Faces Uncertain Future Despite Romney Overhaul," *National Journal*, Vol. 2 (July 11, 1970), p. 1467.

gaged. To assure the necessary consistency and commitments among federal programs, Nathan proposed "an Executive Office staff located close to the President to monitor and coordinate the Government-wide Model Cities system, while administration of the program remains in HUD."[11]

President Nixon asked his newly created Cabinet-level Council for Urban Affairs to review the Model Cities Program. A Committee of the Council began to hold weekly meetings to discuss model cities under the chairmanship of Daniel P. Moynihan, who served as Council Secretary. Romney and Hyde made several presentations, but the early meetings were inconclusive. Hyde then prepared a more elaborate statement explaining how model cities carried out a number of points in the President's "New Federalism" and how the program differed from others. Taking advantage of his abilities as an advanced amateur painter, Hyde did some art work himself for a visual display. The Committee was finally persuaded that model cities should be retained, endorsed Hyde's presentation, and recommended Presidential approval of the program.

A report was prepared by the Committee for consideration by the President and the full Urban Affairs Council. This recommended new priorities for the program: "To improve the effectiveness of federal urban development programs by making them more responsive to local planning and coordination; meaningful involvement of state government as a contributing partner in the process; more effective enlistment of private efforts and voluntary organizations by removing the arbitrary neighborhood boundaries of the program." Among the Committee's other proposals were the establishment of city-wide citizen advisory boards, explicit acknowledgment that complete elimination of blight and poverty in model neighborhoods was beyond the government's immediate means, earmarking of funds from departments other than HUD, and designation of the Under Secretaries who were members of the Urban Affairs Council to resolve operational issues. These were significant changes, which the Committee believed would justify Administration support for the program. Its report concluded, "With the adoption of the above recommendations, the Model Cities program should be greatly strengthened by local planning and coordination, more effective Federal coordination, state involvement and private participation."[12]

Hyde and Romney reported to the full Urban Affairs Council at its April 7

[11] Richard P. Nathan, "The Model Cities Program," Bureau of the Budget staff paper, February 5, 1969.
[12] "Report of the Committee on Model Cities of the Council for Urban Affairs," April 7, 1969.

meeting, which was chaired by President Nixon. Several members of the Cabinet indicated strong support for the program, but the President was not persuaded. He raised a series of skeptical questions on how model cities differed from other programs, whether it was just another social program like those of OEO, or whether it was just another categorical program. Romney pressed for an early decision on whether the President wanted to continue it. Hyde offered, if the President was still not satisfied, to organize a flying field trip for several agency representatives to see how the Model Cities Program was working. President Nixon did not resolve the issue at the meeting; instead, he and Moynihan withdrew to continue the discussion in an adjoining room.[13]

Six More Studies

The next morning, White House aide John Ehrlichman called Hyde to say that the President wanted to go ahead with the field trip. A team of representatives from HUD, HEW, OEO, the Department of Labor, the Department of Transportation, and staff members of the Urban Affairs Council was organized quickly to visit three cities involved in the program (study #1). They gave strong reinforcement to the findings of the Model Cities Committee.

Our general conclusion is that the Model Cities program has gotten off to a successful start, and that if it is administered carefully, with revisions along the lines suggested in the Model Cities Committee report, it could result in strengthening and improving the process by which the federal government helps local governments address their social and environmental problems.

More significantly, they recommended to the White House that

The President's message on Model Cities should stress that his examination of the program reveals that local governments have worked harder to make it work than has the federal government, and that his administration of the program will be aimed at putting the federal house in order, so that local governments can be better assured of Federal support in the Model Cities program.[14]

With the endorsement of the Urban Affairs Council, the Model Cities Program appeared to have enough Administration backing to proceed. HUD had requested $675 million in supplemental funds ($75 million less than the Johnson budget), and President Nixon accepted this figure for his fiscal 1970 budget.

---

[13] Interview with Floyd Hyde, November 22, 1972. For another account of the meeting, see Rowland Evans, Jr., and Robert D. Novak, *Nixon in the White House: The Frustration of Power* (New York: Vintage Books, 1972), pp. 38-41.
[14] Council for Urban Affairs, "Model Cities Study Trip," April 19, 1969.

Secretary Romney held a press conference on April 28, at which he announced that the program would proceed with the changes recommended by the Committee of the Council for Urban Affairs. Its study had shown that the program's goals were sound, but critical deficiencies in its administration would now be corrected. Romney noted that the Council for Urban Affairs would assume direct responsibility for interdepartmental policy in regard to the program.

At this point in the news conference, he went well beyond his prepared text in claiming Presidential support.

Now, this is a very important thing in connection with the effectiveness of this program, unless this program has the backing and direction of the President, unless the President himself is supporting the program, and unless he's backing the policies under which the program is going to be carried out, it is not likely the program is going to be a success. And the fact that the policies that had been developed have the President's backing, and the fact that he will continue to participate in the policy making aspects of this program, is a very important aspect of making it a success.[15]

In a further move to build support for the program, Floyd Hyde published in May 1969 a report on the first year of experience in Atlanta, Dayton, and Seattle (study #2). The case studies on which the report was based had been prepared under contract to HUD as part of a continuing monitoring and assessment of what was happening in the local programs. The report was detailed and avoided sweeping judgments. In several respects it was critical of HUD's administration of the program and called attention to the unreality of certain of its regulations. But the report gave a favorable impression of the local efforts and concluded that they represented "a modest success" in dealing with very difficult problems. In all three cities, the evaluators found that a reasonable start had been made in improving coordinated planning among federal, state, and local agencies, in involving residents and working out their conflicts with local government, and in obtaining aid from private industry.[16]

Despite Hyde's efforts and Romney's assurances, support from the White House was not yet secure. Earlier, President Nixon had seriously considered killing the program. His chief White House aide on urban policy, Daniel P. Moynihan, advised him to continue it, but his argument reflected no enthusiasm for

[15] Secretary Romney, transcript of news conference (Policy Statement on Model Cities), April 28, 1969.
[16] HUD, *The Model Cities Program: A History and Analysis of the Planning Process in Three Cities* (Washington, D.C.: U.S. Government Printing Office, 1969). The report was prepared by the consulting firm of Marshall Kaplan, Gans and Kahn, of San Francisco.

the program as such. Moynihan hastily reviewed a number of early plans from the cities and concluded from these that the program had little substantive value. Nevertheless, he believed that closing it down could prove disastrous. He sensed that model cities had spread a network of promises in black communities, had encouraged many influential people to become involved, and had created a real constituency. Further, he was persuaded that model cities had become the symbol of the new Administration's commitment to deal with urban problems. An Administration that wanted to restore faith in government and keep the peace in the cities ran the risk of serious trouble if it disregarded the commitment that model cities had already made.[17]

Moynihan's advice apparently had some impact on the President's decision to retain the program. In this analysis of the national commitment to model cities, it is important to note that the keeping of a commitment—and not the merit of the program—was the key consideration underlying this decision. At the same time, this basis for continuation would not justify vigorous Presidential leadership or even a reasonably high priority for model cities in the future.

Although the program was continued, White House doubts were not yet resolved, and the reviews also continued. The main ones have been mentioned in earlier chapters, and their findings are presented here in summary form.

Interagency Task Force (study #3). At the request of the Urban Affairs Council, an interagency task force chaired by Guy Chamberlin spent two months studying model cities in the field and in Washington during the summer of 1969. Their report, *Strengthening the Federal Response to Model Cities*, was submitted on September 4 and provided another strong endorsement, together with many detailed proposals for making the program work better. Its major conclusion was

The Model Cities program remains the best existing mechanism for focusing the Federal government's attention and resources on solving urban problems. In spite of moving largely on uncharted ground against a variety of formidable obstacles, the program has made the government more responsive to people's needs, advanced the concept of balanced citizen participation and local government involvement, and helped to reduce the redundancy of Federal programs.[18]

White House Task Force (study #4). Immediately afterward, on September 15, President Nixon appointed Edward C. Banfield to head a new White House task

[17] Lilley, "Urban Report," p. 1474; Evans and Novak, *Nixon in the White House*, pp. 42-43; and interview with Daniel P. Moynihan, October 10, 1972.
[18] Inter-Agency Staff Report, *Strengthening the Federal Response to Model Cities: An Interagency Report*, September 1969.

force that would review the Model Cities Program once again and make recommendations for its future. Banfield, then a professor of government at Harvard University, had a reputation as a severe critic of federal programs. He selected a task force consisting mainly of academicians and public officials and arranged for briefings by federal staff members and others knowledgeable about model cities.

The task force report, which went to the President on December 16, once more endorsed the goals and concept of model cities and once again made many suggestions for improved administration. It criticized the federal government for giving the program too much regulation and too little support. Its conclusions on the program's operation were that

Despite over-regulation and under-support, the model cities program has made a useful contribution. It has succeeded in making some city halls more aware of the special problems of their poor neighborhoods; it has brought some mayors and citizens groups into mutually advantageous relations; it has given some encouragement to the improvement of management methods, and, especially in the larger cities, it has given rise to some projects that are both new and promising. . . . In short, the model cities program is better than what went before. We think that if the cities are given greater freedom and more substantial support the program will be a great deal better still.[19]

Among the recommendations were that HUD should reduce and simplify its requirements and review procedures, that the President make it "unmistakably clear" to heads of other agencies that he attaches importance to the Model Cities Program, that he direct these agencies to set aside at least 25 percent of their nonformula grant funds for model cities use, and that all federal agencies should regard model cities plans as sufficient to meet their requirements for grant applications.

Brookings Institution Evaluation (study #5). Also late in 1969, the Brookings Institution published an independent analysis of the Model Cities Program, conducted by James L. Sundquist and David W. Davis of the Brookings staff. Sundquist and Davis interviewed federal officials, visited a dozen cities involved in the program, and studied detailed chronologies of first-year planning in four other cities. They were favorably impressed.

The model cities structure is probably as well designed on paper as a system can be for serving the several goals that are sought—coordination, participation, and conflict resolution.

[19] U.S. President's Task Force on Model Cities, *Report, Model Cities: A Step Towards the New Federalism* (Washington, D.C.: U.S. Government Printing Office, 1970), pp. 9-10.

We recommend, therefore, that the federal government as a whole—and state and local governments as well—accept the model cities structure as the basic scheme for coordinating program planning and execution in urban slum areas.[20]

Sundquist and Davis qualified their recommendation by noting that the concept had not yet been proved fully through experience.

We argue only that the *potential* of the program has been demonstrated, if one looks at all the hopeful portents; and national policy—in relation to a flexible program such as this one—can be made on the basis of potential.

While Presidential reviews progressed, efforts continued from within the government to build support for the program. Robert Mayo, Director of the Budget Bureau, sent a memorandum to John Ehrlichman in the White House, pointing out the importance of the program to the Administration. He argued that it could be useful as a vehicle for decentralizing responsibility to local government, strengthening local elected officials, improving the delivery of public services, and helping to overcome the problems of local government fragmentation created by the federal aid system. Revenue sharing, the favored Administration strategy, would not eliminate the need for model cities.

Perhaps revenue sharing would avoid all these problems if it replaced all categorical programs. But it won't. Grant consolidation would help minimize some of the problems. But we are running into congressional difficulties. The categorical programs are here to stay. One of our prime goals is to mold them to fit our objectives.[21]

Floyd Hyde pursued his own efforts, also, with a memorandum to Ehrlichman on December 2. He argued that the Model Cities Program was a logical adjunct of the "New Federalism" that Nixon wanted to achieve. Further, he reminded Ehrlichman of the steps that he had already taken with the program to meet the President's charge to the Council for Urban Affairs—steps to involve the states, cut paper requirements, and decentralize responsibility. Then he asked for White House support.

What is needed is a clear recognition of the role that Model Cities can play in support of these Administration objectives, and a decision to utilize Model Cities for this purpose. It would give meaning to my efforts to change Model Cities from an interesting if somewhat academic exercise into a useful tool for blunting

[20] James L. Sundquist and David W. Davis, *Making Federalism Work* (Washington, D.C.: Brookings Institution, 1969), p. 118.
[21] Executive Office of the President, Bureau of the Budget, memorandum for Mr. John Ehrlichman, Subject: The Model Cities Program, November 4, 1969, p. 3.

the headlong rush of the previous decade toward government centralization in America.[22]

Council for Urban Affairs Review (study #6). Instead of that long-sought commitment, still further reviews were in prospect under the wing of the Council for Urban Affairs. Beginning in February 1970, the Subcommittee on Model Cities held a series of meetings at Blair House. Professor Banfield attended an early meeting and took the occasion to deliver his personal views on model cities, which differed markedly from the report of his own task force. In his judgment, there was little that the federal government could do to solve urban problems, and certainly the Model Cities Program would not accomplish much.

The subject under consideration, however, was not the federal government and the urban problem but what to do with the existing Model Cities Program. Secretary Romney presented a "hard sell" position on February 27. The themes by then were familiar. The Model Cities Program was the only current plan that could deal with a number of serious shortcomings in the delivery of federal grants-in-aid to the inner city. He and Hyde had transformed model cities from a Great Society program to a New Federalism program. Further action was needed, involving interagency and intergovernmental relations. Romney asked the President to take several specific steps to support the program. But most important, he recommended a Presidential message on model cities that would endorse the reshaping of the program as a vehicle of the New Federalism and inform federal and local officials that the President stood fully behind it.[23]

Constituents to the Rescue

While the Blair House meetings were still in session, a far more critical test of the President's commitment was shaping up. A proposal was circulated within the Administration that could have crippled model cities by diverting virtually the entire $575 million appropriation for fiscal 1971 into a fund to help southern school districts in their efforts to desegregate. Word was leaked to the press: a *New York Times* article on April 25 reported that John Ehrlichman had asked HUD to consider the feasibility of taking $500 million out of the model cities budget.[24] Floyd Hyde now found himself literally fighting for the life of the

[22] Floyd H. Hyde, memorandum for Mr. John Ehrlichman, Assistant to the President for Domestic Affairs, Subject: Model Cities Role in the "New Federalism," December 2, 1969.
[23] Secretary of Housing and Urban Development, "Briefing to the Urban Affairs Council on Model Cities," February 27, 1970.
[24] "Nixon May Divert Model Cities Aid for Schools' Use," *New York Times*, April 25, 1970, p. 1.

program. He met with Ehrlichman on May 7 and followed up with a letter on May 12: "Because of the extreme importance that we in the Department attach to this issue in the light of current events and the rising tensions in our cities, I feel compelled to set down my views with utmost candor."

Hyde argued that the Administration would pay high political costs if it gutted the program. The cities at large and the minority groups would perceive that their own priorities and the commitments made to them were being scrapped in order to accommodate some southern school districts. Youth would interpret the move as the neglect of urban problems in order to support the Vietnam War. HUD's credibility with Congress, which had met the President's full 1971 budget request for model cities, would be seriously impaired. Hyde also protested at public statements that had been made by spokesmen of the Administration who explained that the fiscal 1971 funds were not needed for the model cities.

The threat to the program was serious enough that Hyde did not have to fight this battle alone. His letter to Ehrlichman reminded the White House that the most outspoken criticism of the proposed fund diversion had come from Republican mayors. By this time, the Model Cities Program had developed a constituency of its own. Local and regional citizens' groups called and visited their Congressmen. The National League of Cities-U.S. Conference of Mayors quickly mobilized those mayors whose cities were in the program. They were urged to contact the White House and their state governors, stressing their need for the money and arguing that an arbitrary switch of funding with no local consultation was totally inconsistent with the New Federalism. Staff of the National League of Cities believed that at least fifty of the mayors contacted the White House and that several governors who had been invited to the White House to review the Cambodia invasion and college unrest also pressed the President to keep the money for model cities.[25]

Interested Congressmen also rallied around the program when cities in their own districts were threatened. Political ideologies gave way to the protection of constituencies. Even Barry Goldwater sent a letter of concern about the funding for Tucson. The combination of interest groups was apparently strong enough to preserve the program: on May 14 President Nixon met with Romney and told him there would be no change in the budget for 1971.

The Urban Affairs Council Subcommittee, meanwhile, continued to discuss George Romney's proposals at its meetings at Blair House but backed away from

[25] William Lilley III, "Washington Pressures/National League of Cities-U.S. Conference of Mayors," in *The Pressure Groups* (Washington, D.C.: *The National Journal*, 1971), p. 102.

those that would have nailed down firm commitments of program funds from other agencies. In June, the White House circulated a draft "Model Cities Action Paper" that had resulted from the Subcommittee deliberations. After discussions with department and agency heads, the report was to be put into final form for submission to the President.

The June draft presented the President with three options for the future direction of the program. One was to let it coast; but the study group argued that in view of the extensive high-level review to which the program had been subjected, a decision to let it coast would have the same political and programmatic effect as a decision to kill it. Another option was to make basic short-term improvements in its administration and to experiment with planned variations in some of the more competent cities. The third was to institute "bold new approaches" program-wide. Arguing that not all cities were performing well enough to take part in planned variations and that the cost of the program-wide new approaches could not be met out of existing budgets, the group recommended the second strategy. To free some funds, they proposed that a few poorly performing model cities should be dropped from the program. They concurred with the proposals Romney had made at Blair House to decentralize review authority to regional offices, eliminate plan reviews by the White House and the Secretary of HUD, and consult with individual mayors on all federal grants going into model neighborhoods. On the critical matter of obtaining funding commitments from other federal agencies, the draft recommended reliance on interagency consultation and Budget Bureau monitoring, rather than the establishment of more specific targets or earmarking procedures.

In the cities selected for planned variations, the study group proposed that federal program and project reviews should be eliminated wherever possible, that programs should be permitted to operate on a city-wide basis rather than only in the model neighborhood, that the mayor should be given a veto on all applications for federal aid affecting the model cities area, and that special incentive grants should be offered to encourage state support for model cities efforts. When the action paper was redrafted later in the summer, it adhered generally to these recommendations and added a call for a public statement of support from the President. The paper was submitted to the White House by the Subcommittee on Model Cities.

HEW gave particularly strong support to the case for White House commitment in a separate memorandum from Secretary Elliot Richardson to John Price, Special Assistant to the President. The memorandum, bearing the marks of

Sidney Gardner's views, presented a thoughtful rationale for the use of the program to improve the effectiveness of federally funded service programs in the cities and to redress some of the inequalities in service levels between the inner city and the suburbs. Recognizing the Administration's growing commitment to programs that would provide income rather than services, the memorandum nevertheless argued that cash grants to consumers would not necessarily enable them to obtain the services they needed and that the delivery of services would also require federal attention. Richardson cited HEW's experiences with nursing homes in the Medicaid program as a case in point. He concluded: "Model Cities, in our view, has the potential for serving as one of the most important elements of the Administration's entire intergovernmental strategy."[26]

The White House nevertheless continued to delay any direct sign of commitment to the program. Early in September, it decided to release the Banfield task force report that had been held back since the previous December. Floyd Hyde, still battling to save the program, suggested a title for the cover that might imply acceptance of the program by the Administration: "Model Cities: A Step Towards the New Federalism." The covers were printed hastily, and John Price of the White House staff agreed to appear with Hyde for a White House news conference releasing the report on September 10. Questions from the press were sharp. Asked why it had taken nine months to release the report, Price answered, "I think it was simply to whet your appetite. In fact, the *New York Times* at the time of the filing of the report, did carry a lead story which had the contents of it. We have no logical reason for not having released it until now." Asked about the recommendation that the President should make unmistakably clear to the heads of the urban agencies the importance he attached to the program, Price gave as strong an answer as he could.

> I told you at the outset of my remarks that we had convened the meeting at Cabinet level of the interested departments. It wasn't just one meeting. We have held several meetings on this at his direction. So, there is significant Presidential interest in making this program work more efficiently to solve the kinds of problems that are outlined here.[27]

Although the White House decision to proceed with the planned variations strategy was made known to HUD in the fall of 1970, the next steps, including

[26] Secretary of Health, Education, and Welfare, memorandum for the Honorable John R. Price, Subject: "HEW Position Papers on Model Cities Directions," July 17, 1970.
[27] Office of the White House Press Secretary, transcript of the White House Press Conference of Floyd H. Hyde and John R. Price, September 10, 1970.

the selection of cities, were mired in numerous delays while the Administration contemplated major changes in federal aid programs for cities. Before acting on planned variations, the White House made an attempt to terminate the entire Model Cities Program. The Administration had been developing plans for the consolidation of a series of urban aid programs, including model cities, into a special revenue-sharing fund for community development and had intended to set the date of December 31, 1971, for the termination of the model cities supplemental funding. After that, if Congress acted favorably on special revenue sharing, cities would be able to use a part of their community development grant to continue the Model Cities Program if they wished, but the decision would be theirs. In February 1971, staff members of the National League of Cities-U.S. Conference of Mayors learned that letters to announce the funding cutoff after December 31 had been prepared for George Romney's signature and were about to be sent out to the mayors.

Mayors of participating cities who were active in the National League of Cities-U.S. Conference of Mayors interpreted this impending move as an attempt to pressure them into support of the special revenue-sharing plan. What worried them further, they doubted whether Congress would act promptly on this legislation and they feared a loss of federal aid. They contacted Vice President Spiro Agnew, who had special responsibility for maintaining contact with local government leaders, and he quickly arranged a series of meetings with officials of HUD, the Office of Management and Budget, and the Vice President's staff. The Administration then backed down and agreed to set no firm termination date; and it also agreed to request a supplemental appropriation to continue funding model cities through the end of fiscal 1972 if Congress failed to adopt the proposed revenue-sharing legislation by December. The mayors themselves, in addition, approached key Congressmen to ask them to exempt the Model Cities Program from the grant consolidation for community development.[28]

Finally on July 29, 1971, the President issued a statement announcing the selection of twenty cities for planned variations. He presented the new approach as an interim measure pending Congressional action on the Administration's revenue-sharing proposals. The latter would accomplish "needed basic changes" in

[28] Patrick Healy, Executive Vice President, National League of Cities, and John J. Gunther, Executive Director, U.S. Conference of Mayors, letter to Vice President Spiro Agnew, March 8, 1971; "White House Drops Intention to Freeze Model Cities Funds," *New York Times*, February 19, 1971, p. 20; "Nixon Drops Plan to Cut Off Funds for Model Cities," *New York Times*, February 28, 1971, p. 1; interview with John Sasso, Executive Secretary, Model Cities Directors Association, August 22, 1972.

the federal grant system. Meanwhile, planned variations would "convert a portion of present Model Cities grants into a test of what can be accomplished under the revenue sharing approach to intergovernmental relations."[29] That was as strong an endorsement as the program was ever to receive from the President.

Appraising the White House Role

Why had two and one-half years of reviews produced so little commitment in the White House? Several reasons have been advanced. The Great Society label was hard to shake off and made the program politically unappealing. It contained within it the seeds of mushrooming demands on the federal budget; as cities studied their needs and developed five-year action plans to cope with all the problems of poverty areas, they were certain to ask for more and more federal help. Further, the inner city was not a promising source of strength for Nixon no matter what he did. Although the conception of the program did indeed have much in common with the New Federalism, the flow of resources through the newly decentralized mechanism ended up in the hands of Democratic voters. As Hyde's aide Warren Butler put it, "We've got the right constituency and the wrong process for the liberals: and we've got the wrong constituency and the right process for the conservatives."[30]

Despite the lack of a strong commitment from the White House, the Nixon Administration nevertheless gave a measure of support to the program. The timing of the program was such that the Johnson years had been devoted mainly to early planning. Operations did not begin until the spring of 1969. The Nixon Administration as a result spent far more on model cities than did the Johnson Administration. Planning grants made by the Johnson Administration totaled $22 million. From 1969 through mid-1972, the Nixon Administration allocated $1.6 billion to the cities in supplemental grants.

Although the Nixon White House did not make an arm-twisting effort to induce federal agencies to spend for model cities, Moynihan in 1969 went through a procedure very similar to Califano's of the previous year. Only three or four weeks after the inauguration, he made phone calls to the newly appointed Cabinet members, expecting to find them at this early stage highly responsive to the President. He discovered they had already picked up the perspectives of their respective departments and gave evasive replies. In asking for earmarked funds, he proposed no specific targets but urged them to "give till it hurts." None re-

[29] Office of the White House Press Secretary, Statement by the President, July 29, 1971.
[30] Lilley, "Urban Report," p. 1467.

fused directly, but all offered to set up committees to look into the matter or promised to get back to him later. He organized one pledge meeting to coordinate earmarking plans and, on arriving, failed to find a familiar face in the room. Every agency head had sent a deputy. To gain full cooperation would have required a great expenditure of time and effort by the White House, which neither the Johnson nor the Nixon Administration was prepared to give. In neither case, to our knowledge, was anyone penalized for failure to cooperate; and both Administrations raised roughly the same amount of earmarked funds from the federal agencies.

The White House contributed to the maintenance of the Model Cities Program, but it acted unevenly and with many reservations. The dedication of a few convinced supporters such as Floyd Hyde, and Sidney Gardner of HEW, provided much of the impetus that kept the entire federal effort moving. To those who had to persuade, cajole, and connive in order to make the program work, the silence from the White House was deafening. Gardner, a former aide to Mayor Lindsay, had worked hard and effectively within HEW to obtain funds for model cities. In November 1969, he wrote to Banfield that whatever cooperation had been achieved among federal agencies "has come about with a virtually total lack of awareness or involvement on the part of the White House."[31]

In truth, model cities probably had as much Presidential support under Nixon as is characteristic for most federal programs. The problem was that the Model Cities Program was not an average federal program. It was more dependent than most upon White House backing, for reasons already noted. First, its ultimate beneficiaries—the urban poor, the blacks, the Chicanos, and Puerto Ricans—did not have much influence with Congress. To win appropriations and legislative support, the President would have to deal with Congress. Second, the federal agencies had their own programs and constituents to look after; they would not do much for model cities unless they felt the program had Presidential backing.

If model cities could not succeed without exceptional White House commitment, perhaps the designers of the program should have thought of that in 1965. There was always the high risk that the President would find other priorities. And in the event of a change of Administration, how likely is it that any incoming President would want the same program to serve as the centerpiece of his urban policy? Programs do spawn bureaucracies and constituencies that can keep them going after an initial input from the White House, and perhaps the Wood

---

[31] Sidney L. Gardner, Director, Center for Community Planning, HEW, memorandum to Edward C. Banfield, November 25, 1969.

task force had expected this to happen. As it turned out, the interest groups around the program were strong enough to prevent its premature death but not to assure its good health. Under Nixon, it had financial support but not enough evidence of political will to inspire confidence, give hope, or encourage wavering bureaucrats to take risks on its behalf.

By mid-1972, even Floyd Hyde was making plans to fold the Model Cities Program into revenue sharing for community development while trying to preserve an important role for the City Demonstration Agencies and their citizen structures. By that time, the mayors had succeeded in persuading both the Senate and House to exclude model cities from special revenue sharing in their versions of the community development legislation. Nevertheless, Hyde fashioned a strategy for encouraging cities to merge their community development and model cities funds. He proposed establishing a fixed termination date for the Model Cities Program in each city five years from the beginning of the first action year. Funds would be withdrawn from "poor performers" and offered instead as incentives to other cities to make their programs city-wide and to help them to merge these with their other activities funded through special revenue sharing. The end of the program was clearly in sight, together with a plan for transition to the Administration's preferred urban aid policy.[32]

The Congressional Role—Spreading the Resources

The long and difficult passage of the model cities legislation through Congress, followed by very small early appropriations, made it evident that Congress was at first no more than a reluctant partner in this venture. Yet Congressional action began to change the nature of the program to make it more capable of meeting essential political requirements. As the character of the program changed, Congress became increasingly committed to it. The main issue at stake in this process of adjustment between White House intentions and Congressional pressures was the original conception of model cities as a program to concentrate federal resources in a limited number of poverty neighborhoods. Such concentration ran counter to Congressional politics. The way to win Congressional commitment was to compromise this goal of the program.

The Wood task force in 1965 called for "the concentration of available and special resources in sufficient magnitude to demonstrate swiftly what qualified urban communities can do and can become." The task force recommended that

[32] Floyd Hyde, memorandum for James Falk, Special Assistant to the President, Subject: Future of Model Cities Program, June 27, 1972.

66 cities be selected for the program: 6 with populations over 500,000, 10 with populations from 250,000 to 500,000, and 50 with populations below 250,000. This breakdown represented best judgments about a balanced distribution among regions and size classes and about the number that would be well qualified to use the new program, tempered by a sense of what was politically desirable and what would be a reasonable cost limit for the entire venture. On the basis of certain assumptions about what the cities would do and hasty calculations of the likely costs for different kinds of activities, the task force staff came up with rough cost estimates. It advised the President that the demonstration program for 66 cities would cost $2.3 billion over five years, of which the federal share would be approximately $1.9 billion. This estimate included only activities supported out of the Model Cities Program itself; other federal aid programs were expected to contribute substantially more.

President Johnson's message to Congress did not specify the number of cities to be included but recommended appropriations of $2.3 billion over a six-year period. Secretary Weaver's presentation to Congress reiterated the cost estimate of $2.3 billion for supplemental grants for five years of operations, plus additional grants for a preliminary year of planning.

But there was more to the program than supplemental funds. In his testimony to the House Subcommittee, Secretary Weaver made it clear that the estimate of $2.3 billion was only for supplemental grants. With the addition of other federal aid programs, plus local contributions and private undertakings, he estimated a total program impact of $5-10 billion. In short, the supplemental funds were expected to have a significant multiplier effect, particularly on the channeling of additional federal resources into poverty neighborhoods. The estimate of $2.3 billion was based on the participation of 60 to 70 cities, something that was clear to Congress from Weaver's testimony. As Chapter 3 indicates, Congressional reactions from the outset focused on making as many cities as possible eligible for the program. The Senate Committee reported out a version of the Administration's bill in which significant changes had been made in response to this interest (after consultation with the White House). The Administration had asked for an authorization of $12 million in planning funds for fiscal 1967 to cover 60 to 70 cities. To this the Senate Committee now added authorization for an additional $12 million in planning funds for the following year. This change gave HUD quick warning that the 60 to 70 cities they had in mind were to be only the beginning. A second round of 60 to 70 cities was to be selected in fiscal 1968, raising the total number close to 140. (In August 1968, Congress added authorization for still another $12 million in planning funds—and thus a third round–in fiscal 1969.) The promise of a second round remained in the legislation that emerged from the 89th Congress.

In addition to expanding the number of cities, Congress moved to block another route toward concentration of resources. The Wood task force and the White House had counted heavily on drawing together grant-in-aid funds from other federal programs and using them in the model neighborhoods. Congressmen were sensitive to the prior claims of other constituencies on these funds and to the political consequences of diverting aid from other recipients into the poverty areas. As noted earlier, both the House and Senate Committees reporting out the bill gave clear warning that they did not intend to change the flow of funds under existing grant-in-aid programs or to provide special priority in those programs for model cities participants.

When the Administration tried nevertheless to channel other grant funds into the Model Cities Program, Congress reasserted its own position and pressed agency officials to curtail such interagency transfers. According to HEW sources, the Senate Appropriations Subcommittee for HEW and Labor made known their unhappiness over the reservation of HEW funds for model cities use. The subcommittee traditionally maintained close ties with administrators and users of the programs it funded and objected to the shifting of these funds to a program removed from its control and influence.[33]

Despite this increase in the number of cities and opposition to bringing in funds from other programs, Congress made no corresponding increase in funding authorization for model cities. Instead of the six-year authorization of $2.3 billion sought by the White House, Congress authorized total appropriations of $900 million in supplemental grants for two years starting in 1968, plus $24 million for two rounds of planning and $250 million in special urban renewal funds. Congress expanded the number of cities and failed to authorize the full six-year program. The level of funding they authorized ($400 million for 1968, $500 million for 1969) was consistent with the Administration estimate of $2.3 billion over six years. But it would have to be spread to twice as many cities as the task force and the White House had originally wanted to include. The will to concentrate funds was a good deal weaker than the will to spend money in poverty areas.

HUD officials got the message. By the time the Johnson Administration left office, 150 model cities had been chosen. They were located in all regions of the country, in 46 states, the District of Columbia, and Puerto Rico. Five counties

[33] Lilley, "Urban Report," p. 1476.

and an Indian reservation were among the participants. All but three of the nation's cities with populations over 500,000 and almost 90 percent of all cities over 250,000 were included.[34] The goal of resource concentration at the national level was impossible to sustain; the Nixon Administration did not even speak of this as one of the purposes of the program.

The other side of the coin, however, is that Congressional revision of the program was critical in creating a constituency that could protect and maintain it over time. The Nixon Administration's attempts to divert model cities funds to southern school districts and to terminate the entire program at the end of 1971 have already been noted. On both occasions, the Administration reversed its course under political pressure. On still another occasion, the President sliced HUD's budget request for model cities for fiscal 1972 from $575 million to nothing at all.[35] In an attempt to forestall 1972 budget cuts, Hyde reminded Romney of the successful intervention of model cities constituents to prevent the loss of funds to southern school authorities.

Extreme resistance was expressed not only by the Mayors in the program, which would be expected, but by Governors (Republican Governors in particular), Senators and Congressmen. Indeed far greater concern and interest in the program was demonstrated than most of us realized, including myself.[36]

Congress eventually appropriated $150 million, which together with unallocated earlier appropriations made possible continued outlays at the same rate that prevailed before 1972.

Once model cities took on the shape of a federal grant-in-aid program benefiting large numbers of communities, the alliance of mayors, governors, and Congressmen could be mobilized. The price for securing these sources of strength, however, was a considerable departure from the earlier stress on a national concentration of resources.

Commitment from the Cities

A Willingness to Cooperate
The Model Cities Program counted heavily on commitment at another level as

[34] Secretary of HUD, "Briefing to the Urban Affairs Council on Model Cities," February 27, 1970.
[35] "Congress Clears HUD Appropriations," *National Journal*, Vol. 3 (August 7, 1971), p. 1671.
[36] Floyd H. Hyde, memorandum to George Romney, "Proposed Reduction in Model Cities Outlays and Budget Authority for FY '72," November 10, 1970.

well—in the cities themselves, where municipal neglect and inaction had compounded the problems of urban poverty. The program was premised on the ability to find cities that were now prepared to channel extra resources into poverty areas so as to begin closing the gap between these neighborhoods and the rest of the community. This would be in marked contrast to the ways in which cities had used federal aid under the urban renewal program; there the objective had generally been to attract tax-paying development to slum areas rather than to improve them for the benefit of their low-income residents.

The initial applications were promising. Cities appeared, in their proposals, to be defining neighborhoods of genuine need and were acknowledging openly that they had shortchanged these neighborhoods through the years. A few excerpts from the first-round applications submitted early in 1967 illustrate the purgetrial confessional tone of these documents.

This is not to say that the City has, in its 160 years of development, been totally insensitive and unresponsive to the needs of its people. But it is true that its sensitivity has been limited, that its response to human problems has been inadequate, and that this neglect and inaction has resulted in the most difficult and crucial problems facing the City of Detroit today. [Detroit, Part II, p. 32.]
. . . not only are the public facilities of the area too small to accommodate the number of people living in the area, but they are too deteriorated and lack the technical conveniences commonplace to contemporary society. . . . Educational facilities are overcrowded and many lack fireproofing. Little space is available for contemporary teaching techniques, such as libraries, physical education, and counseling. . . . Only one Public Assistance Office and one Child Welfare Office serve the entire area, yet one-half of the city's public welfare cases are located here. [Philadelphia, Part III, Section D, p. 1.]
Concomitant with the severe housing problem is the generally poor condition of related facilities and the inadequacy of municipal housekeeping services. In many areas streets and sidewalks are cluttered and in need of repair, vacant rubbish-strewn lots and yards abound. . . . Although the City has made efforts to close the gap, capital improvements within these areas are generally inadequate, older and in poor condition. [New York, Part III-A, p. 1.]
Public facilities in the model area, including sewers, libraries, neighborhood facilities and schools, are also obsolete or inadequate. Again, a lack of city funds to correct these deficiencies, combined with public apathy, are the major causes of their present condition. [New Haven, Part II, p. 2.]

City applications also gave evidence of a willingness to use the model cities funds in areas where the poor were concentrated. This was in contrast both to the neglect of such areas in the past and to the more recent failures of city school departments to spend federal Title I funds for elementary and secondary education on the poor children for whom the aid was intended. Perhaps the competitive nature of the Model Cities Program, in which cities had to establish a convincing case for participation, prompted more than usual attention to the statutory requirements. The residents of the 150 model neighborhoods included in the program by 1970 were 55 percent black and 14 percent Spanish-speaking. Their average unemployment rate was more than 10 percent. Thirty-two percent of the families had annual incomes below $3,000, and more than 30 percent of the housing units were substandard.[37]

The Banfield task force obtained its own reading of the mayors' attitudes toward model cities in 1969. Task force members interviewed mayors and city managers in several parts of the country. The sample was small, and the results were merely suggestive, but almost all those interviewed indicated strong support for the program. One question that the mayors were asked was whether they would prefer the present Model Cities Program or one that would give the city 20 percent less money but complete freedom in spending it; another question asked which would do more for the poor of the city, model cities or increased welfare payments. Replies reported to the task force from seven or eight cities all favored model cities over these alternatives. The two local chief executives on the task force, Mayor Richard Lugar of Indianapolis and City Manager David Rowlands of Tacoma, concurred.

An interview with Barney Frank, aide to Boston Mayor Kevin White at the time, provided some insight into the reason why the mayors were attracted to model cities. The mayor wanted to have programs that would help the black poor and respond to pressures from the black community, but in the normal course of events he would have been compelled to spread funds around the city in response to pressures from other neighborhoods. Having a federal requirement that model cities funds be spent in a single poverty neighborhood took political heat off the mayor. Further, he did not have strong personal commitments to particular projects or priorities in the model neighborhood and was glad to have an elected neighborhood board make these decisions. A program that did not impose federal requirements would not be able to cope with the needs of the model cities area: its funds would have to be divided among too many competitors. As between model cities and bigger welfare payments, only the poor on welfare would benefit from the latter. The working poor, on the other hand, were likely to gain substantial benefits from model cities; probably they would be the main beneficiaries. The Model Cities Program was also helpful to the may-

[37] Secretary of HUD, "Briefing to the Urban Affairs Council . . . ," pp. 5-6.

or as part of a strategy to build up new agencies and institutions that could handle innovative programs and that would be more responsive to the mayor than established municipal departments. "The existing agencies are encrusted and loaded with unproductive people," according to Frank. "Their employees won't hustle for anybody, and least of all for the poor and the blacks."[38]

Sundquist and Davis's evaluation of early model cities experience touched on the same themes. They found mayors welcoming the Model Cities Program for the chance it might offer them to win some measure of control over the "independent satrapies" of community government.[39] By the same reasoning, however, municipal departments were less likely to cooperate; yet their commitment would be needed, too, if the conditions of life were to be improved in model neighborhoods.

The programs that cities proposed for their model neighborhoods also gave evidence of mayoral commitment to the objectives of concentrating resources and using them for comprehensive local programs tailored to the needs of low-income residents. The projects that were envisioned were a clear departure from the narrowly restricted range of most HUD programs. Even in contrast to OEO's Community Action Program, city proposals stretched far to give attention to the full range of slum problems. The analysis by the Urban Institute of thirty-five city plans showed a mixture of expenditures on capital investments (34 percent of the total budget) and services to residents (45 percent), in contrast to the emphasis on "hardware" of most HUD programs. Cities also indicated a willingness to coordinate the activities funded through model cities supplemental grants with the activities supported out of other sources. In total, the thirty-five plans contemplated using model cities funds to cover 54 percent of their anticipated first-year budgets.[40]

Participating city governments showed an early commitment to the goals of the program by making several noticeable changes in their activities that affected the model neighborhoods. Marshall Kaplan, Gans and Kahn, in their HUD-sponsored evaluation of the initial planning year in eleven cities, found that the proportion of local expenditures going into the model neighborhoods had increased by a small margin in most cases over that year. Further, this evaluation found sustained resident involvement in Model Cities Program planning and also found equal attention being given to social, economic, and environmental problems in

---

[38] Interview with Barney Frank, aide to Mayor Kevin White, Boston, November 11, 1969.
[39] Sundquist and Davis, *Making Federalism Work*, p. 112.
[40] The Urban Institute, "Survey Research Related to the Evaluation of the Model Cities Program: Second Quarterly Progress Report" (Washington, D.C., 1969), pp. 125-149.

the planning process. All three findings constituted departures from past practice in the eleven cities.[41]

That many mayors had made a political commitment to the program was demonstrated when they intervened to prevent the Nixon Administration from diverting program funds to southern school districts. They had rallied earlier in the fall of 1969 to block an attempt by the Office of Management and Budget to cut spending for the program below the level of Congressional appropriations. As noted above, the mayors also blocked a plan to close the Model Cities Program ahead of schedule by folding it into the proposed plan for urban community development revenue sharing.[42]

Local Concentration of Effort

Although Congressional action had ruled out a concentration of federal resources in a limited number of cities, the responses of city governments still held open the possibility of focusing model cities funds within selected neighborhoods where they might make a substantial impact. With national concentration increasingly difficult to achieve, HUD officials used their leverage with the cities to work for local concentration.

The legislation required programs to operate within poverty neighborhoods but did not limit their size: "A city's program would have to be of sufficient magnitude to make a substantial impact on the physical and social problems and to remove or arrest blight and decay in entire sections or neighborhoods. . . ." Similarly, HUD's first program guide to the cities, distributed in December 1966, also did not define a suggested size for the model neighborhood. When early inquiries and informal proposals first reached Washington, however, Assistant Secretary Ralph Taylor and his staff discovered that cities were proposing to select large downtown areas, sometimes including more than 20 percent of the city's total population. In February 1967, Taylor instituted a new policy limiting the model neighborhood to 10 percent of the city's population or 15,000 people—whichever was larger. The reasoning behind this move was twofold: to concentrate program resources and to take political pressure off the mayors to spread the funds to many neighborhoods.[43]

With the change of national administrations, there was a minor erosion of the

[41] HUD, *The Model Cities Program: A Comparative Analysis of the Planning Process in Eleven Cities* (Washington, D.C.: U.S. Government Printing Office, 1970), pp. 57, 61, 62. This report was prepared by the firm of Marshall Kaplan, Gans and Kahn.
[42] Interview with John Sasso, Executive Secretary, Model Cities Directors Association, National League of Cities-U.S. Conference of Mayors, August 22, 1972.
[43] Marshall Kaplan, Gans and Kahn, *Development of the Model Cities Program*, pp. 19-20.

limited concentration that had still been possible with 150 cities and the funds that were available. Although the Nixon Administration did not add more cities to the program, Romney and Hyde eliminated the 10 percent limit on the population size of the model neighborhood in April 1969. Aware of complaints and pressures from neighborhoods that had not been selected, HUD was now prepared to give the mayors greater freedom in defining boundaries. Whether, on balance, the mayors welcomed this freedom or missed the prop that the earlier requirement had given them, it is difficult to know. In any event, they were encouraged not to open their programs to the entire city but to draw somewhat more generous boundaries if that course of action seemed justified. Additions to the model neighborhood still had to meet statutory requirements as poverty areas, and the cities were warned to expect no additional supplemental funds as a result of any boundary expansion.[44]

The Results: Budget Levels and Program Limits

This complicated mix of White House support, Congressional redefinition of the program, and city government acceptance of the major HUD policies set the conditions affecting the flow of federal aid into model neighborhoods. After moving the program away from the earlier idea of national concentration, Congress gave it consistent financial support, despite increasing pressures to hold down domestic spending. Johnson and Weaver originally asked for appropriations of $2.3 billion for model cities over a six-year period. From 1967 through mid-1973, Congress in fact appropriated $2.3 billion in supplemental grants for the program, plus $412.5 million in urban renewal funds earmarked for use with it (see Appendix C).

Although these appropriations honored the original commitment, they had to cover twice the number of cities the Administration originally had in mind. Further, with Congressional and bureaucratic opposition to sending federal dollars from other grant programs into the model neighborhoods, the model cities appropriations had a much smaller total financial impact than the White House and HUD expected. Weaver, in his Congressional testimony, estimated that model cities funds would generate from two to four times as much in additional federal, local, and private resources going into the model neighborhood. The actual

[44] U.S. Congress, Senate, Subcommittee on Housing and Urban Affairs, Committee on Banking and Currency, *Hearing: Progress of the Model Cities Program*, 91st Cong., 1st Sess., June 6, 1969, pp. 21-23.

multiplier, however, according to experience through 1971, was no greater than one and probably less. A survey of the funding generated by the Model Cities Program that was undertaken in March 1971 by the Model Cities Service Center of the National League of Cities-U.S. Conference of Mayors reported supplemental grants of $481 million, other federal and state funds of $375 million, and local contributions of $108 million in 106 cities.[45] And this survey does not distinguish between federal-state projects added to the neighborhood by the Model Cities Program and those slated for the area for other reasons and actually representing only a "maintenance of effort." The massive federal assistance originally promised to participating cities turned out to be "fairy gold," as government officials in Britain characterize funds to be made available some time in the vague future.

Despite these obstacles to national concentration of resources, Taylor's decision to limit the size of locally defined model neighborhoods and the cities' acceptance of his 10 percent limitation effectively magnified the impact of model cities allocations. The Urban Institute's analysis of the first-year budgets for thirty-five cities provided some perspective on the degree of resource concentration that could still be achieved. If these cities had been able to carry out all the projects for which HUD funding was approved, the average program cost per family would have been $497, with categorical grants accounting for 54 percent of the total.[46] The per family figure is greater than the degree of concentration achieved through earlier antipoverty programs, where the most generous community action efforts allocated from $200 to $300 per poverty family, and most allocated far less. The model cities budget average of $497 per family worked out to $121 per capita in the thirty-five cities. In the mid-1960s, average per capita expenditures for all municipal services in the central cities of the thirty-seven largest metropolitan areas were $325.[47] Thus model cities added a boost of about one-third more than the big cities were spending on the average for all public services.

As the Model Cities Program reached nationwide operation, this level of per capita funding seems to have been sustained or increased slightly. By fiscal 1971, virtually all 150 cities had begun their first action year. HUD estimated the population of the model neighborhoods as approximately 6 million people. Alloca-

[45] Model Cities Service Center *Bulletin*, Vol. 2 (June 1971), p. 17.
[46] The Urban Institute, "Survey Research Related to the Evaluation of the Model Cities Program: Second Quarterly Progress Report" (Washington, D.C., 1969), pp. 125-149.
[47] U.S. Advisory Commission on Intergovernmental Relations, *State and Local Finances: Significant Features of 1967 to 1970* (Washington, D.C., 1969), p. 70.

tions of supplemental grants were $503 million in 1971 and an estimated $617.5 million in 1972. For these two years, the average national allocation was $93 per capita. If supplemental funds constituted half the typical model cities budget, program costs were thus $186 per capita. This was not the significant concentration of resources that the Wood task force had in mind, but it was a noticeable boost over usual local government expenditures for the model neighborhoods.

This level of federal aid was enough to pay for new or improved services to model neighborhood residents: educational programs, child care, health services, manpower training, seed money for housing development corporations. It could not cover the much higher costs of major capital facilities or of direct income assistance. Thus the model cities budget had the effect of limiting local programs primarily to what has been termed the "service strategy," which was typical of most of the Great Society programs aimed at helping the poor. Many observers of these programs have strongly condemned the service strategy as an ineffective way of dealing with the problems of poverty. It assumes that poor people can be given help that will equip them to raise their incomes. But service programs for the poor tend to provide only weak and partial assistance against massive problems. Critics have urged instead that public programs deal directly with the problem of poverty by supplementing the incomes of poor people.[48] In this view, once people are relieved of the struggle for existence on a poverty budget, they will be better able to take advantage of job training and other programs that can open doors to regular employment at decent wages.

The "income strategy," which has won increasing acceptance in the federal government as well as among researchers in social policy, costs much more money than service programs. The Nixon Administration's Family Assistance Plan, as presented in 1969, called for a basic federal benefit level of $1,600 per year for a family of four, and to many critics this figure was far too low. Compared with model cities allocations on the order of $500 per family, it implied a level of funding of a totally different order of magnitude. The Family Assistance Plan, with full national coverage, would have cost $4 billion per year on top of another $4.2 billion the federal government was already spending on public assistance.[49]

Even the modest level of appropriations for model cities, on the order of $600

[48] See Lee Rainwater, "The Lessons of Pruitt-Igoe," *The Public Interest*, No. 8 (Summer 1967), pp. 116-126.

[49] Daniel P. Moynihan, *The Politics of a Guaranteed Income* (New York: Vintage Books, 1973), p. 232.

million per year, was maintained only through the repeated efforts of a newly emerging constituency that countered White House reluctance to ask for appropriations.

Model Cities and the Total Urban Aid Budget

The national will to concentrate resources in urban poverty areas has to be measured also against the national will to channel funds to the cities at large, without special reference to poverty groups. Total federal aid to the cities has never been very great. During the Senate debate over the model cities legislation, Senator Fulbright pointed out how small the program's authorizations were in comparison with other federal expenditures.

Day after day, with respect to programs like the one before us, we grudgingly grant money; but the funds provided for in this bill are little more than what the Senate added beyond the requests of the Defense Department in the bill we considered yesterday. We voted over $58 billion to build arms, and yet this bill goes to some of the sources of our trouble.[50]

Senator Ribicoff's well-publicized hearings on the federal role in urban affairs, conducted in 1966, occasioned estimates at that time of how much federal money was going to the cities. According to HUD's analysis, total federal aid to urban areas in 1966 was $28.4 billion, or, excluding the face value of residential mortgage insurance and guarantees, $16.8 billion. These figures were based on very generous assumptions about the impact of federal programs on urban areas and counted in such items as military facility costs, Veterans Administration hospitals, and the cost of federal buildings.[51]

By 1971, federally prepared estimates on spending in urban areas ranged from $19 billion to as much as $44 billion. The high figure once again represented HUD's calculations, counting loan insurance and guarantees at face value and defining all communities over 2,500 as urban. A more realistic view of federal aid to cities, however, ought to exclude the loan insurance and guarantees, as well as federal administrative expenses for programs, funds spent outside the cities that may nevertheless help them (such as flood control projects of the Corps of Engineers), grants to support state agency administration, programs of direct

[50] *Congressional Record*, Senate, August 19, 1966, p. S19170.
[51] U.S. Congress, Senate, Subcommittee on Executive Reorganization, Committee on Government Operations, *Hearings: Federal Role in Urban Affairs*, 89th Cong., 2nd Sess., August 15-16, 1966, Part 1, pp. 178-181.

aid to individuals regardless of residence (Veterans Administration services, public assistance), and numerous others. In a rough attempt to estimate federal aid to urban areas on this more restricted basis, staff members of Floyd Hyde's office figured the total as some $10 billion in 1971.[52] (Hyde circulated this estimate within the Administration in an effort to correct the impression that massive federal aid was going to the cities.) The HUD share of this total was $2.6 billion.

In comparison with either the total urban aid budget or the HUD share of it, model cities expenditures were small. From 1967 through 1972, appropriations averaged approximately $390 million per year: 15 percent of HUD's total urban aid contributions and less than 4 percent of the federal total.

Still another yardstick is provided by general revenue-sharing allocations to state and local governments. President Nixon's original (1969) proposal was to build up to a nationwide distribution of some $5 billion over a six-year period.[53] Treasury Department estimates of how the plan would work showed that even after six years, at the maximum level of revenue sharing, a majority of communities in the Model Cities Program would receive less than under their model cities supplemental grants (see Table 9.1, columns 1 and 2 for illustrative cases). Further, they would not be under a mandate to spend it in poverty neighborhoods. Although a few cities would have fared better under the Administration's revenue-sharing plan, most notably New York, the model cities funding was generally more than substantial in comparison with the revenue-sharing alternative conceived early in the Nixon Administration.

As eventually enacted in 1972, however, general revenue sharing provided for a more generous distribution of funds: $5.3 billion in the first year, and $30.2 billion over a five-year period.[54] Revised allocation formulas also increased the share for city governments. As a result, the first-year entitlements for calendar 1972 were in most cases greater than the first-year model cities grants that had been made in 1969 (see column 3 of table). Typically, the revenue-sharing allocations were about twice as great as the model cities funding—still greater in New York and Philadelphia, but still less than model cities had provided in Atlanta and San Antonio. Yet even where revenue sharing exceeded model cities grants by a factor of two or three, local political pressures could be counted on to

[52] "The Basis for Analysis of Federal Aid Programs for Urban Impact," staff paper, Office of the Assistant Secretary for Model Cities, 1971.
[53] U.S. President, *Message to Congress Proposing a Program for the Sharing of Federal Revenues with the States*, August 13, 1969.
[54] Under the State and Local Fiscal Assistance Act of 1972.

Table 9.1
Federal Grants to Selected Cities under Model Cities and General Revenue Sharing (annual grants in millions of dollars)

City	1 Model Cities First-Year Supplemental Grant[a]	2 Nixon Administration General Revenue-Sharing Proposal[b]	3 Actual General Revenue-Sharing Allocation, 1972[c]
Atlanta	7.2	4.0	6.0
Baltimore	10.6	7.0	23.2
Boston	7.7	10.7	17.4
Chicago	38.2	20.9	61.1
Denver	5.8	5.1	11.6
Detroit	20.5	13.1	35.9
New York	65.0	157.0	198.1
Philadelphia	3.3	21.1	43.1
San Antonio	9.6	2.5	8.3
St. Louis	5.2	7.3	12.2

Sources:
[a]U.S. Department of Housing and Urban Development, Model Cities Administration.

[b]U.S. Department of the Treasury, Office of the Assistant Secretary for Economic Policy, *Federal Revenue Sharing with State and Local Governments: Allocations to Major Counties, Cities and Towns* (July 1970). Figures shown are the maximum allocations, effective during the sixth year of the plan.

[c]"Revenue Sharing Payments: Notice of Allocations," *Federal Register*, Vol. 37, No. 244 (December 19, 1972); and U.S. Department of the Treasury, Office of Revenue Sharing, *2nd Payment: Entitlement Period 2* (Washington, D.C.: U.S. Government Printing Office, 1973). The sum of these two payments covered the period January 1-December 31, 1972.

make far less available for spending in the model neighborhood, which usually represented no more than a tenth of the city's population. Thus the amounts targeted for poverty neighborhoods under model cities remain significant even in comparison with the more recent provisions for general revenue sharing.

If the money spent for model cities was not sufficient to make dramatic living improvements in living conditions or to induce municipal agencies to reorient their programs, the explanation must be partly in the small share of urban aid devoted to model cities and partly in the low level of overall national commitment to the cities. Even if we assume that the model cities appropriations of $390 million per year represented only half of all federal aid to the model neighborhoods, the 6 million residents received far less than more favored, more affluent, and less numerous groups that had established their claims to federal subsidies. Direct cash payments to feed-grain producers totaled some $1.5 billion per year; wheat and cotton producers each received about $900 million. The mineral industries then received federal tax subsidies on the order of $1.3 billion per year in the form of depletion allowances and deductions on exploration and development costs.[55] The entire general revenue-sharing fund of $5 billion per year for all state and local governments was less than the current cost of federal agricultural subsidies.[56] With the pressures against any concentration of funds as strong as they showed themselves to be, the way toward more substantial national commitments to urban poverty areas must involve a substantial increase in the flow of federal resources to the cities at large.

Coping with the Failure of Reform:
Underspending by the Cities

Although evolving relations among the White House, the Congress, and the federal agencies produced reasonable support for concentrated city service programs, the terms on which that support was available still left the cities with formidable problems of management. If the federal government had succeeded in reforming its grant-in-aid system, most cities would have had the administrative capacity to start organizing a wide range of activities in keeping with the program's comprehensive mandate. Funding would have been available on a priority basis without burdensome application and review procedures from any of several federal agencies sponsoring a few hundred grant-in-aid programs.

Instead, the cities were still under a directive to be comprehensive and responsive to the full range of citizen needs, but they had to negotiate their own way through the swampland of complicated and often conflicting federal programs to get the necessary resources. Further, HUD pressed them to combine model cities funds with support from other federal agencies. In addition, they had to contend with HUD's own regulations and reviews, which were a far cry from the simplicity and flexibility model cities was supposed to provide.

The failure of federal aid reform, described in Chapters 4 through 8, left the cities ill equipped to do what was expected of them. As a result, one of the ironies of the model cities experience is that despite the widespread conviction that appropriations were inadequate, the cities proved unable to spend even those funds that were allocated to them. In 1970, actual outlays in the model cities amounted to only 18 percent of the supplemental funds that HUD had

[55] U.S. Congress, Joint Economic Committee, *The Economics of Federal Subsidy Programs*, 92nd Cong., 1st Sess., January 11, 1972, pp. 88-90, 171-172.
[56] Ibid., p. 87.

committed. The rate of actual expenditures increased year by year but in 1972 still equaled only 54 percent of the HUD commitment. In fiscal 1973, HUD expected the rate to reach 75 percent.[57]

A number of reasons explain this slowness of cities to spend their model cities funds. The federal government unquestionably bears prime responsibility. In most cases, cities had to wait many months after the submission of their plans to HUD before they received approval, the contract was signed, and a letter of credit was issued. During the interval, which could last up to eight months, key staff members sometimes left their jobs, residents lost interest, and then new working relationships had to be developed from scratch when the funds became available. Similar delays were created by the lengthy amendment process that HUD required when cities decided to change their plans.

In many cases, the cities failed to develop detailed project plans when they filed their proposals with HUD. Without such detailed plans in hand, they were later unable to negotiate with the local operating agencies that were to carry out model cities projects under contract. Sometimes, too, detailed plans had to be reviewed by citizen groups as they were developed, which could cause fresh delays.

In some cases, the cities were tied up in their own cumbersome administrative procedures, which made it impossible to set new projects in motion without lengthy local government reviews. A study of the reasons why New York City was able to spend only half of its first-year model cities grant of $65 million revealed many horror stories, among them the following: purchasing a piece of equipment required 71 specific actions by 10 city agencies; hiring a person required 56 steps by 5 different agencies; a contract could not be signed until 12 agencies had examined the papers in 17 different steps.[58]

Another frequent source of delay was provided by the complexity of mixing supplemental grants with categorical funds from other federal programs. With HUD encouragement, the cities planned to mix funds in support of local projects. After they had received their HUD commitment, many cities found, however, that they had missed funding deadlines for other programs, that their plans were not sufficiently developed or in the proper format for consideration by other federal agencies, or that they did not have high enough priority to get the

[57] HUD, *Justification for 1973 Estimates: Community Development*, prepared for House of Representatives Committee on Appropriations (February 1972), p. B-8.
[58] "$65 Million U.S. Slum Aid Snarled in City Red Tape," *New York Times*, November 11, 1971, p. 1; "Lindsay Defends Model-Cities Aid," *New York Times*, November 12, 1971, p. 1.

grant they needed. HUD would not allow a city to spend supplemental funds on a jointly funded project until there was a firm commitment that the other support would be forthcoming.

In addition, the recalcitrant city agencies, which Mayor White's aide had mentioned, often had to be brought in as local programs moved into operation. Then the limited authority of the mayor and the model cities agency became all too evident. The lure of generous federal funding from categorical programs as well as from HUD had been expected to overcome agency resistance. But the federal failure to deliver a coordinated interagency response, detailed in Chapter 5, meant that the carrot was a good deal less appetizing than HUD and the mayors had anticipated. Parallel dramas were being played out in Washington and in the cities. HUD was failing to bring in the resources of the other federal agencies; correspondingly, the model cities agencies were failing to bring in the municipal agencies whose funding pipelines ran directly back to the other federal departments.

By 1971, Roland Warren's study of organizational behavior in the Model Cities Program had pushed him to harsh conclusions.

The [local] agencies concerned themselves with Model Cities principally for two related purposes: to prevent any threat to their own domains and their own viability, and, where possible, to benefit from the program by increasing their budgets or enlarging their domains. That is the nature of all organizations. To expect them to do otherwise is like expecting human beings voluntarily to stop breathing. . . . if we had been serious about it, we would have needed a budget at least four times as large. That would have been the minimum for the program to have a serious possibility of making some appreciable impact.[59]

No simple conclusion can be reached about the ability of the cities to spend federal funds effectively on the problems of poverty neighborhoods. Large numbers of them applied to participate in the Model Cities Program; both their plans and their planning arrangements were consistent with the purposes of the program. Along the way, the mayors endured many local controversies with citizen groups and undoubtedly paid a political price for their support of the program. They became increasingly active and effective in protecting the program in Washington. But their commitment was slow to produce tangible results. The cities, like the federal government, and partly because of the federal government, could not reorient their own agencies quickly enough. Perhaps what the program offered was sufficient incentive to win mayoral commitments but not sufficient

[59] Roland Warren, "The Model Cities Program: An Assessment," *Social Welfare Forum, 1971* (New York: Columbia University Press, 1971), pp. 153-154.

incentive and federal reform to make the new commitment meaningful through prompt local action.

Reform, Redistribution, and the Future

In retrospect, the model cities experience does give evidence of a continuing if limited national commitment to the goals of the program. At the White House, the Nixon Administration was clearly less supportive than the Johnson Administration had been, but the basic commitments were nevertheless kept. Despite reservations, President Nixon retained the program, was about as successful as his predecessor in earmarking funds from other federal programs, and eventually spent model cities funds at a rate that was consistent with the target figures the Johnson Administration had originally given to Congress. Efforts from within the White House to divert funds from model cities or to close the program prematurely were reversed as interest group pressures made themselves felt. The latter experience does not attest to unwavering commitment within the White House but rather to the fact that White House commitments reflect a political context. This context of interest group politics was sufficient to maintain the program. Beyond that, it could not generate the degree of interest in the White House that would have been required to bring about massive changes in the federal aid system. Neither Johnson nor Nixon gave the program the massive support needed for that end, but both used limited leverage on the federal departments.

Congress did not support the original conception of model cities as an experimental program to concentrate resources in a small number of cities. They redefined it to make it a national program, doubling the number of cities at once and making plans to increase the number still further in the future. But having reshaped it in this way, Congress was willing to support it over the years and to keep the faith in terms of appropriations. There was no evidence of Congressional willingness to channel funds from other federal aid sources into local Model Cities Programs as an established priority, and considerable evidence to the contrary. Thus the Congressional commitment was largely to a conception of model cities as another categorical program rather than as a device for reforming other grants-in-aid.

Within the federal bureaucracies, the program had both its dedicated friends and its dedicated enemies. A sequence of HUD Secretaries and other officials fought ably on behalf of the program. Similarly, the HEW Center for Community Planning and a number of officials in the Budget Bureau gave consistent and effective support to the program. The change of Administration, with resultant changes in personnel, did not alter or even interrupt the commitment from these key sectors of the federal bureaucracy. Neither did they have much impact in changing the coolness or hostility with which the program was regarded by other federal agencies whose cooperation was sought.

The mayors of participating cities played a significant role in maintaining a national commitment. Acting mainly through the National League of Cities-U.S. Conference of Mayors, they protected the program against a number of threats and came to the rescue when funding was in jeopardy. Local citizen groups also supported it but were less influential than the mayors.

In short, there was enough continuing support for the program to justify the assertion that the national commitment was kept. That commitment, however, was to a series of objectives that corresponded only roughly to the original purposes of the program. One purpose had been to concentrate federal resources in neglected urban poverty neighborhoods, particularly those where blacks and other minorities lived. Although this commitment to help the poor and the minorities was kept, less and less was said about it over the years. The model neighborhoods were predominantly poor and predominantly minority, but, increasingly, the program was presented as one to help "cities." On top of this, the concentration of federal resources that had originally been intended was watered down by the spread of the program to twice the number of cities and then by the failure to earmark a significant amount of money from other federal aid programs. Further, the cities proved unable to spend even these limited funds as quickly as they became available.

A second underlying purpose of the program had been to reform the federal grant-in-aid system by making it more responsive to local priorities, more flexible, and more subject to control by local elected officials. The White House showed continuing interest in this conception of the program, as did HUD officials. Over the years, federal descriptions of the program came to emphasize its goals of decentralizing responsibility to the cities, building city competence, and advancing the New Federalism. And to most other members of the supporting coalition, grant-in-aid reform was an important purpose. But it was also a source of continuing opposition from those federal agencies responsible for administering the categorical programs. To the extent that efforts to redirect the categorical programs spanned both the Johnson and Nixon Administrations, the commitment was kept. But because of the reluctance of other federal agencies to go along, the results showed only the most marginal progress. The Nixon Administration had its own strong commitment to this goal, which was independent of the Model Cities Program, and it soon moved toward revenue sharing as a more promising approach to accomplish its ends.

To a pessimist, the model cities experience may indicate that the country had just enough commitment to its purposes to mount a halfhearted program that could not possibly produce impressive results. To an optimist, the experience may indicate that there is a sufficient base of national concern for both a more equitable distribution of resources to the poor and for the reform of the federal aid system to sustain other and less quixotic approaches in the future.

Chapter 10
Epilogue: Back to the Drawing Board

The gap between promise and performance was conspicuously large in the Model Cities Program. Looking toward future federal efforts to cope with the problems of cities, we consider it important to distinguish among three different sources of shortcomings in the program. Some faults arose from flaws in the initial conception and design, such as the failure to investigate statutory and funding limitations in other grant-in-aid programs that were expected to be readily available for use in the model neighborhoods. Others arose from ineptness in administration, such as the imposition of unrealistic and counterproductive planning requirements on the cities. Still others, however, resulted from the nature of the federal government itself, the behavior of its executive departments, and the politics of its grant-in-aid system.

Designers of future programs may conceivably be smarter and more thorough than the Wood task force, and administrators of future programs may conceivably be more sophisticated and adroit than the successive teams that guided the Model Cities Program within HUD. If so, perhaps they can avoid some of the errors in design and implementation that plagued the model cities effort. But no matter how clever the designers and administrators, they will still have to deal with the formidable and deep-seated factors that shape the behavior of federal agencies. These factors, in our opinion, will continue to set sharp limits on what the federal government can accomplish. Giving them proper recognition will mean inventing a strategy quite different from that of the Model Cities Program.

Last of the Grand Designs?

The Wood task force, President Johnson, and top officials at HUD all promised to bring together massive federal resources for a concerted series of demonstrations that would meet the complex needs of people living in poverty neighborhoods. When the time came, neither HUD nor the White House was able to deliver on this promise. Too many hands controlled the federal resources. From the outset, the designers of the Model Cities Program knew that the necessary components would have to be assembled from separate executive agencies, each subject to the claims of different constituents and different Congressional committees. But they assumed that the White House had sufficient power to find the resources and to give strong central direction to the entire federal establishment.

The power of the White House turned out to be unexpectedly limited. Its ability to cajole and persuade reluctant Congressmen to vote for the Model Cities Program proved far superior to its ability to move reluctant federal administrators to support model cities policies. Funds appropriated for other grant-in-aid programs were simply out of the range of White House staff members, whose phone calls rarely reached beyond generating admonitions or memos from departmental secretaries to staff deep in the bureaucracy. The latter were well protected by civil service regulations, by detailed, often obscure statutory and administrative criteria governing their "own" programs, and by the support of strong constituencies likely to outlast any occupant of the White House.

Even the clear interest of so powerful a political leader as Lyndon Johnson was not enough to produce a unified federal response. One might conclude that the answer to problems of urban poverty is a still greater concentration of power in the White House, so that a future President can intervene more effectively on behalf of the poor. But after Watergate and after Vietnam, the dangers of excessive White House power are all too obvious. The most likely prospect for the future is that authority will continue to be dispersed within the federal government and among the levels of government in the federal system. The White House, as before, will surely be able to step in from time to time to put out fires or to resolve disputes in domestic programs, but continued effective surveillance to maintain a unified policy seems as unlikely as ever. Even if an expansion of Presidential power were politically feasible and desirable on other grounds, however, our analysis of the institutional constraints involved suggests that it would be of only marginal value to domestic efforts such as model cities.

Out of Partisanship—Unity?

If the White House cannot harness the federal system to make it work consistently toward a defined strategy for the cities, what about the prospect for accomplishing the same purpose through direct interagency negotiations? Downs's theories of bureaucracy, noted in Chapter 1, suggested some of the likely patterns of agency behavior. Lindblom went a step further and contended that agencies pursuing their own interests can nevertheless arrive at joint decisions that are helpful, reasonable, and wise through a process of "partisan mutual adjustment."

The Model Cities Administration and the top leadership of HUD did not follow a consistent strategy for handling interdependencies among federal agencies. At times, particularly early in the program, HUD officials pursued what Anthony Downs termed the "superman style"; that is, they made comprehensive proposals that gave minimal attention to the conflicting interests and probable behavior of other affected bureaus. But when results were not forthcoming, they switched readily to the "shrinking violet" syndrome, narrowing their own purposes and actions so as to affect fewer external agencies. MCA officials and the top HUD leadership sometimes took different stances simultaneously, until the third or fourth year of the Nixon Administration, when almost everyone concerned with model cities followed the shrinking violet approach. Congress, in turn, reflected precisely the ambivalence about bureaucracies that Downs depicted, in restricting HUD's ability to coordinate the programs of other agencies. Members of Congress wanted to see improved coordination among urban programs, but at the same time they feared a concentration of power within any single executive agency. As a result, they refused HUD even the modest device of an office of the federal coordinator for each of the participating model cities; and they stated their intention to permit no change in the priorities or operations of other grant-in-aid programs, at the same time that they called on the Secretary of HUD to find some way to secure the interagency coordination necessary for the success of model cities.

Within this confused but typical federal context, HUD's real powers were chiefly those of persuasion in its negotiations with other federal agencies. Lindblom's analysis of these negotiations as instances of partisan mutual adjustment is accurate as a description, but his normative judgment of how productive they can be bears no resemblance to the actual outcome. The results showed far more partisanship than mutuality or adjustment. Concerted actions among agencies were rare, and protracted efforts to obtain earmarking of grant funds brought only marginal success. Attempts at joint policy making to rechannel federal aid for the model neighborhoods, simplify grant application procedures, review city plans, and provide technical assistance were no more successful. The meetings of the established interagency groups—the WIC (Washington Interagency Committee) and the RICCs (Regional Interagency Coordinating Committees)—had a depressing quality of futility that is difficult to capture in words. At a low point in the deliberations of the Banfield task force on model cities, after several informants had described the dismal nature of these meetings, one task force member broke the silence with the announcement that he had just been gripped by a terrible fear that after his death he might be reincarnated as a member of an RICC or a WIC.

Several explanations can be advanced for the failure of partisan mutual adjustment to lead to unified action. The agency negotiators themselves were highly constrained by circumstances that blocked ready compromise: statutory restrictions on the operation of their programs, weak control from Washington over the operations of field offices, and above all the politics of the grant-in-aid programs. The redistributive goals of model cities meant that HUD was continually, if implicitly, asking other agencies to divert some resources from their traditional clients to a new constituency of the urban poor. These requests went against the grain of normal agency behavior, Congressional grant-in-aid politics, and ultimate reliance for support on established interest groups that benefited from existing programs.

Added to these already compelling factors was the lack of a consensus on effective strategies for dealing with the perplexing problems of urban poverty. Without any underlying agreement on objectives or priorities, movement toward unified action was even more difficult. The Wood task force was concerned with finding solutions to problems of urban poverty; and HUD officials were subsequently concerned with advancing the particular solutions embodied in the Model Cities Programs. But the other negotiators were more likely to concern themselves with defending the claims of their existing clients, protecting their own control over programs, and advancing their careers within established bureaucracies. Few were overtly hostile to model cities; some were even sympathetic but unable to do much to help; and most pursued their own interests under a veneer of cooperation.

Thus Lindblom's partisan mutual adjustment was no more productive of a coordinated, unified strategy for the cities than was the central direction attempted by the White House. In both cases, the reasons are deep seated and unlikely to change in the near future. The national motto, *E pluribus unum*, simply does not apply to relations among federal agencies.

Yet the notion of concentrated, coordinated, unified policies to solve domestic problems dies hard. As recently as 1971, the federal Environmental Protection Agency gave serious consideration to a Model River Program, which called for the coordination and concentration of the country's antipollution efforts to clean up a single river as a demonstration of what might be achieved through a massive combination of money and talent.[1] Wisely, the idea was dropped. Even more recently, critics have pointed to the lack of consistency and coordination in fields such as energy supply and nutrition and have called for unified federal efforts behind a single strategy.

If the designers of future urban policies take away any single lesson from mod-

[1] "U.S. Kills Its Own Cleanup Plan for the Passaic River in Jersey," *New York Times*, September 5, 1971, p. 26.

el cities, it should be to avoid grand schemes for massive, concerted federal action. Setting aside the notion of a tightly unified federal approach, however, does not rule out other constructive measures more consistent with political and bureaucratic realities. In this concluding chapter, we propose less grandiose ways of continuing to help the urban poor within the framework of the federal aid inventory as it exists today.

The Current Federal Aid Inventory

Despite widespread disillusionment with both the promises and performance of the Great Society, domestic federal programs have continued to grow in both variety and dollar volume. Designers of future federal urban policy have a richer starting base than the inventors of model cities did in 1965. Yet few recent analysts have reviewed the contemporary federal inventory to consider how it can be adjusted to meet the continuing needs of those who remain disadvantaged. The main components of this still evolving collection of aids consist of income support programs for individuals, general revenue sharing, special revenue sharing, and the remaining categorical programs.

Income Provision

The War on Poverty began in 1964 with programs that stressed the provision of services and the initiation of efforts to organize and mobilize the poor. Within a few years, the limitations of this "service strategy" became increasingly evident, and reformers turned their attention to finding ways of remedying income deficiencies. Both the Johnson and the Nixon Administrations took steps to improve the operation of the chaotic welfare system. Although a grand design to replace public welfare with a family assistance plan failed during the Nixon Administration, partial reforms were implemented.[2] The federal government now provides uniform income assistance (supplemental security income) for the elderly, the blind, and the disabled; state governments supplement this aid with their own resources. Families with dependent children still remain under the earlier system of federal-state public assistance grants, which continue at or below minimum subsistence levels in many states. The net effect of these changes has been to provide more uniform and more adequate income for those poor who are outside the labor force.

[2] See Daniel P. Moynihan, *The Politics of A Guaranteed Income* (New York: Random House Vintage Books, 1973).

During the same period of time, federal provision of other cash and in-kind benefits has expanded considerably in such fields as medical care payments, food stamps, student aid, child care, and housing subsidies. In the latter field, an unprecedented growth in the volume of federally assisted housing was terminated abruptly after 1972, but the Administration has begun to move tentatively toward a system of direct cash payments to the poor for housing expenses.

Thus, although the ideal of a single system for federal income guarantees has eluded the reformers, a piecemeal collection of income and in-kind grants now deals more adequately with the income deficiency of the poor than was the case in 1965; but there are still many inequities in the system, and income transfers to families with dependent children remain low.

General Revenue Sharing

In 1972, Congress enacted a major component of President Nixon's New Federalism with the passage of the State and Local Fiscal Assistance Act. Under its terms, the Treasury Department will provide $30 billion to state and local governments over a five-year period. These general revenue-sharing allocations are virtually free of federal strings and can be used for tax relief or to fund any of the normal local government activities. For most cities, as noted earlier, the annual allocation is at least as great as model cities grants, and it applies to every local government in the country.

Special Revenue Sharing

Paralleling general revenue sharing, President Nixon's New Federalism also placed great emphasis on a series of special revenue-sharing measures to give state and local governments considerable flexibility in spending federal grants within broad functional categories of activities. An important forerunner of this concept was the Partnership for Health Program, enacted in 1966, which offered flexible block grants in place of a series of earlier categorical public health grants. The Nixon Administration's proposals were to consolidate existing categorical grants in urban community development, rural development, education, manpower, transportation, and law enforcement. The resulting special revenue-sharing grants were to be usable for any of the activities formerly covered by the consolidated categorical aids; some federal regulation was still to be maintained but far less than in the categorical programs.

Of the six proposals, two were enacted by the time of this writing: special revenue sharing for manpower in 1973 and community development revenue sharing, which was included within the Housing and Community Development Act of 1974. The community development measure, which has greatest relevance to this discussion, encompasses the Model Cities Program; urban renewal; grants for water and sewer projects, open space, urban beautification, historic preservation, and neighborhood facilities; and loans for public facilities and for housing rehabilitation—all formerly administered as separate HUD programs. Thus the measure contains essential components of any new strategy for improving disadvantaged urban neighborhoods.

Special revenue sharing for community development incorporates four potential advances over the separate programs that preceded it. First, it offers far greater flexibility in the uses of federal funds to meet local needs. The new grants are usable for the same range of purposes as the categorical programs they replace, but the local community can draw upon a single block grant for any of these purposes instead of applying for separate project allocations restricted to specific uses. A second source of flexibility results from the elimination of prior requirements for local matching shares in each project. Third, the administrative regulations are considerably simplified: a single application and review process replaces seven sets of complicated and extensive program requirements. Finally, aid allocations are based on a statutory formula using three measures of need. This allocation method should offer greater predictability of future budgets, as well as greater equity among communities, than the former reliance on the vagaries of grantsmanship ability and political influence.

The allocation arrangements, however, present problems as well as advantages. If Congress appropriates the full amount authorized by law, funds available for new commitments will remain at about the same level as the total for the previous community development programs in 1972 and 1973.[3] Increases to the maximum authorized level of $3.0 billion dollars by 1976 and 1977 will barely keep pace with current rates of inflation. So the total federal aid budget for community development will remain about what it was in the recent past; but it will be divided differently.

[3] New commitments for these programs were $2.47 billion in fiscal 1972 and $2.36 billion in fiscal 1973. See Barry M. Blechman, Edward M. Gramlich, and Robert W. Hartman, *Setting National Priorities: The 1975 Budget* (Washington, D.C.: Brookings Institution, 1974), p. 38. Total disbursement limitations for community development revenue sharing are $2.55 billion for fiscal 1975, $3.0 billion for 1976, and $3.05 billion for 1977. See U.S. Congress, House Subcommittee on Housing of the Committee on Banking and Currency, *Directory of Recipients: Housing and Community Development Act of 1974*, 93rd Cong., 2nd Sess., 1974, pp. 1-2.

Unlike general revenue sharing, the funds will not be spread to all 38,000 units of general state and local government in the country. Instead, they will be concentrated in about 500 "metropolitan cities" (central cities and other cities with a population of 50,000 or more within metropolitan areas) and some 50 "urban counties."[4] These communities will be entitled to formula allocations, provided they meet program requirements. Other state and local general government units are eligible to apply for limited funds remaining after the metropolitan cities and urban counties receive their formula grants.

The formula itself takes into account population, overcrowded housing, and the extent of poverty, with the poverty factor given double weight. Many cities— particularly those that have been aggressive consumers of federal aid—will be entitled to substantially less under the formula than they have been accustomed to receiving. During the first three years, additional funds will be provided above the formula entitlements to maintain the average level of funding these communities have had for the past five years under the prior categorical programs. Subsequently, these transitional awards will be reduced and then eliminated after fiscal 1979. Although transitional grants will cushion the shock, the fact remains that the flow of federal aid for urban development activities will change drastically as a result of special revenue sharing.

Cities both large and small that have given high priority to community development programs and have been winners in the competition for federal aid, will sustain deep cuts in their allocations, while other communities will be eligible for major increases in federal aid. Congressional estimates, assuming a continued level of appropriations at $3.0 billion from 1976 through 1980, show a new pattern of federal aid flowing to the various regions of the country as well as to individual cities. In Connecticut, total aid to eligible communities will be cut in half from 1975 to 1980, while Massachusetts cities will have their aid cut by a third.[5] Nevada communities, in total, will see a fourfold increase in federal aid; Puerto Rico will increase its aid two and a half times; and aid will double in Arizona, Florida, Louisiana, Nebraska, Nevada, South Carolina, and Utah.

Among the individual cities, the big losers include New Haven, which will be cut by 80 percent from 1975 to 1980, and Akron, Boston, Minneapolis, and Washington, D.C., which will all be cut by approximately two-thirds. The big

---

[4] U.S. Congress, House Subcommittee on Housing of the Committee on Banking and Currency, *Compilation of the Housing and Community Development Act of 1974*, 93rd Cong., 2nd Sess., 1974, p. 355.
[5] State totals and city estimates from House Subcommittee on Housing, *Directory of Recipients*.

winners include Miami, Omaha, and Phoenix, which will receive six to seven times as much aid in 1980 as in 1975, and Memphis, which will get two and a half times as much. Among the largest cities, New York will get an increase of 60 percent, Chicago 50 percent, and Los Angeles 30 percent; while Baltimore, Cleveland, Detroit, Philadelphia, Pittsburgh, and San Francisco (in addition to Boston and Washington) will all lose substantially, and St. Louis will stay about the same. A by-product of greater fairness in distribution, then, will be less federal aid for community development in most of the largest and oldest of the hard-pressed central cities, which used to command a disproportionate share of whatever was available. While these communities are struggling to adjust to cutbacks, many other cities will have to build new administrative and political capacities to spend their rapidly growing budgets for urban development.

Although the law is very specific in controlling the allocation of funds among cities, it provides no comparable requirements for the distribution of aid within cities. It does contain vague and general criteria to encourage the use of special revenue sharing for low- and moderate-income groups and to cope with the problems of slums, but monitoring will be difficult. There is no formula requiring measurable concentrations of resources for the urban poor. The likely impact of current program requirements in community development revenue sharing is discussed more fully later in this chapter.

Remaining Categorical Grants

General revenue sharing was enacted with the understanding that it would supplement and not replace existing categorical programs. Subsequent impoundment of grant funds by the Office of Management and Budget and the imposition of a moratorium on housing subsidy programs raised serious questions about Administration intentions on this score. Nevertheless, expenditures for categorical aid programs have continued to increase, and taken together they amount to a far greater share of the federal budget than general revenue sharing. The major categorical programs, dating from the early 1960s, were continued and even expanded under the Nixon Administration. Although individual cities suffered from cutbacks, the total volume grew from $1.7 billion in 1963 to an estimated $35.7 billion in 1973. Of the 1973 total, $20 billion went for direct aid to individuals in cash or services, while the remaining $16 billion represented grants to state and local government.[6]

[6] Charles L. Schultze, Edward R. Fried, Alice M. Rivlin, and Nancy H. Teeters, *Setting National Priorities: The 1973 Budget* (Washington, D.C.: Brookings Institution, 1972), p. 11.

Even if Congress acts promptly to consolidate a number of these programs into special revenue-sharing grants, the remaining volume of categorical programs will be too great to ignore. Designers of future urban policies should continue efforts to improve the administration of these programs and to direct their resources into the areas of greatest need, particularly the slum neighborhoods of cities.

Are the Goals of Model Cities Still Valid?

During the 1960s, problems of the urban poor and minority groups had high visibility. Since then, the public and the communications media have revealed a short attention span for any problems that cannot be solved in a few years. As a mood of disenchantment settled over the unmet promises of the Great Society, many people began to question not only the effectiveness of federal programs but also the worthiness of their objectives. Poverty neighborhoods and their problems no longer hold center stage in most current discussions of national priorities.

Yet the needs that model cities addressed are still largely unmet and still responsible for denying millions of people the chance to live in a decent environment with reasonable access to social and economic opportunity. The poverty population has barely diminished since the mid-1960s. According to conservative federal definition, the number of people below the poverty level declined only from 28.5 million in 1966 to 24.5 million in 1972. Further, very little of that modest decline has occurred in recent years: between 1968 and 1972, the number of people in poverty dropped by less than one million.[7]

Although the incidence of poverty is relatively unchanged, it is still relevant to consider whether recent changes in federal policy are likely to achieve the purposes of the model cities through other means. To a casual observer, the growth of income transfer programs and of in-kind benefits might appear to do away with the need for efforts such as model cities. But this conclusion can result only from a misreading of the purposes of the Model Cities Program. It was never intended to address the problem of insufficient income; neither its funding levels nor its methods of operation provided for direct cash transfers to poor families. To meet the problems of inadequate environments and inadequate public services, it aimed at a redistribution of public resources, not private incomes. Income strategies are at least as important and may well deserve higher priority, but they

[7] Blechman, Gramlich, Hartman, *Setting National Priorities*, p. 167.

deal with different needs. Income transfers still do not permit disadvantaged families to buy public goods or community services; these must be provided primarily by local government, and model cities attempted to redirect municipal expenditures to help close the gap in services and community facilities between poverty neighborhoods and the rest of the city. Differences between income and service approaches should not, however, obscure the pressing need for public action on both fronts. Although our own recommendations deal with policies for community development and public services, we believe concurrent action should be taken to improve the system of cash transfers to the poor, either through a guaranteed annual income or through a rationalization and extension of the present series of cash and in-kind programs.

There is one sense in which income strategies could conceivably reduce the need for attention to slum neighborhoods. If the poor were able to raise their income by a substantial amount, they might be able to move to better neighborhoods that already receive a fair share of municipal resources. Many families have, in fact, been able to move away from the worst inner city neighborhoods, which have been experiencing absolute losses in population accompanied in some cases by the abandonment of older housing. But very large numbers of people continue to live in these neighborhoods, and even if current rates of out-migration persist, major concentrations of the poor will remain there for years to come. For these people, federal and state income support programs do not provide enough to cover the higher cost of housing in better areas, and the increasing instances of abandonment only add further decay to their present environment.

Thus the deterioration of poverty neighborhoods has become still more striking in recent years than it was earlier. In New York, some analysts have observed that the city no longer has a housing shortage; it now has a neighborhood shortage. Whole neighborhoods have been neglected to the point where they are basically unlivable, even though some of the housing within them is still of reasonable quality. The more mobile residents have already left, but a majority stay on because they have no alternative.

Although New York is one of the more extreme examples, similar trends are in evidence in many parts of the country. Even new housing built under federal subsidy programs has run into a great deal of trouble because of adverse neighborhood conditions. Where the neighborhood setting itself is substandard, new rental projects have had high vacancy rates and other management problems, and low-income homeowners have been abandoning subsidized houses. Under these conditions, the provision of modest income supplements, whether in cash or as housing subsidies, can accomplish little toward meeting the country's social housing objectives. Those who argue the case for utilizing income or cash assistance strategies as the solution to low-income housing problems are giving fresh attention to the need for concomitant action to improve living conditions in older neighborhoods. If the Administration proceeds to develop a national program of direct cash assistance for housing, it will be necessary to reinvent something similar to model cities as a way of providing decent community services and rehabilitating the neighborhoods where poor people are most likely to spend their housing dollars.[8]

Are Other Programs Replacing Model Cities?

If income maintenance strategies cannot cope with the problems that gave rise to model cities, are other federal programs doing anything to supply the resources that model cities failed to deliver? The evidence does not permit a firm judgment on this score but it suggests very strongly that the answer is "no."

Among the categorical grant-in-aid programs, the most relevant are those that provide assistance for community development—the physical equipment of cities—and for education and manpower, which provide key services for low-income groups. Although federal expenditures for these programs have generally increased since the 1960s, their growth has been curtailed during the past few years. Measured in terms of current outlays, education grants alone have risen consistently since 1972 at a rate sufficient to keep pace with inflation. Community development outlays dropped in 1973 below the 1972 level, although a slight increase was anticipated for fiscal 1974. In the case of manpower, grant expenditures in 1974 and 1975 were expected to fall below the levels of 1972 and 1973. Current outlays, however, reflect appropriations and commitments made in the past. By a more significant measure, new obligations incurred, there will be reductions in federal activity in all three areas between 1973 and 1975. As of 1974, absolute reductions in new obligations were anticipated for community development and manpower, while the increase estimated for education was less than the amount needed to keep pace with inflation.[9]

These current cutbacks in federal grant programs almost certainly mean that

[8] See Arthur P. Solomon, *Housing the Urban Poor* (Cambridge, Mass.: M.I.T. Press, 1974), pp. 194-197.
[9] Blechman, Gramlich, and Hartman, *Setting National Priorities*, pp. 34-41.

fewer resources are being made available to the urban poor for the kinds of activities that model cities attempted to support. The only way the poor could be receiving more at a time of budgetary restriction would be if program administrators have been diverting funds from their customary clients outside poverty areas in favor of new low-income recipients. Everything we have learned about federal agency behavior during the implementation of the Model Cities Program indicates that this possibility is too remote for even hypothetical consideration.

Aside from categorical programs, the other possible federal replacements for model cities are general revenue sharing and special revenue sharing for community development. In the case of general revenue sharing, the evidence is very difficult to gather. Revenue-sharing dollars can be substituted for local revenues at will, so that a city can, for example, reduce its own expenditures on services for the poor by $100,000, replace these funds with $100,000 of revenue-sharing money, transfer the money it has saved to renovate a riding stable for the wealthy, and report that its revenue-sharing allocation has gone to services for the poor. To complicate matters further, city reporting of revenue-sharing expenditures is generally in categories that say nothing about who received the benefits. A reported use of revenue sharing for "capital expenditures," for instance, could mean anything from school construction in an affluent neighborhood to the purchase of a new garbage truck to improve sanitation services in the slums.

One persuasive survey, which covered cities with populations over 50,000 during the spring of 1973, found that cities generally reported spending their revenue-sharing allocations in a pattern similar to that of their normal budgetary decisions. As an indicator of spending for the poor, the survey found that cities reported spending only 1.6 percent of their new funds for social services for the poor and aged, and only 1.1 percent for health services; in all, they reported spending a slightly smaller proportion of revenue-sharing funds for health and welfare needs than was the case in their normal expenditure pattern.[10] A more extensive Treasury Department analysis, covering expenditures in some 33,000 units of government through June 1973, reported a similar finding that only 3

[10] David A. Caputo and Richard L. Cole, "The Initial Impact of Revenue Sharing On The Spending Patterns of American Cities," paper presented at the annual meeting of the Southern Political Science Association, 1973, p. 10, cited in Jeffrey L. Pressman, "Political Implications of the New Federalism," paper prepared for the Metropolitan Governance Research Committee, Resources for the Future/Academy for Contemporary Problems, Columbus, Ohio, May 17, 1974, p. 16.

percent of revenue-sharing funds went for social services for the poor and aged.[11]

The annual revenue-sharing allocations to cities are great enough, as has been noted, to permit most of them to continue funding model cities activities at the same levels as provided in the past by the model cities grants. But to do so would require city governments to concentrate a disproportionate share of their new funds in the model neighborhood—an unlikely event, in view of typical political pressures to spread budgetary resources to many different neighborhoods and particularly to take care of the best-organized and most influential local groups.

In our judgment, neither general revenue sharing nor the categorical grant programs are replacing model cities, nor are they likely to do so in the near future. If the federal government is to honor even a limited commitment to meet the needs of urban poverty areas, it will have to find a different approach. The potential contribution of special revenue sharing for community development is discussed later in this chapter. As presently established, it, too, is not likely to do the job. With appropriate changes, however, it could be the central component of a strategy for assisting the urban poor.

Redirecting the Current Federal Inventory

Dealing with the complex problems of urban poverty and blighted neighborhoods must be a continuing responsibility of government, not one to be completed by any single program. Strategies to assist the urban poor therefore must be woven into the many separate activities of government that have an impact on living conditions and economic opportunities. Experience with the Model Cities Program can help define an approach drawing on the federal aid inventory as it exists today. Unfortunately, very few people, either in the federal government or outside, appear to be considering the relevance of each of the current forms of federal aid either to one another or to the total inventory. As a result, important opportunities to use the system to meet national commitments may well slip away unnoticed. In the late 1970s, we may still be searching for effective federal strategies for the cities, while the new forms of aid each develop an independent life that will make them less flexible and more resistant to change than they are at the present time.

[11] National Clearinghouse on Revenue Sharing, *Revenue Sharing Clearinghouse*, May-June, 1974, p. 2.

Model cities itself had much in common with the newer forms of federal aid, both general and special revenue sharing. It loosened the federal strings on grants-in-aid and was an early step toward the deregulation of categorical programs, which has been the dominant trend since then. But model cities showed that deregulation did not have to lead to the abandonment of national objectives. The blockages it encountered revealed a number of political requirements that must be met to achieve effective programming, both at the national and the local level. Congress demonstrated a willingness to maintain a steady if limited flow of appropriations for the urban poor, provided that these funds were spread to a large number of cities across the country. The nation's mayors came forward repeatedly as a constituency committed to the program and to its major purposes, provided that their political needs were also taken into account.

Model cities also showed the way toward a style of federal administration and review that could reconcile local flexibility with national purposes. Although the federal reviews in the Model Cities Program were far too burdensome in relation to what they accomplished, they did move the cities into action on the issues that mattered most: defining project boundaries to include the poor and disadvantaged minority groups, concentrating available federal and local resources within these areas, strengthening the role of the mayor, and giving the residents a voice in planning and operating the projects that affected them. It should now be possible, through less cumbersome federal administration, to establish a better balance between national purposes and local freedom and effectiveness.

At the same time, model cities confirmed that further attention is needed to bolster the mayors' political ability to help the poor, improve the capacity of local governments to manage complex programs, and to strengthen mayoral control over federal resources going into their cities. The key to strategic use of the present aid system is an understanding of the mayors' situation. They are under pressure to spread available resources among many neighborhoods and many groups: the need to distribute aid broadly is as much a fact of local political life as it is in Congress. If the mayors are to give special attenion to the poor out of proportion to their political strength, they need special justification. One form of this justification can be the provision of additional and substantial resources that mayors can use flexibly to take care of their other constituents who also have legitimate needs. Another form can be a federal requirement that makes certain aid available only if a major share goes to poverty areas.

Our study of the model cities experience indicated that many mayors willingly accepted the requirement that program funds were to be used for poverty neighborhoods. This restriction actually permitted them additional freedom of maneuver when they wished to do something for the poor and the blacks, because they did not have to take the full political heat for such a decision. In effect, the federal government shared responsibility with the mayors for a politically troublesome act. This insight was confirmed subsequently when the U.S. Conference of Mayors pointed to the lack of such a requirement as one of its major objections to the Nixon Administration's proposal for community development revenue sharing. The mayors wanted to see the inclusion of a provision requiring cities to use these revenue-sharing funds to meet national goals for housing, slum clearance, and the improvement of community facilities.[12] And officials at HUD were amazed with their own discovery that the mayors "actually *want* guidelines" in community development revenue sharing.[13]

Another salient feature of the mayors' situation, noted in Chapter 4, is their characteristically loose and limited control over important municipal agencies, particularly those that bring in sizable federal grants. The model cities strategy of rechanneling all aid for the model neighborhood through the mayor's office or the CDA was a promising attempt to remedy this weakness. But even where certification procedures were adopted to provide for mayoral review, as in the case of certain HEW programs, most mayors were not able to take advantage of it because their staffs were too small and too busy. The lack of strong managerial capacity in city hall was further reflected in the inability of cities to spend even their limited supplemental grant allocations within a reasonable time.

A Three-Part Approach

The basic components of the present federal inventory—general revenue sharing, special revenue sharing, and the remaining categorical grants—are surprisingly capable of responding, in combination, to the political and administrative needs highlighted by the model cities experience. What is needed is a deliberate federal strategy that recognizes the continuing, special claims of poverty populations to a fair share of national resources, and a willingness to deploy the three types of federal aid according to this strategy.

General revenue sharing offers a ready source of funds, at a predictable level, virtually free of restrictions on its use, unencumbered by federal reviews, and allocated nationwide directly to general local governments rather than to specific

[12] "Mayors Back Plan on Fund Sharing," *New York Times*, June 18, 1973, p. 11.
[13] Pressman, "Political Implications . . . ," p. 48.

municipal agencies or to special authorities. Because this funding comes direct from the Treasury Department and is allocated by statutory formula, it is in no way dependent upon cooperation or coordination among federal agencies managing grant-in-aid programs, nor are there opportunities for Washington bureaucratic pressures to shape local decisions on expenditures. Thus general revenue sharing is ideally suited to meeting the needs of local interest groups as they are expressed through normal political channels and budgeting processes.

The availability of general revenue-sharing funds should make it possible for both Congressmen and local officials to argue persuasively that they are giving proper recognition to their "majority" constituents and even that they are taking care of needs not previously covered by categorical programs. They are now in a better position than ever to make a case for allocating other federal funds to priorities that reflect national commitments as well as local needs, particularly needs related to the poor. With general revenue sharing already on the books and providing visible benefits to the population at large, political leaders are well equipped to defend other federal aids intended for the still pressing needs of poverty populations.

Special revenue sharing for community development, in principle, could satisfy many of the political and administrative requirements that the Model Cities Program was unable to meet: that is, availability to all urban communities rather than a few selected for "demonstrations," local flexibility in the use of federal aid, a single channel for federal aid flowing through local elected officials, simplified federal reviews with reliance mainly on performance criteria, and predictable levels of funding to cover several years of operations.

In terms of the three-part strategy we propose, special revenue sharing could, and should, incorporate clear performance criteria similar to those used in model cities, requiring that most, or all, of the funds be used to benefit low-income groups and poverty neighborhoods. Administrative regulations should not prescribe program content or sponsorship, but they should require an explicit role for residents in allocation decisions and program operations. These criteria would provide political shelter for mayors who want to respond to the needs of the poor, but they should also assert a compelling national interest to override the reluctance of other mayors who do not recognize special obligations to the poor and the minorities.

Community development revenue sharing, as enacted, is a big improvement over the categorical programs it replaces, but neither the law itself nor HUD's first administrative regulations reflect some of the key lessons of model cities and of other programs of the 1960s. The performance criteria calling on local governments to focus their programs on eliminating slum conditions and meeting the needs of low-income residents are weak and ambiguous and likely to give rise to conflicts of interpretation between local and federal officials.

The original Nixon Administration proposal would have permitted local governments alone to decide priorities for the use of the federal aid funds. Both the Senate and House committees rejected this "no strings" approach and insisted that special revenue-sharing dollars should be used to achieve national as well as local objectives. The Senate bill thus contained a clear requirement that no more than 20 percent of a city's funds could be used for "activities which do not directly and significantly benefit low- and moderate-income families or blighted areas."[14] In an irony of legislative draftsmanship, the Senate-House Conference Committee replaced this provision with a phrase that recalls "maximum feasible participation," the notoriously troublesome language of the Economic Opportunity Act of 1964. Thus the final legislation requires participating communities to give "maximum feasible priority" to activities that benefit low- or moderate-income families or help prevent or eliminate slums or blight. Because judgments will vary as to what is feasible and what is maximum, we expect this phrase, like its 1964 predecessor, to lead mainly to "maximum feasible misunderstanding," as Daniel Patrick Moynihan concluded in the earlier case. The Senate language, in contrast, was far less ambiguous and more readily subject to verification.

Congress not only adopted an ambiguous compromise on priority uses for the funds but further departed from the notion of minimizing federal regulation by mandating a complicated application and review process that must be repeated every year. The law requires each eligible community, prior to receiving funds, to submit an annual application that has many unfortunate overtones of the early model cities planning requirements. Each application must contain a three-year plan identifying community development needs, a comprehensive strategy for meeting them, short- and long-term objectives, and a one-year program of activities to meet community development needs, plus a program to eliminate or prevent slums, blight, and deterioration and provide improved community facilities and services, as well as a housing assistance plan giving special emphasis to the needs of lower income people. A program budget and several local certifications are also required before the Secretary of HUD can make an initial grant. Subsequently, cities are required to submit an annual performance report on

[14] House Subcommittee on Housing, *Compilation of the Housing and Community Development Act of 1974*, p. 301.

their activities. HUD will review annual performance for conformity to a city's own application and to federal requirements, with the authority to reduce or terminate grants in cases of unsatisfactory performance. HUD's initial administrative rules expand and elaborate upon the legislative requirements for the yearly application and its three plans; they further require a midyear amendment if the city wants to revise its community development program in any significant way.[15]

We believe these planning requirements are excessive and are likely to prove harmful. Clearer performance criteria, accompanied by a simple requirement that the city define its own targets after receiving its initial grant and followed by a strong postaudit role for HUD based on actual performance, would offer better prospects for safeguarding national purposes while limiting wasteful paperwork. The present law and administrative rules run a high risk of achieving the worst of two worlds: a proliferation of annual local submissions and federal reviews, yet little real federal influence over local priorities on issues of national importance. The major beneficiaries may well be private consulting firms, which are already promoting their services to help cities prepare the required documents.

Similarly, performance criteria on the role of poverty area residents in community development decisions and operations are weak and diffuse and suggest a return to the very limited city-wide citizen advisory boards used in connection with urban renewal more than a decade ago. The law requires a city applying for funds to supply assurances that it has provided citizens with information on its program, held public hearings, and provided citizens "an adequate opportunity to participate in the development of the application." HUD's administrative rules state the performance standards that the Secretary will use to determine whether cities are complying with federal policy. In the case of citizen participation, they call for the city to specify "when and how citizens will have an opportunity to participate in the development of the application prior to submission;" "when an how technical assistance will be provided to assist citizen participants to understand program requirements;" and to develop a process "which permits citizens likely to be affected by community development and housing activities, including low- and moderate-income persons, to articulate needs, express preferences . . . , assist in the selection of priorities, . . . and have . . . complaints an-

[15] U.S. Department of Housing and Urban Development, Office of Assistant Secretary for Community Planning and Development, "Community Development Block Grants: Notice of Proposed Rulemaking," *Federal Register*, Vol. 39 (September 17, 1974), pp. 33482-33498.

swered in a timely and responsive manner." The city is not asked to show that these standards have been met, but merely to "indicate progress made toward meeting the performance standards."[16]

These criteria reflect a very limited conception of resident participation, far more limited than the one implemented with some success by Floyd Hyde in the Model Cities Program. Even the key elements of independent technical assistance and reimbursement for the expenses of participation are missing. The Senate version of the bill included explicit requirements for involving residents of community development areas in the execution of community development activities and providing adequate resources for their participation. The conference report amended these provisions to make it clear that "involving residents in the execution of community development activities and providing resources for their participation is discretionary with the applicant."[17] The failure to define a clear and measurable role for residents, together with the suggestion that HUD's performance standards can be met by superficial citizen involvement, is likely to generate confusion and controversy, and to confront federal officials with a need to make many ad hoc judgments about local performance.

Finally, community development revenue sharing is off to a disappointing start in terms of the frequently declared objectives of strengthening local government capacity by concentrating authority over federal aid expenditures in the hands of elected officials and by assuring them of continuity of federal funding at predictable levels. Neither the legislation nor the administrative rules set performance standards for the active involvement of local elected officials in community development programs, nor do they even offer encouragement to this end. The House Committee report on the legislation states that a principal objective is "to strengthen the ability of local elected officials to determine their community's development needs, set priorities, and allocate resources to various activities." After noting that elected officials should clearly be in charge of managing block grant funds, the Committee states that the day-to-day conduct of community development programs, including entering into contracts with HUD, may be delegated to one or more agencies of the local government, such as a redevelopment agency.[18] The Senate Committee report envisions a possible delegation to special agencies of not merely operating responsibilities, but even advance plan-

---

[16] Ibid., p. 33494.
[17] House Subcommittee on Housing, *Compilation of the Housing and Community Development Act of 1974*, p. 300.
[18] Ibid., pp. 355-356.

ning and program preparation: ". . . units of local government may designate one or more public agencies to develop, negotiate, and carry out the community development program in whole or in part." Further, the local public agency could be a special district.[19] The law itself states simply that the chief executive officer of a state or a unit of general local government may designate one or more public agencies to undertake a community development program in whole or in part.

This readiness to accept a delegation of authority from elected officials to special-purpose and semi-independent agencies suggests, once again, not a continuation of promising directions explored in the Model Cities Program, but rather a return to the earlier pattern of urban renewal. Nor are the financial arrangements conducive to strengthening community development programming as an ongoing responsibility of local government. HUD's proposed administrative rules would have the Secretary authorize no more than a one-year grant contract for communities whose applications are accepted.[20] This abbreviated contract period is a direct outcome of Congressional intent. The Senate bill called for a two-year application period, but the Conference Committee accepted a House amendment calling for communities to submit a three-year plan but only a one-year funding application.[21]

Thus the change in federal aid policy accomplished through the enactment of special revenue sharing for community development may produce little more than a redistribution of funds among cities. The objectives of reducing federal reviews, strengthening local government, and reconciling national purposes with local flexibility have all been compromised even at the outset. Early attention is needed to legislative amendments as well as revision of administrative regulations.

Residual categorical programs are declining in favor as a method for delivering federal aid, but they still account for most of the current inventory. Serving mainly a series of well-established interest groups, they offset by a very large margin any special aids intended for the poor and the less powerful. Together with general revenue sharing, they should be useful in establishing the case for compensatory efforts under special revenue sharing. Despite the attempt under model cities sponsorship to simplify their management and permit their use with

[19] Ibid., p. 618.
[20] HUD, Office of Assistant Secretary for Community Planning and Development, "Community Development Block Grants," *Federal Register*, p. 33490.
[21] House Subcommittee on Housing, *Compilation of the Housing and Community Development Act of 1974*, p. 229.

increased flexibility, they remain encrusted with layers of unnecessary nonstatutory administrative criteria, and they require complicated and time-consuming application and review processes.

With the model cities experience fresh in mind, we cannot be optimistic about prospects for changing the nature of categorical programs or for putting them to new uses. Nevertheless, reforming them may become more feasible as the recognition of their inadequacies becomes more widespread. Further, client groups and Congressmen, anxious to protect their favorite programs against growing demands for consolidation into newer forms of special revenue sharing, may agree to simplification and reform as the price for keeping them alive. Enactment of the Joint Funding Simplification Act of 1974 is a sign of continuing Congressional interest in grant reform, but not a very promising one. The act attempts to streamline federal aid procedures by simplifying reviews and making administrative practices more uniform. It has few teeth, however, and relies once more on the voluntary cooperation of agency heads.

If constituents, Congressmen, and administrators do become more amenable to change in the categorical programs, we envision three ways in which they can contribute to the tripartite approach. First, the need remains for demonstration and evaluation efforts to test urban programs. The Model Cities Program accomplished little on this score because its goals were too ambitious and too comprehensive to permit reasonable evaluation of the results; the program mushroomed too quickly from the notion of selected demonstrations to a national scale; and demonstrations and evaluation issues received only low priority. The narrower, single-function categorical programs have the potential to serve as better laboratories for trying out new ideas. Within this more focused context, a portion of categorical funds should be set aside for demonstrations of specific strategies to achieve carefully defined objectives. Further to avoid the errors of model cities in this respect, demonstrations should not be undertaken without an agreed-upon plan for independent evaluation of the results.

Second, because the resources tied up in categorical programs are so vast, efforts should be made to open the application channels to new clients that are not now served, particularly to city governments that want to use them in conjunction with special revenue-sharing funds for poverty neighborhoods. The Model Cities Program tried and failed to achieve this objective by working at the federal level to secure earmarking and guideline revisions for large numbers of programs at once and without Congressional support. If reform becomes more feasible through Congressional and administrative action, there may be important opportunities to reshape aid programs one at a time to make them more accessible to poverty groups.

Third, if changes in the allocation procedures for categorical programs become acceptable politically, these programs should be used as incentives to induce and reward national commitments to the poor. That is, cities whose use of other federal aids demonstrate genuine progress in meeting the needs of the poor should receive special priority in the award of categorical grants.

Federal reviews should differ for the three types of assistance. General revenue sharing requires no advance application but does require a subsequent reporting of expenditures; the Treasury Department's Office of Revenue Sharing is responsible for monitoring these expenditures to ensure compliance with the minimum restrictions contained in the legislation. But because local transfers of funds are easy to accomplish among categories of expenditure, federal review has very little meaning. Remaining categorical programs, at the other extreme, still require the local sponsoring agency to file an application, which is then reviewed prior to a decision on funding. This process, as noted, has grown into a major industry consuming vast quantities of paper, manpower, time, and energy.

Special revenue sharing, in our conception, must have some federal review, but we believe the form of this review can be almost as simple as that of general revenue sharing, while still giving fair assurance that national purposes are met. Cities should receive their initial allocation of community development funds as a matter of entitlement, with no prior application and review process. They should, however, then be required to submit a brief statement of their objectives for the use of these funds consistent with the statutory performance criteria determining who the beneficiaries are and establishing a role for residents in program decisions. Federal postaudits should focus on the consistency of this statement with the legislation and the consistency of subsequent expenditures with the statement. If this review is to have meaning, federal officials will have to make judgments about local performance—we know of no way to avoid it. If a city's performance is incompatible with the national objectives stated in the legislation, its subsequent funding should be reduced.

Making Programs Work

Although even a simple review process may provide an opening wedge for bureaucratic overregulation, this risk is unavoidable if we are to attempt to honor national commitments at all. One of the great dangers in making federal urban policy is the tendency for pendulum motion to follow current fashions, such as moving from excessive regulation to no regulation. Both the three-part approach we propose and the federal role it implies reflect a considerable reduction in ambitions from the style of the 1960s with its massive national efforts to do everything from putting a man on the moon to winning a fast victory in the War on Poverty. If model cities was the last of the grand designs for an urban policy, we now propose a small design rather than none at all.

Small designs, admittedly, are not likely to capture the headlines or grip the public imagination. But headlines and public awareness alone do not implement programs, as we learned in the 1960s. A more important requirement is that large numbers of people must have a stake in program outcomes. The Model Cities Program was too isolated from the concerns of most Americans, particularly after the civil disorders subsided and the conditions of poverty areas no longer posed a threat to the stability of society. Then the extreme pluralism of the nation asserted itself once more, and active interest groups again concerned themselves with the pursuit of their own special objectives, to the detriment of the less organized and less influential minorities. The strategy we now propose, *if presented in its entirety*, offers substantial benefits to the majority while still reserving one special type of aid for the minority.

The question remains, however, whether our pluralistic system, with its constantly shifting coalitions and political alliances, is capable of giving sustained attention to any problem that can be resolved only over a long period of time. Robert Wood, observing the rapid waning of interest in the urban development goals that were widely proclaimed as recently as 1968, has commented sharply on our "disturbing tendency to *replace* goals rather than to *fulfill* them."[22] Before we had a chance to make much progress in coping with the "urban crisis," we replaced it with the "crisis of the environment," complete with the national purification rite known as Earth Day. The problems of environmental pollution will not be solved in a short time, either, and now we are on to the "energy crisis."

To break this inane cycle, we can only suggest patient attention to the less spectacular task of adapting existing institutions and shaping new programs to meet legitimate national needs, while building a base for politics that aim at the gradual achievement of results. The alternative is continued neglect of past commitments, masked by the rhetoric of newly discovered crises and the proclamation of bold new goals.

[22] Robert Wood, "Housing and Environmental Escapism," *Journal of the American Institute of Planners*, Vol. 36 (November 1970), p. 422.

Appendix A
A Chronology of Key Events in the Model Cities Program

October 1965	President Johnson appoints a Task Force on Urban Problems, chaired by Robert Wood, Head of the Political Science Department at M.I.T.
December 22, 1965	The Task Force on Urban Problems issues a "Report to the President" recommending the establishment of an experimental program in approximately 66 cities of varying sizes, focusing on deteriorating residential sections in each city. The purpose of the program, to run for five years, would be to concentrate resources where they are most needed, coordinate the various activities under way to resolve urban blight, and mobilize local leadership and area residents in fighting urban decay.
January 26, 1966	President Johnson sends a message to Congress on "City Demonstration Programs" that incorporates most of the task force recommendations.
January 27, 1966	Draft legislation is introduced in each branch of Congress embodying President Johnson's recommendations—H.R. 12341 and S.2842. An intensive lobbying effort ensues.
May 1966	H. Ralph Taylor, an urbanist with extensive experience in urban renewal efforts, is appointed Assistant Secretary for Demonstrations and Intergovernmental Relations, one of four divisions of the Department of Housing and Urban Development. The major "demonstration" to be included would be the Model Cities Program if it is passed by Congress.
October 20, 1966	A special HUD task force, chaired by William Rafsky, issues a "Report to the Secretary on the Demonstration Cities Program," presenting suggestions for its implementation if it is passed by Congress.
November 3, 1966	President Johnson signs the Demonstration Cities and Metropolitan Development Act into law—PL.89-754. At the signing ceremony the President refers to the newly established program for the first time as the "Model Cities Program."

December 1966   HUD issues a document "Improving the Quality of Urban Life: A Program Guide to Model Neighborhoods in Demonstration Cities," providing the first official interpretation of the Model Cities Program. The "Program Guide" follows closely the recommendations made in the "Report to the Secretary . . . " the previous October. It contains suggestions on the content of the model cities application and the comprehensive plan that participating cities are expected to prepare.

January 1967   The Model Cities Administration is established by HUD Secretary Weaver to administer the program. MCA will be under the direction of Assistant Secretary Taylor. Over the next two months MCA is staffed, and Walter Farr appointed its director. Farr has served previously with the Agency for International Development. MCA will retain responsibility for program policy decisions, while HUD's regional offices will be responsible for operational decisions and technical assistance. Coordination between MCA and the regional offices will be achieved through the establishment of "desk officers" in MCA who will deal with the Assistant Regional Administrator for Model Cities in each regional office. The regional offices will maintain liaison with participating cities through the assignment of a HUD model cities "leadman" for each city who will report to the ARA for Model Cities.

January-February 1967   HUD conducts regional briefing sessions on model cities for mayors and other interested local officials.

February 1967   Informal proposals for model cities grants begin arriving in Washington. They suggest that selected target areas are too large and frequently include substantial portions of central business districts. This prompts MCA to issue instructions to regional offices to limit target areas to include no more than 10 percent of a city's population or 15,000 people, whichever is larger. All applications must be submitted by May 1, 1967.

April 1967   The "Model Cities Planning Application Review Process" is established. Planning applications will be reviewed by the Washington Interagency Review Committee, chaired by Assistant Secretary Taylor. To ensure interagency coordination, representatives from the Departments of Labor and Health, Education, and Welfare, and from the Office of Economic Opportunity are included on the committee.

May 1, 1967   Application due date. HUD has received a total of 193 applications from cities ranging in size from 1,200 to over 8 million (New York City).

July 1967   The application review process is completed, with most decisions being made in Washington and most of the work done by MCA. Recommendations on cities to be selected are presented to HUD Secretary Weaver. MCA officials anticipate that announcements will be made in August, and they begin to develop program guidelines and evaluate their internal organizational structure. Commitments are held up, however, pending Congressional appropriations.

November 16, 1967   A total of 63 cities are announced as successful applicants for the Model Cities Program. (An additional 12 cities are added in March 1968.)

October-December 1967   The first formal Model Cities Program guidelines are issued in the form of "CDA Letters" (CDA refers to the City Demonstration Agencies that are to be established to administer the program in each participating city). CDA Letter No. 1 describes the sequential planning process that cities are expected to follow in preparing their Comprehensive Demonstration Plan. It also encourages cities to "think big" in requesting additional federal monies over the five-year life of the program. CDA Letter No. 2 presents administrative and fiscal requirements. CDA Letter No. 3 presents the requirements for resident involvement in the program. In addition, a revised "Program Guide" is issued in anticipation of a second round of applications from interested cities. The revised guide emphasizes the need to establish clear linkages between problems described in program applications, to involve local residents in developing the application, and to describe the contemplated administrative structure for the program. These changes in emphasis have resulted from an in-house evaluation of the content of the first round of applications.

December 7, 1967   An Inter-Agency Agreement is formally approved by HUD, HEW, the Department of Labor, and OEO, regarding the Model Cities Program. It provides for the establishment of several coordinating and policy groups at both the Washington and regional levels. In Washington, the Washington Inter-Agency Committee, chaired by Assistant Secretary Taylor, will be responsible for making all policy decisions for the program; while a series of working groups, chaired by MCA Director Farr, will be established below it as needed. In each region a Regional Inter-Agency Coordinating Committee will be established, chaired by the Assistant Regional Administrator for Model Cities, which will be responsible for operating decisions and the provision of technical assistance to participating cities. Each city will also have a Local Inter-Agency Working Group, chaired by its HUD model cities leadman, which will monitor local progress.

January 1968   MCA announces April 15 as the deadline for a second round of model cities applications. The application review process is revised, with more authority delegated to the HUD regional offices and the newly established RICCs. In addition, more emphasis is placed on the basic capability of applicant cities rather than on the contents of the application itself.

April 15, 1968   A total of 168 applications are received for Model Cities Programs, 83 of them from cities that were rejected as first-round applicants. MCA and the regional offices begin reviewing immediately.

April 29, 1968	Several unrelated activities are transferred from Assistant Secretary Taylor's office, and his title is changed to Assistant Secretary for Model Cities and Governmental Relations, the latter activity now relating almost exclusively to efforts to achieve state involvement in the program.
Summer 1968	MCA hires several consulting firms to evaluate the Model Cities Program and prepare materials to assist participating cities.
July 1968	CDA Letter No. 4 is issued, clarifying the planning requirements established in CDA Letter No. 1 and requiring the submission to HUD of Part 1 of the Comprehensive Demonstration Plan two-thirds of the way through each participating city's planning year.
September 6, 1968	Another round of model cities applications is approved. On September 6, a total of 33 cities are designated. On October 14, another 17 are approved, with 22 more following on November 22, and 3 more scattered over the ensuing month, for a total of 75.
October 29, 1968	A formal agreement between HUD and OEO is signed recommending coordination between Model Cities and the Community Action Programs at the local level. The agreement recommends the sharing of policy board memberships and coordination of citizen participation, administrative, and program activities. A broader agreement on coordination among HUD, OEO, HEW, and Labor is signed on December 10, 1968, calling for the coordination of resident groups, planning, and program activities in model neighborhoods. On December 19, 1968, OEO agrees to provide $4 million in its funds for training and technical assistance to model neighborhood residents, to be conducted in conjunction with its local Community Action Programs.
October-November 1968	Three more CDA Letters are issued. They provide guidelines for such subjects as relocation planning, budgets

for supplementally funded projects, and ground rules for the local expenditure of supplemental funds.

November 1968

HUD regional offices are authorized by MCA to offer first-round cities that appear to be within four months of submitting their Comprehensive Demonstration Plans 175 percent of their supplemental grant if they submit these plans before the end of 1968. A total of 16 cities submit their plans before the end of the year.

December 23, 1968

Seattle, Washington, is announced as the first city to have its Comprehensive Demonstration Plan approved. A total of 8 more cities are approved before President Nixon's inauguration in January 1969.

January 1969

President Nixon is inaugurated. George Romney, Governor of Michigan, is named Secretary of HUD. Floyd Hyde, Mayor of Fresno, California, is named Assistant Secretary for Model Cities and Governmental Relations. The Administration undertakes the first in a series of studies of President Johnson's Great Society programs, including model cities.

February 1969

CDA Letter No. 8 is issued, presenting requirements for administrative and fiscal procedures during the model cities action period.

April 28, 1969

HUD Secretary Romney holds a press conference in which he provides the first Administration comments on model cities. He announces that the Urban Affairs Council will henceforth assume all responsibility for interdepartmental responsibility concerning the program; involved departments will receive categorical funds earmarked specifically for model cities; the 10 percent or 15,000-people restriction for model neighborhoods is eliminated so that minor boundary changes can be effected; the requirement for comprehensiveness will henceforth be construed to mean a comprehensive attack over the five-year life of the program rather than within each action year; and CDAs are urged to devote

April 28, 1969
(cont.)

greater efforts toward involving states and private and voluntary organizations in their programs. The Secretary also announces that as a result of White House action the regional boundaries of all federal departments concerned with urban problems will be standardized to facilitate greater coordination among them.

May-June 1969

Approved Model Cities Programs begin receiving their first action year supplemental grants. HUD adopts the policy of incremental sign-offs, under which those first-year projects that meet with federal approval can begin immediately, while those that require further work will be delayed while they are revised by the CDAs. Completed Comprehensive Demonstration Plans continue to be submitted and reviewed. By June 30, 35 plans are approved.

August 22, 1969

MCA revises program submission requirements for a second round of cities. The Comprehensive Demonstration Plan is shortened and simplified. A five-year statement of goals and fiscal needs is no longer required. Part 1 is shortened and redesignated as the midplanning statement. A description of the actual planning process is to be added.

Summer 1969

MCA issues a series of consulting contracts to provide technical assistance to participating cities in specific programmatic areas and in the planning and implementation process.

Summer 1969

Robert Baida replaces Walter Farr as director of the Model Cities Administration. Baida has been serving as Deputy Assistant Secretary for Model Cities and remains in this position, assuming Farr's duties, upon the latter's resignation from HUD.

December 1969

The President's Task Force on Model Cities, chaired by Professor Edward Banfield of Harvard, issues a report "Model Cities: A Step Toward the New Federalism." The report is moderately supportive, recommending that the program be continued and simplified. It also recommends the establishment of revenue sharing and consolidation of categorical grants. (The report is not released to the general public until August 1970.)

February 1970

MCA establishes the policy of reprogramming. Having found that first-round cities in their first action year have been spending funds quite slowly, HUD devises reprogramming as a means for speeding up the expenditure rate. Essentially, each CDA is to estimate how much money will remain unspent at the proposed end of its action year if the present or anticipated rate of expenditure is maintained. The CDA is then to develop new, quickly implementable projects to spend this money.

March 1970

MCA issues stringent requirements for evaluation activities by CDAs. For almost a year, MCA has been exhorting CDAs to prepare adequate evaluation plans and hire sufficient evaluation staff. Now they inform all cities currently in their first action year that their funds will be cut off at the end of the fiscal year if they do not have an approved evaluation plan and evaluation staff by that time. Second-round cities, which are still in the planning stage, are required to include an acceptable evaluation plan in their Comprehensive Demonstration Plans.

April 1970

The White House considers a proposal to divert $500 million of the model cities funds to provide special assistance to southern school districts facing problems of racial desegregation.

May 14, 1970

Secretary Romney meets with President Nixon and announces the President's decision not to transfer model cities funds to the school boards. This decision follows a campaign by mayors, governors, and members of Congress to block any diversion of model cities funds to other uses.

Summer 1970   HUD begins the reorganization of its regional offices. Model cities leadmen are assigned to HUD area offices and become part of area teams. The Assistant Regional Administrators remain in the regional offices, as do the various programmatic specialists who have provided participating cities with technical assistance.

September 1970   MCA announces an experimental set of "planned variations" within the Model Cities Program. Cities selected on the basis of their high level of performance are invited to Washington to discuss three possible variations: expansion of model neighborhood boundaries city-wide; chief executive review and comment on all categorical grants coming into the city; and waivers of administrative regulations in federal programs operating as part of the model cities plans. A total of 12 cities are contacted. Several more are contacted a few months later and respond with proposals, but HUD takes no immediate action.

November 1970   MCA issues a series of guidelines to separate CDA planning functions from the operation of specific model neighborhood projects. These regulations prevent CDAs from taking on operational responsibilities for projects and limit their participation on the governing boards of operating agencies.

February 1971   The Administration prepares to announce the termination of the Model Cities Program as of December 31, 1971. After that date any funding for the program will have to come from the special revenue-sharing plan for urban community development that the President has proposed to Congress as a successor to several categorical grant programs administered by HUD.

February 18, 1971   Representatives of the National League of Cities and U.S. Conference of Mayors meet with officials of HUD and the Office of Management and Budget. The Administration agrees as a result to set no firm termination

	date for model cities and to request a supplemental appropriation for continued funding if Congress fails to enact the special revenue-sharing plan by December 1971.
Spring 1971	HUD undergoes an internal reorganization in anticipation of President Nixon's program on special revenue sharing. The Model Cities and Urban Renewal Administrations are combined and placed under an Assistant Secretary for Community Development. Assistant Secretary Floyd Hyde is named to this position. Similar shifts occur in all HUD regional offices.
Spring 1971	MCA requires all model cities to develop a resident employment plan that provides for the systematic recruitment, training, and employment of model neighborhood residents.
July 29, 1971	President Nixon announces the start of the planned variations experiment in 20 selected cities.
August 24, 1972	President Nixon announces the continuation of planned variations in 20 cities for a second year.
January 8, 1973	Secretary Romney announces a White House decision to suspend a number of HUD programs. Model cities funding is to be suspended after June 30, 1973, in anticipation of Congressional approval of special revenue sharing for community development. HUD regional offices inform participating cities not to expect funding beyond their current action year.
August 22, 1974	President Ford signs Housing and Community Development Act of 1974. Title I of the act consolidates the Model Cities Program, urban renewal, and a series of other community development programs administered by HUD and replaces them with a new program of block grants for community development, beginning January 1, 1975. Communities participating in the Model Cities Program will receive block grants large enough to permit

August 22, 1974   them to complete five action years at the prior average
(cont.)   annual level of model cities funding, plus a declining
                    percentage of this amount for a subsequent three-year
                    period.

Appendix B
Sequence of Events for Participating Cities Leading up to First-Year Action Grant

First-Round Cities

1. HUD issues a document, "Improving the Quality of Urban Life: A Program Guide to Model Neighborhoods in Demonstration Cities," in December 1966, which provides cities with the initial description of the Model Cities Program and a rough idea of what an application should include.

2. Interested cities are invited to regional briefings on the program by HUD officials in January-February 1967. Applications are due by May 1.

3. Regional offices inform interested cities that model neighborhoods should be primarily residential in character and should contain no more than 10 percent of the city's population or 15,000 people, whichever is greater.

4. Cities develop applications and submit them to HUD by May 1.

5. No announcement is made until November 1967, when 63 cities are announced. An additional 12 cities are approved the following March.

6. Each approved city receives a "Discussion Paper" from the HUD regional office, presenting it with the required revisions in its application, the proposed work program, and planning year budget. In almost all cases, cities receive a much smaller planning grant than requested. They have 45 days to respond.

7. Once the response to the "Discussion Paper" is completed and approved by HUD, each city receives approval to begin drawing funds from its planning grant. It must submit monthly financial reports and bimonthly progress reports.

8. Two-thirds of the way through the planning year, each city is required to submit a draft Part I of its "Comprehensive Demonstration Plan." This is reviewed by the Regional Inter-Agency Coordinating Committee, comments are made, and the city is expected to respond to these comments while at the same time completing its plan.

9. At the end of the planning year the completed plan is submitted to HUD for review. This may take from two months to a year, depending on the quality of the document. Revisions are requested and reviewed upon receipt. The plan is finally approved, possibly with some reservations on certain activities, and the city receives its supplemental grant.

Second-Round Cities

1. HUD issues a revised "Program Guide" in December 1967, for cities interested in submitting a second-round application.

2. In January 1968, the deadline for second-round applications is announced as April 15.

3. Cities develop applications and submit them by April 15.

4. A total of 75 cities are designated, a few at a time, over the course of three months at the end of 1968.

5. Each approved city receives a "Discussion Paper" from the HUD regional office. This time, however, cities are informed in advance of the size of the planning grant they can expect, so that they do not have to make drastic revisions in their budget. In addition, they are given 90 days in which to prepare a response.

6. Once the response to the "Discussion Paper" is approved by HUD, cities are authorized to draw on their planning grant. The same reports are required as for the first-round applicants.

7. In August 1969, cities are notified that the planning guidelines have been modified. Part I has been simplified and shortened, but must be submitted to HUD midway through the planning year. Part II (five-year projections) has been eliminated.

8. As many cities approach the end of their planning year, HUD informs them that they must develop detailed evaluation plans as part of their "Comprehensive Development Plan" (CDP).

9. At the end of the planning year, the CDP is submitted to HUD and reviewed. In comparison with first-round procedures, the reviews are generally shorter in duration and more lenient in their criticisms.

Appendix C
Model Cities Funding, 1967-1973 (millions of dollars)

	Fiscal Year (ending June 30)	President's Request	Congressional Appropriation
For planning grants	1967	$ 12.0	$ 11.0
	1968	12.0	12.0
For supplementary (operating) grants	1968*	400.0	200.0
	1969*	500.0	312.5
	1970	750.0	575.0
	1971	575.0	575.0
	1972	−0−	150.0
	1973	515.0	500.0
Totals through 1973		$2,764.0	$2,335.5

*Congress appropriated an additional $100 million for fiscal 1968 and $312.5 million for fiscal 1969 for urban renewal funds, which were to be used as part of the Model Cities Programs.
Source: U.S. Department of Housing and Urban Development, Office of the Assistant Secretary for Community Development.

Appendix D
Cities Participating in the Model Cities Program
(as of December 31, 1971)

(cities with planned variations designated by *)

City and State

Alabama
Huntsville
Tuskegee

Alaska
Juneau

Arizona
Gila River
*Tucson

Arkansas
Little Rock
Texarkana

California
Berkeley
Compton
*Fresno
Los Angeles City
Los Angeles County
Oakland
Pittsburg
Richmond
San Diego
San Francisco
*San Jose

Colorado
Denver
Trinidad

Connecticut
Bridgeport
Hartford
New Haven
New London
Waterbury

City and State

Delaware
*Wilmington

District of Columbia
Washington, D.C.

Florida
Dade County (Miami)
*Tampa

Georgia
Alma/Bacon County
Athens
Atlanta
Gainesville
Savannah

Hawaii
Honolulu City/County

Idaho
Boise

Illinois
Carbondale
Chicago
*East St. Louis
Rock Island

Indiana
Gary
*Indianapolis
South Bend

Iowa
*Des Moines

Kansas
Kansas City
Wichita

City and State

Kentucky
Bowling Green
Covington
Pikeville

Louisiana
New Orleans

Maine
Lewiston
Portland

Maryland
Baltimore
Prince Georges County

Massachusetts
Boston
Cambridge
Fall River
Holyoke
Lowell
Lynn
New Bedford
Springfield
Worcester

Michigan
Ann Arbor
Benton Harbor—Benton Township
Detroit
Genesee County (Flint)
Grand Rapids
Highland Park
*Lansing
Saginaw

City and State

Minnesota
Duluth
Minneapolis
St. Paul

Missouri
Kansas City
St. Louis

Montana
*Butte
Helena

New Hampshire
Manchester

New Jersey
East Orange
Hoboken
Jersey City
*Newark
*Paterson
Perth Amboy
Plainfield
Trenton

New Mexico
Albuquerque
Santa Fe

New York
Binghamton
Buffalo
Cohoes
Mt. Vernon
New York City
    Central and East Harlem
    South Bronx

City and State

New York (cont.)
Central Brooklyn
Poughkeepsie
*Rochester
Syracuse

North Carolina
Asheville
Charlotte
Highpoint
*Winston-Salem

North Dakota
Fargo

Ohio
Akron
Cincinnati
Cleveland
Columbus
*Dayton
Martins Ferry
Toledo
Youngstown

Oklahoma
Lawton
McAlester
Tulsa

Oregon
Portland

Pennsylvania
Allegheny County
Bradford
*Erie

City and State

Lancaster
Philadelphia
Pittsburgh
Reading
Scranton
Wilkes-Barre

Puerto Rico
San Juan

Rhode Island
Pawtucket
Providence

South Carolina
Rock Hill
Spartanburg

Tennessee
Chattanooga
Cookeville
Nashville/Davidson County
Smithville/DeKalb County

Texas
Austin
Eagle Pass
Edinburg
*Houston
Laredo
San Antonio
Texarkana
*Waco

Utah
Salt Lake County (City)

City and State

Vermont
Winooski

Virginia
*Norfolk
Richmond

Washington
*Seattle
Tacoma

Wisconsin
Milwaukee

Wyoming
Cheyenne

Source: U.S. Department of Housing and Urban Development, *Justification for 1973 Estimates: Community Development*, prepared for House of Representatives Committee on Appropriations (February 1972), pp. B-10 to B-13.

INDEX

Publications of the Joint Center for Urban Studies

The Joint Center for Urban Studies, a cooperative venture of the Massachusetts Institute of Technology and Harvard University, was founded in 1959 to organize and encourage research on urban and regional problems. Participants have included scholars from the fields of anthropology, architecture, business, city planning, economics, education, engineering, history, law, philosophy, political science, and sociology.

The findings and conclusions of this book are, as with all Joint Center publications, solely the responsibility of the author.

Published by Harvard University Press

The Intellectual versus the City: From Thomas Jefferson to Frank Lloyd Wright, by Morton and Lucia White, 1962

Streetcar Suburbs: The Process of Growth in Boston, 1870-1900, by Sam B. Warner, Jr., 1962

City Politics, by Edward C. Banfield and James Q. Wilson, 1963

Law and Land: Anglo-American Planning Practice, edited by Charles M. Haar, 1964

Location and Land Use: Toward a General Theory of Land Rent, by William Alonso, 1964

Poverty and Progress: Social Mobility in a Nineteenth Century City, by Stephan Thernstrom, 1964

Boston: The Job Ahead, by Martin Meyerson and Edward C. Banfield, 1966

The Myth and Reality of Our Urban Problems, by Raymond Vernon, 1966

Muslim Cities in the Later Middle Ages, by Ira Marvin Lapidus, 1967

The Fragmented Metropolis: Los Angeles, 1850-1930, by Robert M. Fogelson, 1967

Law and Equal Opportunity: A Study of the Massachusetts Commission Against Discrimination, by Leon H. Mayhew, 1968

Varieties of Police Behavior: The Management of Law and Order in Eight Communities, by James Q. Wilson, 1968

The Metropolitan Enigma: Inquiries into the Nature and Dimensions of America's "Urban Crisis," edited by James Q. Wilson, revised edition, 1968

Traffic and The Police: Variations in Law-Enforcement Policy, by John A. Gardiner, 1969

The Influence of Federal Grants: Public Assistance in Massachusetts, by Martha Derthick, 1970

The Arts in Boston, by Bernard Taper, 1970

Families Against the City: Middle Class Homes of Industrial Chicago, 1872-1890, by Richard Sennett, 1970

Publications of the Joint Center for Urban Studies

The Political Economy of Urban Schools, by Martin T. Katzman, 1971

Origins of the Urban School: Public Education in Massachusetts, 1870-1915, by Marvin Lazerson, 1971

The Other Bostonians: Poverty and Progress in the American Metropolis, 1880-1970, by Stephan Thernstrom, 1973

Published by The MIT Press

The Image of the City, by Kevin Lynch, 1960

Housing and Economic Progress: A Study of the Housing Experiences of Boston's Middle-Income Families, by Lloyd Rodwin, 1961

The Historian and the City, edited by Oscar Handlin and John Burchard, 1963

The Federal Bulldozer: A Critical Analysis of Urban Renewal, 1949-1962, by Martin Anderson, 1964

The Future of Old Neighborhoods: Rebuilding for a Changing Population, by Bernard J. Frieden, 1964

Man's Struggle for Shelter in an Urbanizing World, by Charles Abrams, 1964

The View from the Road, by Donald Appleyard, Kevin Lynch, and John R. Myer, 1964

The Public Library and the City, edited by Ralph W. Conant, 1965

Regional Development Policy: A Case Study of Venezuela, by John Friedmann, 1966

Urban Renewal: The Record and the Controversy, edited by James Q. Wilson, 1966

Transport Technology for Developing Regions: A Study of Road Transportation in Venezuela, by Richard M. Soberman, 1966

Computer Methods in the Analysis of Large-Scale Social Systems, edited by James M. Beshers, 1968

Planning Urban Growth and Regional Development: The Experience of the Guayana Program of Venezuela, by Lloyd Rodwin and Associates, 1969

Build a Mill, Build a City, Build a School: Industrialization, Urbanization, and Education in Ciudad Guayana, by Noel F. McGinn and Russell G. Davis, 1969

Land-Use Controls in the United States, by John Delafons, second edition, 1969

Beyond the Melting Pot: The Negroes, Puerto Ricans, Jews, Italians, and Irish of New York City, by Nathan Glazer and Daniel Patrick Moynihan, revised edition, 1970

Bargaining: Monopoly Power versus Union Power, by George de Menil, 1971

Housing the Urban Poor: A Critical Evaluation of Federal Housing Policy, by Arthur P. Solomon, 1974

Publications of the Joint Center for Urban Studies

The Politics of Neglect: Urban Aid from Model Cities to Revenue Sharing, by Bernard J. Frieden and Marshall Kaplan, 1975

The Joint Center also publishes monographs and reports.

DATE DUE			
OCT 11 2004			